TEXTBOOK BEATLES:
VOLUME 1

GREGORY ALEXANDER

TABLE OF CONTENTS

INTRODUCTION

Being a true Beatles geek, expert, super-fan or aficionado involves more than listening; reading is a big part, too. As a committed Fabs fanatic over multiple decades, I've spent many a day and evening with their music blasting out of my speakers while my nose was buried in the pages of some overview of the group, breakdown of their songs, first-person tale of their times, fanciful satire of their story, exhaustive chronicle of their recording sessions, survey of their instruments, interview with some Beatles person or encyclopedic biography of the individual members or band as a whole. Whenever I might have thought I'd heard or read it all, I was wrong.

So every Sunday morning as I listen to Terri Hemmert's "Breakfast with the Beatles" show on WXRT-FM Chicago, I stop whatever I'm doing (making coffee, cracking eggs…) and turn up the volume upon hearing the voice of Greg "Professor Moptop" Alexander. That means it's time for one of his "Beatle University" segments, in which he explores the background, influences, sessions and meanings of a Beatles song—or takes a look at some other topic, such as novelty songs about the group or the impactful works of artists the Beatles revered, such as Chuck Berry and Carl Perkins.

As much as I think I know about the Beatles, I always learn something new from Professor Moptop. So when I heard he was writing a textbook, I was ready to fill out my application for Beatle University. Now I've seen the book, and, in the words of John Lennon: Well well well! (Sorry, but "yeah yeah yeah" would've been too on the nose.)

A splendid time is guaranteed on every page (OK, I can't always restrain myself), with each patented Professor Moptop lesson delivered in his expert, conversational voice. This boy (sorry again) has an encyclopedic knowledge about the Beatles, and his words sing. You can open up this book anywhere and get sucked in by the stories you realize you didn't know; it's the equivalent of an online deep-dive where you keep clicking from one fascinating topic to another. And when you take a break from reading, you can marvel at all of those amazing picture sleeves and records presented in full color and wonder how he got his hands on so much cool art.

If I had this book when I was a kid, my parents would've had to drag me away from it to come down for dinner every night. Textbook Beatles is fab all around, and if you're anything like me, I've got a feeling you've got some appropriate music to play as you…yes…dig it.

Personally, I hope he'll be writing more in a week or two.

—MARK CARO, EVANSTON, IL - 2018

CHAPTER 1:
THE DAWN OF TIME...

IN MUSIC HISTORY THERE ARE FEW DAYS, IF ANY, THAT CAN BE CONSIDERED MORE IMPORTANT THAN JULY 6, 1957, THE DAY JOHN LENNON WAS INTRODUCED TO PAUL MCCARTNEY BY A MUTUAL FRIEND.

VAN VAUGHAN ISN'T A HOUSEHOLD NAME, but the world would be a very different place without his presence. Vaughan was McCartney's childhood friend and schoolmate at the Liverpool Institute where both graduated at the age 11. For a brief period Ivan would play bass in Lennon's band, and he introduced the future partners to one another.

After "retiring" from music, Vaughn would study at University College in London, becoming a teacher. Throughout their success John and Paul would remain friends with Ivan, planning to put him in charge of a communal teaching style of school which never materialized.

Sometime in early 1957 or possibly Christmas 1956, John Lennon was given a gift of a guitar. While it is unclear who bought the guitar for him, John received it while in the care of his stern but loving Aunt Mimi.

Mary Elizabeth "Mimi" Smith was Lennon's mother's sister who was granted custody of John when Julia Lennon was deemed unfit to care for her infant son. Mimi was the oldest of five sisters and, much like her nephew would grow to be, she was unapologetic and vocally truthful.

Mimi was critical of many of Lennon's personal decisions and associations and highly dismissive of his musical aspirations, famously telling him "The guitar's all right John, but you'll never make a living out of it." Despite these differences John and Mimi had a close relationship, and he showed her a respect that he rarely gave anyone.

She was vehemently against him starting a band, disliking "John's little friend" Paul and "hating" George because of his accent and Teddy Boy look. When John began dating Cynthia, Mimi was cold and unpleasant towards her as well, strongly disapproving of their marriage and threatening to never speak to John again.

John would remain extremely close to his aunt throughout his life, reportedly calling her once a week without fail.

John Lennon with Nigel the dog

him profoundly for the remainder of his life.

In December 1938 Julia Stanley married Alfred Lennon. None of her four sisters were present as she didn't inform her family of the union, which was disapproved of, and in early 1940 Julia became pregnant with her first son, who would be John. Alfred was not present for his son's birth in October as he was away at sea at the time.

Alfred was said to always be joking and he never held a job for very long, spending long stretches of time away while working as a merchant sailor during World War II. He deserted in 1943.

After Julia and Alfred split up she became involved with a series of men. Her sister Mimi worried about the care of the young child, and as a result contacted Liverpool's social services. Julia unwillingly gave her sister custody of John, whom Mimi and her husband George Smith raised.

John would stay in occasional contact with his mother, becoming especially close with her during his early teen years. He would visit Julia, and she encouraged him to explore his love for music and art, teaching him some rudimentary skills on banjo and ukulele. It is possible, although not confirmed, that Julia also bought him his first guitar.

Another trait that John and his aunt shared was an inconsistency in their opinions. Mimi stated that she was "horrified to see John performing" but on other occasions she was "delighted" or "pleased as punch" to see her nephew singing. She also claimed to be the one who bought John's first guitar, which is likely untrue.

Julia Lennon was John's mother who was tragically killed when he was a teenager, affecting

Mimi was notoriously strict with the high-spirited youth. She referred to John's love for music as a "dead end" and never allowed a record player in the house. John would go to his mother's and play the records he wanted to hear. Julia and John both enjoyed the music by various artists, even Elvis, as she was a very open-minded free spirit.

Julia enthusiastically attended a 1957 Quarrymen show, clapping loudly and was seen "smiling, swaying, and dancing" throughout the entire performance.

Tragically on the night of July 15, 1958, at the age of only 44 years old, Julia was killed after being struck by an off-duty policeman who had been drinking.

Lennon was devastated by the death of his mother and friend, causing the traumatized teen to become very violent and angry. The tragedy, however, brought John closer to his friend Paul, who also lost his mother at a young age. John never really reconciled with the death of his mother, even after he achieved fame and acceptance on an international level.

By March 1956, at the height of the skiffle resurgence in Liverpool, Lennon formed his own band. They were briefly called the Black Jacks, but only for "about a week," according to him.

Skiffle was a style of music which fused jazz, folk, country, and blues and was popular in the United States in the early part of the 1900s. The genre gained interest in the 1950s in England.

Lonnie Donegan, frequently called the King of Skiffle, was one of the most popular artists in post-war England with his American country-fueled act. He scored hits with covers of Lead Belly and Woody Guthrie songs. With continuing success in England as well in the United States, Donegan became a model of how to succeed for the young Beatles. Once again they were thinking of the U.S. as a holy land beyond their wildest fantasies.

Pete Shotton, who played the washboard in the Quarrymen, was a friend of John's who attended the Quarry Bank High School in Liverpool. He is likely the one who suggested the name Quarrymen from a line in the school song that goes "Quarry Men, strong before their birth."

Lennon insisted that Shotton join his band, even though the two were both very novice musicians. They would quickly recruit other skiffle-loving schoolmates of similar ability including Colin Hanton on drums, Rod Davis on banjo, and Eric Griffiths on guitar.

The Quarrymen in Liverpool, July 6, 1957.
Left to right: Eric Griffiths, Colin Hanton, Rod Davis, John Lennon, Pete Shotton, and Len Garry

John's mother Julia taught Lennon and Griffiths some elementary skills on the banjo and how to tune their guitars.

Bill Smith played the tea-chest bass with Lennon's group, but his tenure as a band member was brief, primarily due to his disinterest in rehearsals. He was replaced by Len Garry or Vaughan.

Depending upon who was available or willing to show up, either Garry or Vaughan would handle the bass duties. Nigel Whaley would also take the role on occasion, also acting as the band's manager, although it appears that Lennon was the clear leader of the band.

It is also rumored that for a brief period, possibly one performance from a day when the band played two shows, they were called Johnny and the Rainbows.

After playing several small engagements and unsuccessfully auditioning for "Mr. Star Maker," the band performed at the Woolton Garden Fete at St. Peter's Church in Liverpool. This was a large social event for an area that didn't have many entertainment opportunities. The Quarrymen played twice on this occasion, once in the early afternoon and again in the evening.

McCartney recalls seeing the band perform on this

Clockwise from top left: Mimi and George Stanley; John Lennon and his mother Julia Stanley; Ivan Vaughan (left) and Pete Shotton; Aunt Mimi and John Lennon

day (likely in the afternoon) and hearing John sing the Dell-Vikings' "Come Go With Me," although Lennon was said to have made up most of the lyrics on the spot, only properly performing the chorus.

As the band members were setting up their instruments for their second performance of the day, Vaughan, then a student at the Liverpool Institute, introduced the 15-year-old McCartney to Lennon.

After a bit of chatting, Paul was asked to show his ability on one of the out-of-tune and right-handed guitars. McCartney tuned the instrument and played it upside down, which immediately impressed the skeptical young Lennon.

Paul is said to have performed Eddie Cochran's "20 Flight Rock," Gene Vincent's "Be Bop a Lu La," a medley of Little Richard tunes, and Jerry Lee Lewis' "Whole Lotta Shakin' Goin' On" for this occasion as an informal audition for the band. There was a piano in the room which Paul played as well, possibly on the Little Richard tunes, and likely on the Jerry Lee Lewis song.

Paul's ability to play both the guitar and the piano while singing and knowing the words was of great interest to John, who even at an early age realized that the other members of his band lacked potential. Lennon recognized that Paul was quite a

MUSIC THAT INFLUENCED THE QUARRYMEN

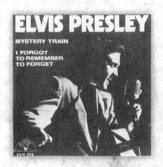

natural performer, and was appealing to the eye as well, which would hopefully attract birds (ladies) to their performances.

Paul also recalls John being slightly drunk on ale on this occasion.

While Vaughan's role in the history of the band is insurmountable, his tenure as an actual bandmate was extremely brief. He filled in only occasionally and likely never played with the band after McCartney became a member.

After the show the Quarrymen, along with Vaughan who did not perform with that band that day, lied their way into a Woolton pub where they discussed the young lefty possibly joining the band.

He likely kept it to himself but John was a bit conflicted about letting Paul join his band because even though it would make the Quarrymen better, it could possibly result in John not remaining the best member of the band which he led.

Ultimately Lennon decided that having a young, good looking, and talented band member on his side would be better than dooming the band to failure without him.

Remarkably on this historic day, a man in the audience recorded a portion of the show.

Bob Molyneux dragged his Grundig tape recorder to the event and captured a brief bit of history. It is likely but unconfirmed that he taped the first show, which was forgotten about until he rediscovered it 1994, selling it to Sotheby's auction house.

Although the quality of the audio is well below professional grade, the crude recording captures a young Lennon enthusiastically performing a Donegan song, "Puttin' on the Style," as well as Elvis Presley's "Baby Let's Play House."

"Puttin' on the Style," which was the current No. 1 in England on the day John and Paul met, is a great example of what was popular when the band began, and what they each enjoyed separately before being joined together.

These early influences shaped them individually,

thus eventually contributing to the Beatles' collective sound.

As the "King of Skiffle," Donegan inspired a young George Harrison to take up guitar, and Ringo Starr would enter the world of music as a member of the Eddie Clayton Skiffle Group, which had a fair amount of Donegan songs in their repertoire. Lennon thought the music didn't sound all that hard to play, so he decided to take up banjo, and ultimately guitar.

American singer, songwriter and folk guitarist Woody Guthrie

Likewise, in November 1956 Paul attended a Donegan performance at the Empire Theater in Liverpool and decided he wanted to trade in the trumpet he received for his 14th birthday the previous June for a guitar.

Another artist the individual Beatles were listening to and influenced by during this key time in their history was Elvis Presley. The wide-eyed young Beatles paid close attention to style, and no other artist captured this as well as Elvis. His early music left an indelible mark on the tastes of all four individual Beatles in their youth, thus played an essential role in the formation of the Beatles.

As the band took shape, the Beatles continued to

The Quarrymen, November 23, 1957.
Left to Right: Colin Hanton, Paul McCartney,
Len Garry, John Lennon, Eric Griffiths

on October 18, 1957 when they played the Conservative Club at New Clubmoor Hall in Liverpool. McCartney played lead guitar that evening. His first night jitters were said to have caused his performance to be noticeably uneven, specifically on "Guitar Boogie," a 1946 instrumental hit for American country and western performer Arthur Smith. American country was yet another favorite style of music that all four of the individual Beatles found themselves drawn to at a young age, another example of their open minds in terms of what music they enjoyed.

McCartney also told guitar virtuoso and inventor Les Paul that one of the first shows he performed with the Beatles began with them singing "How High the Moon," although beyond McCartney's recollection this is unsubstantiated.

Paul was said to have been very embarrassed about his disappointing debut with the band, and in an attempt to win back Lennon, he showed him a song he wrote called "I Lost My Little Girl." Lennon then played some of his original songs he had "dreamt up," and a songwriting partnership was instantly born.

The band continued with frequent lineup changes. Davis and Whalley left the group, as did Vaughan, the man who brought the two young songwriters together. Shotton left the group but remained close friends with Lennon, and this also resulted in the washboard being permanently dropped from the lineup. By the end of 1957 the Quarrymen were a five-piece band with Griffiths, Hanton, and Garry joining Lennon and McCartney. ◆

be impressed with his charisma and persona, as well as his success. Not only did emulating Elvis seem like a good way to "get chicks," the Beatles were also big fans of his music. They performed dozens of Presley's songs throughout their career, although none for their official recordings.

A couple weeks after initiating the first meeting between John and Paul, Vaughan bumped into McCartney (who recalls cycling around Liverpool) and told him that the band was very interested in having him become a member. Paul thought about it for a bit before accepting the offer, becoming an official "Quarry Man" in early August 1957.

On August 7, 1957 the band played their first show at the recently opened Cavern Club, located on Mathew Street in Liverpool. Although McCartney was an official member of the band at this point and likely already rehearsing with his new bandmates, he did not perform in the inaugural Cavern Club gig as he was away at scout camp.

McCartney's official debut with the band came

CHAPTER 2:
ENTER GEORGE HARRISON

IN EARLY 1958 A NEW MEMBER OF THE BAND WAS INTRODUCED, A YOUNG SCHOOLMATE OF MCCARTNEY'S NAMED GEORGE HARRISON. PAUL AND GEORGE WOULD RIDE THE BUS TO SCHOOL TOGETHER AND EVEN THOUGH GEORGE WAS A BIT YOUNGER, THE TWO BONDED OVER MUSIC, A PASSION THEY BOTH SHARED AND COULD ENDLESSLY DISCUSS.

SOURCES GREATLY VARY on the specific date and location of the first introduction of George to the rest of the band and its leader John Lennon, although many agree it was February 6, 1957. Harrison was a determined player who had zero experience. He had no band of his own although he was a member of the Rebels with his brother Peter Harrison, who played only one show. Despite this lack of credentials, Harrison impressed Lennon when he was able to play "Raunchy," a 1958 instrumental hit by Bill Justis.

Harrison's love for American guitar-based rock and roll gave him a lot in common with Lennon and although Lennon objected to letting "a kid" into the band, perseverance would pay off and eventually Harrison would become a member. Although he was never officially asked to join, George would hang out at rehearsals and fill in for any missing band member, which was a frequent occurrence.

Griffiths was indirectly fired from the band because they thought there were too many guitarists and they knew George was a superior player with more potential. The young amateur band would simply just not inform Griffiths of rehearsals or shows.

After Whalley and Gary both became ill and left the band at the beginning of 1958, a piano

George Harrison, circa 1950

player named John "Duff" Lowe became an occasional member. Lowe performed on the band's first recording, a cover of Buddy Holly's "That'll Be the Day," and an original Harrison/ McCartney composition called "In Spite of All the Danger."

John, Paul, George, Colin, and Duff performed on this homemade "vanity" recording on (or about) July 12, 1958 at Phillips Sound Recording Services. This "studio" was located in owner Percy Phillips' living room. The two songs they were cut onto 78 rpm shellac acetate and although the band didn't have enough money to take the disc home the day they recorded it, they eventually did raise the funds to get it from Phillips. The deal was that each band member would get to keep the record for a week, and

it ultimately found its way into the sole possession of Lowe, who held onto it for over 20 years. "Duff" eventually sold it to McCartney for an undisclosed price in 1981.

The Beatles would only record one song for official release that was a Buddy Holly number. In addition to that first amateur record, however, there are several recordings that exist of the dozen or so songs that they learned through Holly.

"That'll Be the Day" was a hit for Holly in May 1957. It was actually recorded twice, first in June '56 whern it was ultimately released as the B-side to "Rockin' Around with Ollie Vee" on the Decca label, credited to Buddy Holly. It was recorded again and the credit went to Buddy Holly and the Crickets in order to avoid contractual issues. That second version was recorded in February 1957 and released on the Brunswick label in September, hitting No. 1 in November of that year.

Holly is said to have gotten the title of the song from a phrase that John Wayne used several times in the movie "The Searchers," which is also how the skiffle-turned-British Invasion band the Searchers, originating from Liverpool, took their name.

All of the Beatles were enthusiastic fans of Holly and closely followed his output. John, who was always self-conscious about having to wear spectacles, was especially impressed by the fact that a rock and roller played guitar, sang, led his own band, wrote songs, and wore glasses.

On the Quarrymen's recorded performance of "That'll Be the Day" John sings lead with Paul adding harmony vocals. George likely sings also, but his contribution is hidden by the hisses of the recording. John, Paul, and George all play guitars and, although they are very hard to detect, Hanton and Lowe allegedly play on the recording as well.

Despite its poor quality, the recording displays the

confident and professional level of musicianship that the young and eager band possessed. They clearly rehearsed and took pride in their performance, even if the intention of the recording was just so they could hear themselves.

Not only was the music of the Crickets vital to the creation of the Beatles, but the lyrical content was also a great inspiration. Specifically influential was the frequently used theme of the man as the one in charge, and the woman should follow orders or suffer consequences.

"Crying, Waiting, Hoping" was a song Holly initially recorded in December 1958 as a demo in his Manhattan apartment, accompanying himself on a guitar. After his death the tapes were discovered and given to producer Jack Hansen to finish in what was hoped to be a respectful fashion true to Holly's original intentions.

There were six songs discovered from these final unfinished recordings. The Beatles were drawn to both sides the Holly's posthumous released single "Peggy Sue Got Married," which continued the story of Holly's fictional love interest. A singer referring to a different song of his own was also a quality that the Beatles found endearing. They were aware that bands such as theirs would help preserve the legacy of their hero, whose passing undoubtedly upset them greatly.

After flipping the record over and quickly learning the B-side "Crying, Waiting, Hoping," the Beatles rehearsed the song frequently and were well prepared for the January 1, 1962 recording.

The initial Holly recording had him pausing between the words in the title and was subsequently turned into a call and response song with the background singers playing a very prominent role. Paul and John both added effective background vocals as all the band members began to relax and get more comfortable in the studio including Pete Best, who confidentially contributes on the song. Harrison executed a wonderful reproduction of the solo from the Holly release (played by Don Arnone on the record).

After the auditions the Beatles would perform the song one final time for the BBC on August 6, 1963, this time with Ringo on the drums. On this occasion the song had a different energy which revolves around the drums and their interplay with the singers. Certain early songs have multiple versions recorded and the evolution is clear as their music progressed, specifically on drums.

Paul McCartney, circa 1956 or 1957

It is not known if "Crying, Waiting, Hoping" was ever considered for an official recording by the band for any of their EMI releases.

"Reminiscing" was a song that was written by Buddy Holly to record with King Curtis, who was a favorite saxophonist of the Beatles, even if they weren't aware of it.

"King" Curtis Ousley was raised in Fort Worth, Texas and began playing saxophone in 1946 at the age of 12, taking inspiration from jazz, R&B, and popular music from the '40s and earlier. A well-known and in-demand session man, King Curtis appears on the Coasters' "Yakety Yak," and "A Lover's Question" by Clyde McPhatter, both in 1958, and "Boys" by the Shirelles in 1960, which of course the Beatles would record in early '62.

Sadly Curtis would be stabbed to death in 1971 outside of his New York apartment, leaving behind an extremely impressive but too small body of work.

In late '58 Buddy Holly requested that Curtis fly down to Clovis, New Mexico to record "Reminiscing" with him. It's said that the song was written by Holly, who gave Curtis credit as a "gift" for traveling so far for his session.

Tragedy struck just a few months later when Holly was killed in a plane crash. The recording was shelved until it was released on the posthumous album also titled *Reminiscing*, which was comprised of assorted previously unreleased Holly material and completed under the supervision of Norman Petty with overdubs by the Fireballs.

Holly's influence on the Beatles, particularly in the early, pre-EMI days, is immeasurable. Holly would remain a favorite of the band, even after they developed past his teachings.

"In Spite of All the Danger" was an early Holly-inspired song written by McCartney and credited to McCartney/Harrison, the only such occasion when this combination would occur.

As Paul explains, it was he who wrote the song and George played the guitar solo. The young and naive performers had no idea of royalties, writing credits, ownership, and publishing rights. They seemingly assumed that whoever played the solo on the song got writing credit as well.

It is likely that McCartney worked slowly on the song throughout '58, and it's obvious the band again rehearsed it thoroughly with the understanding that they would have only one chance to get it right as they all gathered around a single microphone.

A young and impressionable Paul was trying very hard to rewrite an Elvis song when he penned "In Spite of All the Danger." Although he admits he indeed had one in mind, he has never revealed which one. Sources vary (as opinions do) on which Presley song it was.

Elvis' "Trying to Get to You," a Sun Records release from 1955, contains the lyric "In spite of all that I've been through" and is widely considered to be the one that Paul "borrowed" for his early composition. "Heartbreak Hotel" from January 1956 and "Love Me" from September of the same year share similar elements as does "It is No Secret (What God Can Do)" from Elvis' 1957 Christmas album.

Ultimately, it's very likely that Paul took features from several different songs, including background "oohs" and "ahhs," and melded them together.

Although the words were written by Paul, the lead singer on "In Spite of All the Danger" was John, still the undisputed front man of the band, with George and Paul doing their best imitation of the Jordanaires.

After recording the song it was left behind, falling out of their act for more interesting covers or originals that they thought were better than Paul's cautious tale of love.

As 1959 rolled around things weren't looking too promising for the youthful gang from Liverpool.

In January after a drunken brawl cost the band any future jobs, Colin Hanton quit by simply getting off the bus with his drums and never contacting the band members again. Through the rest of '59, the three remaining Quarrymen rarely played in public.

George even joined another group, the Les Stewart Quartet. That band was booked to be the resident band at the Casbah Club, which was slated to open in August in the basement of a home of a woman named Mona Best. The space itself was a former coal cellar, and Best was anxious to open the club to give young Liverpudlians a safe place to enjoy themselves and experience live local music.

Ken Brown was a member of the Les Stewart Quartet and was very involved in helping Best set up the teenage social club. Stewart was upset with Brown for missing too many rehearsals and as the argument got more heated Harrison and Brown quit the group, effectively disbanding it.

Harrison then contacted Lennon and McCartney, and along with Brown the four-member lineup performed for the opening night of the Casbah Club on August 29, 1959, possibly with Paul on

drums. Brown was a member of the band for just about a month until an argument over money led him to either leave or get fired.

Harrison, McCartney, and Lennon also helped paint the Casbah Club's walls with a large spider web, dragons, and many flowers as well as stars on the ceiling in preparation for the opening. John's then-girlfriend and future wife, Cynthia Powell, assisted by painting a silhouette of Lennon using white paint on a black wall.

After playing every Saturday night for about two months at the successful underground cellar club, the Quarrymen quit their residency over an argument about money involving Brown getting paid by Best for a show in which he didn't perform. The Quarrymen would eventually perform there again and frequently visit the club.

Shortly after the falling out a group called the Black Jacks, which featured Brown as well as Mona's son Pete, became the resident band.

The remaining three members of the Quarrymen changed their name to Johnny and the Moondogs for a brief time. Under that name they auditioned for "TV Star Search" in Liverpool. The TV talent show was hosted by Carroll Levis, a Canadian-born radio and television personality who moved to England in the 1930s. Johnny and the Moondogs were selected for the finals in Manchester and traveled to perform in the hopes of winning a live spot on Levis' show "Discoveries."

According to Paul, the three singing Moondogs performed "Think it Over" and "Rave On," both Buddy Holly tunes from 1958.

"Think it Over" was written by Holly along with Jerry Allison, drummer from the Crickets, and Norman Petty, who produced much of Holly's work. Petty, along with co-writer Bill Tilghman wrote "Rave On" with Sonny West, who originally recorded the song in February 1958. West and Tilghman also co-wrote "Oh Boy!" which was first released as "All My Love" by West in February 1957. Holly promptly covered the song and renamed it, and the Quarrymen and Moondogs likely performed it frequently, although no recordings are known to exist.

For the TV audition the three performed "Think it Over" with John singing but not playing guitar, because his had either broken or been stolen. Paul stood on one side of him with George on the other, with the necks of their guitars facing opposite directions. Lennon sang lead with a hand on each of his bandmates' shoulders and Harrison and McCartney chimed in with the proper response in their own unique way, although never straying too far from the original.

As Harrison explained, an act would perform and the crowd would cheer, then whoever got the highest score on the "Clap-o-meter" would be declared the winner and would advance to the next round.

Unfortunately the band had to hurry to catch the last bus to Liverpool and never did get to find out how well they scored on the "Clap-o-meter." According to McCartney, however, Lennon was able to get his hands on a new guitar that evening.

In January 1960 the band added a new member in Stuart Sutcliffe. A gifted and talented painter, he was briefly a member of the Beatles in an era where looking good was almost as important as the ability to perform.

Sutcliffe's father, Charles, was a wartime nautical engineer who moved his family to Liverpool when his son was an infant. Charles was frequently away from home for long stretches of time and when he was home he was abusive to his wife, which was witnessed by the observant and sensitive pre-bohemian son.

After an appearance at the Casbah Coffee Club, Lennon convinced Sutcliffe to use the money he won from an art contest to buy a Höfner bass and join the band. Although familiar with several other instruments, Sutcliffe was a novice bass player at best. There are tapes of the band rehearsing from May 1960 which reveal his limitations, as well as the natural ability of the other players.

The artist improved slightly during his tenure and he gained popularity not so much for his elementary performing, but for his image of being cool and wearing Ray-Ban sunglasses, which were new to the Liverpool audience.

Lennon and Sutcliffe became close friends, moving into an apartment together in early 1960. McCartney admitted to feeling envious of their relationship and having to "take a back seat."

Even in the band's earliest conceptions, everybody had their moment to sing a number and shine on "center stage," similar to the formula of Elvis Presley movies and countless other musicals from the era that inspired the Beatles in so many ways. Sutcliffe's "center stage" moment came when he sang "Love Me Tender," which would garner the most applause. This resulted in jealousy from the very competitive McCartney, who was frequently, albeit justifiably, critical of his bandmate's performance.

After deciding to leave the band and stay behind in Germany with his fiancé, Astrid Kirchherr, to focus on his painting and teaching art, Sutcliffe began suffering from terrible headaches. Sadly this led to his death in April 1962 at age 22 which greatly affected Lennon, who had been very close to him since they were introduced by mutual friend Bill Harry at the Liverpool College of Art.

Harry was born in Liverpool and was the founder of *The Mersey Beat* newspaper, Liverpool's premier entertainment source dedicated to local music. At age 13, Harry created his first magazine, a science fiction periodical called *Biped* which was printed on a Gestetner stencil duplicator, a very early version of a photocopier.

While learning a great deal about printing while at Liverpool College of Art, Harry started several other magazines as well, primarily about film and music. After being introduced to rock and roll Harry met Cass and the Casanovas and Rory Storm and the Hurricanes, and began to write about "the scene." Harry surmised that Liverpool was like New Orleans at the turn of the century, but with "rock 'n'

From left: Pete Best, Astrid Kirchherr, Bill Harry, Stu Sutcliffe, Rory Storm and the Hurricanes (bottom right)

roll instead of jazz," which was remarkably prophetic from a 1961 point of view.

Harry attempted to get stories he had written about the rock and roll scene printed, but the local newspapers refused to change their policies, dealing strictly in jazz. In 1961 he formed his own magazine which would cover all music from a wide area surrounding Liverpool. His coverage was similar to that of a policeman's beat, as he had a daily route or specific section he would "patrol."

The Beatles were written about in *The Mersey Beat* so often some joked it should have been called *The Mersey Beatles* instead. The magazine named them the most popular band of the Mersey area in January '62, edging out Storm and his band with their "all-Starr" drummer.

Lennon would present Harry with "a few hundred" drawings, poems, and stories, telling him to use what he wanted and credit the "Beatcomber," similar to the *Daily Express*' "Beachcomber."

Brian Epstein, by then the Beatles' manager, encouraged Harry to make the paper a nationally printed news magazine and subsequently *The Mersey Beat* became *Music Echo*. With worldwide attention being placed on the area the magazine became the standard guide for the entire beat scene.

Epstein promised Harry that he would have complete editorial control of *Music Echo*, but it was soon revealed that Epstein had plans of his own, causing Harry to resign and move to London where he became a public relations agent. Harry would be directly involved with PR for the Kinks and the Hollies. He quickly widened his clientele by adding Pink Floyd, Jethro Tull, Procol Harum, David Bowie, Led Zeppelin, the Beach Boys, Clouds, Ten Years After, Free, Mott the Hoople, and many others to his list. Harry's reputation was such that when Bob Dylan visited England in May 1965 he would request Harry as his personal tour guide.

Nearly a half-century after he published the first issue, Harry was asked by the British Council to revive *The Mersey Beat* to celebrate Liverpool's International Beatle Week, and the magazine returned to publication with a special issue in August 2009. ◆

CHAPTER 3:
NAME CHANGES

AT SOME POINT IN EARLY 1960 STU SUTCLIFFE SUGGESTED A NAME CHANGE TO THE BEATALS, AN INTENTIONAL MISSPELLING OF THE NAME OF THE BEETLES, RIVAL TO THE BLACK REBELS IN THE 1953 MARLON BRANDO MOTORCYCLE GANG FILM "THE WILD ONE."

SHORTLY AFTERWARD THE BAND changed the name to the Silver Beetles (correcting the spelling of Beetles) so it would sound similar to Buddy Holly's Crickets. At first the name was Long John and the Silver Beetles, after the villain in Robert Louis Stevenson's 1883 novel "Treasure Island."

In April 1960 Paul and John would also perform as a duo, calling themselves the Nerk Twins when they performed at the Fox and Hounds, a pub in Caversham owned by McCartney's cousin Betty Robbins and her husband Mike Robbins.

Local booking agent and coffee shop owner Allan Williams began "managing" the band in May 1960. He frequently let them play at his club, the Jacaranda, located near the art college that Lennon and Sutcliffe attended, which was close to the Liverpool Institute where McCartney was a student.

Williams, of Welsh descent, attempted to become a singer while in his teens and landed in Liverpool in 1958. He opened the Jacaranda, a club popular with students from the nearby art colleges. When Lennon and Sutcliffe asked to play "The Jac" they wound up painting and redecorating the building, finally performing there in May 1960. Also in May or June 1960, the Beatles were hired to play behind English Beat poet Royston Ellis, who had previously performed at the Liverpool Institute.

Williams began to book paying shows for the Silver Beetles at other venues as well. He also ran an exotic dance club called New Cabaret Artistes and one dancer would only perform with a live accompanying band. Williams hired the group primarily because he knew they didn't have day jobs and would be readily available. The band was unfamiliar with the "Gypsy Fire Dance" which the dancer suggested; instead they played the "Theme to Harry Lime" (also known as the "Third Man Theme") as the dancers performed. From a musician's viewpoint they weren't thrilled at such an engagement, clearly knowing that

Johnny Gentle with George in the background, Carl Perkins (inset)

in Liverpool.

Brian Kelly (known as Beeky or BK) was the promoter for this and a series of other shows and had booked the band to perform on an upcoming bill with Taylor. After Parnes offered them the job backing Gentle, the band failed to show up for the performance with Taylor, disappointing fans as well as Kelly, who vowed to never hire them again.

With the Silver Beats backing him, Gentle's set included "It Doesn't Matter Anymore" and "Raining in My Heart," both posthumous releases for Buddy Holly, "I Need Your Love Tonight," a 1959 hit for Elvis Presley, "Poor Little Fool," a Rick Nelson hit in 1958, "(I Don't Know Why) But I Do," a Clarence Frogman Henry song from May 1961, and "C'mon Everybody," originally done by Eddie Cochran in 1958. The Silver Beats' initial performance with Gentle came shortly after Cochran was killed in an auto accident that also injured Gene Vincent.

While on the tour Gentle wrote the song "I've Just Fallen for Someone" with help from Lennon, and Adam Faith would record the song in 1962.

Gentle was very pleased with the Beatles as a background band, and surprised them by showing up at the Grosvenor Ballroom in Liscard, Wallassey on July 2, 1960. The amicable reunion featured Gentle joining the band for a few numbers.

During this period George adopted the name Carl Harrison, after Carl Perkins, John became Long John from the Stevenson novel, Paul took the name Paul Ramon (later to become the name of the 1970s punk band the Ramones), and Sutcliffe was Stuart de Staël after French painter Nicolas de Staël.

George taking on Perkins' name is just a small example of the huge impact the rock pioneer had on the Beatles.

Perkins was an American rockabilly singer/ songwriter who immensely influenced the sound

the clientele was not there to hear the music, but to see the other sights. From the view of three young men, however, it was an intriguing invite and it was a paying gig, which was always of interest to the band.

Williams booked the band's first extended engagements in Hamburg and drove the tour van crowded with the band and their equipment. In 1961 band members would have a falling out with Williams over the amount of money he thought he was owed for setting up "the Hamburg thing." He was rather critical of them immediately afterwards, but eventually mended fences and became part of the first wave of Beatlemania nostalgia in the 1970s.

Johnny Gentle was a British pop singer who was touring Scotland in May 1960. The Silver Beetles were selected by Larry Parnes, a successful producer throughout the '50s and early '60s, to be Gentle's backing band. On May 14, 1960 the band performed as the Silver Beats on a bill with the Deltones and King Size Taylor and the Dominoes at Lathom Hall

From left to right: Alan Williams, his wife Beryl, Lord Woodbine (sitting) Stuart Sutcliffe, Paul McCartney, George Harrison, and Pete Best

of the Beatles. McCartney stated "if there were no Carl Perkins, there would be no Beatles." While McCartney's accolades may be slightly overstated, Perkins' catalog of music undoubtedly brought great inspiration to the band.

One quality that consistently impressed the Beatles was the ability of an artist to write, sing, and perform their own music. As they began writing songs of their own, these were the types of songs they were trying to create.

Among the Perkins songs the young Beatles performed live, including some kept well into the recording era, were "Sure to Fall (In Love with You)," "Lend Me Your Comb," "Matchbox" and its B-side "Your True Love," and "Gone, Gone, Gone" (not to be confused with the Everly Brothers song of the same name). They also included two songs that would land on the Beatles' fourth LP, *Beatles For Sale*, "Honey Don't" and "Everybody's Trying to Be My Baby."

"Boppin' the Blues" was a Perkins song the band reportedly did very early in its performing days, although no exact records exist. However, a close look at the song clearly reveals why they might be attracted to it. A 1956 Sun Records single for Perkins, "Boppin'" sings of the blues as the cure for a sickness, placing music on an even greater pedestal. It is a song about dancing which was certain to get the people moving, a frequent request from club owners.

Some of the heroes and/or inspirations of the band drifted away and never returned, others were surpassed, yet the sound of Perkins was one that the band carried with them throughout the years.

Finding the right drummer proved to be an ongoing struggle in the band's early years.

Tommy Moore was a drummer for a very brief time, coming to the band through his ties to

From left to right: The Big Three at the Cavern Club, the Beatles with Tommy Moore, Pete Best (top right)

Williams. The band knew, however, that they desperately needed a permanent drummer.

During Moore's short stint, the Silver Beetles lost the chance to audition to become the backup band for Billy Fury, possibly because Moore was late to show up. Johnny Hutchinson of the Big Three sat in for the first part of the audition until Moore showed up, which was said to have greatly annoyed Lennon.

After their stint with Gentle, Moore was unhappy with the conditions of the tour and left the group, also making it known he was not enjoying the poor treatment he was getting from John Lennon.

Again finding themselves drummer-less, the band played a show at the Garston Baths in Liverpool where John invited anybody who could play drums to join them on stage. A tough and talentless drummer named "Ronnie" decided that he was going to join the band, whether they wanted him or not. Lennon phoned Williams to ask him to come and help defuse the situation, and Lennon never asked for volunteers anymore.

While once again lamenting the fact that they couldn't find a drummer the bandmates heard the sound of beating drums, eventually tracking it down to a space above the National Cash Register Co. offices. The drummer practicing was Norman Chapman, who was asked to join the band. Chapman agreed but had to quit after only a few shows when he was called up for national service.

During some of the periods when the band lacked a drummer, McCartney filled in as best he could. He was said to be competent but needed some training. Paul complained of not being able to sing and play at once, and he much preferred playing a guitar or fill in on bass if Sutcliffe was unable to perform.

In August 1960 the Beatles finally hired a steady drummer.

Pete Best was playing in a band called the Black Jacks with Chas Newby and Bill Barlow, as well as Ken Brown who had joined after leaving the Quarrymen. Black Jacks was also what Lennon briefly called his band before the Quarrymen were officially named, and also the title of a popular skiffle song released by Sonny Stewart and his Skiffle Kings (as the B-side to "The Northern Line") in August 1957. Best's band may have come up with the common term on their own.

As Best's Black Jacks were on the verge of disbanding, it was McCartney who recruited the drummer to join the Beatles instead. Tour time was drawing near and they quickly needed a drummer for their already booked visit to Hamburg, Germany.

Bruno Koschmider was a German concert promoter who saw Liverpool band Derry and the Seniors, also managed by Williams, and hired them to perform at the Kaiserkeller in Hamburg. After a couple of months of successful shows, Koschmider contacted Williams and asked for another band from Liverpool to play the Indra, another club he owned in Hamburg. Williams offered the Beatles.

On August 12, 1960 Best auditioned for the Beatles, not realizing that they already made their choice to hire him and were fearful he would want more money if he knew how important his joining the band was to the upcoming visit to Germany.

Williams auditioned Best by asking him to perform a drum roll, which he did "cleverly enough;" with that he became a Beatle. Best played his first show with the band on August 17, 1960 at the Indra Club in Hamburg.

Best was a member of the band for almost exactly two years, joining in August 1960 and being fired in August 1962 to be replaced by Ringo Starr.

Randolph Peter Best was born in India in 1941 and raised in Liverpool by his mother Mona and his adoptive father Rory Best. Best's biological father was Donald Peter Scanland who died while serving as a marine engineer during World War II before his son was born. Scanland was also the father of Pete's older brother Rory.

The family moved into a very large home located at 8 Hayman's Green, later to be home to the Casbah Coffee Club. The family claims that the Mona pawned all of her jewelry and earthly possessions to gamble on a long shot, a horse named Never Say Die, which paid off and allowed them to purchase the impressive estate with an oversized cellar in 1957.

After his family purchased the large home Best asked his mother if he could have some of his friends over to hang out and listen to records in their basement, complaining that there weren't any locations where he and his teenage friends could socialize. That hangout eventually became the Casbah.

In 1960 Best became friends with Neil Aspinall who rented a room in the spacious house that had the coffee club in the basement. It was Best who suggested to the band that Aspinall become their driver because he was trustworthy and Harrison and McCartney were mutual acquaintances.

Rory Best's family business as sports promoters who also ran the Liverpool Stadium required him to travel frequently. During one of these extended business trips Aspinall and Mona Best began a lengthy romantic interlude which would result in Pete Best's half-brother, Roag, being born.

While Best fit in reasonably well with the band there always was an unspoken separation from the other three members who had a different type of closeness among them.

Best would sing lead on several songs including "Boys" and "Matchbox," which would remain in the act after his departure. He would also take his turn on center stage performing the Elvis song "Wild in the Country," a slow tempo ballad from the 1961 film of the same name.

Best also took the lead on the Joey Dee and the Starlighters' "Peppermint Twist" while Paul played drums, and also sang an unnamed song that McCartney wrote for him, possibly "Dance" or "Twist in the Streets."

As the band began getting more famous each member had his own individual group of fans. The Best crowd was especially loyal, calling him "mean, moody, and magnificent."

After almost two years with Best on board, the Beatles auditioned for EMI records. Producer George Martin was a bit critical of the band's drummer,

Neil Aspinall (inset)

When Best was dismissed, Aspinall threatened to quit his now steady paying job with the Beatles, however Best talked him out of it, telling him to think reasonably.

The August 23 edition of *The Mersey Beat* read "Beatles change drummer," prompting hundreds of upset fans to protest and hold a vigil outside of Mona Best's house and sign petitions in the hopes of getting their drummer back, all to no avail.

Epstein offered to manage a new band built around Best. The drummer declined, joining Lee Curtis and the All Stars, who eventually became Pete Best and the All Stars, hoping to capitalize on the familiar name after Curtis left the group. The All Stars signed with Decca Records and released a single called "I'm Gonna Knock On Your Door" which was not a hit.

Best later moved to the United States, forming the Pete Best Four/Pete Best Combo, and eventually retired from the music business in 1968. He became a civil servant for 20 years, then returned to the music business in 1988, forming the Pete Best Band and occasionally performing and recording.

Four days after firing Best the Beatles traveled to Hamburg and performed there for the first time on August 17, 1960. That began a residency that lasted until October 3.

Their first night was sparsely attended, with the crowd consisting mostly prostitutes and their patrons. The Beatles were told to turn down their amplifiers after the tenant who lived above the club complained.

The Beatles' challenging schedule called for them to play six hours each weeknight, with three 30-minute breaks. On Saturdays they played from 7 p.m. until 3 a.m. with four 30-minute rest periods, and Sunday shows ran from 5 p.m. until 1:30 a.m., with five full 30-minute breaks.

Koschmider allowed the band to reside

suggesting they replace him on the record. Martin had no concern about who performed when they played live.

The band members were questioning their fourth member's abilities as well, wondering if Best was a contributing factor to the failed Decca Records audition. Throughout his tenure Best's drumming remained adequate, though he was frequently criticized by McCartney for not being aggressive enough. The other band members were also very fond of Ringo Starr, not only for his drumming abilities but his personality as well.

Best wasn't in tune with the rest of the band, not quite gelling with the others and failing to inspire the feeling that John, Paul, and George experienced when they performed with Ringo.

On August 15, 1962, Best was told by Epstein that he was out of the group, leaving the drummer devastated.

temporarily in a room behind the screen in a local cinema called the Bambi Kino, which was less than luxurious.

The young, wide-eyed Beatles were very impressed with the city of Hamburg, with its bright lights and grown-up activities.

Before the band's second night at the Indra Club, Williams pressed them to be more energetic in their performance in an attempt to win over the audience. He encouraged them to "make a show" which when translated to German was "Mak Show." This quickly became the band's battle cry during their first stay in Hamburg, and word got out quickly about this new and exciting act in town.

The savage young Beatles played 48 consecutive nights at the Indra Club, using the long show hours as a chance to improve their stage craft. After a series of noise complaints from the woman who lived above the club, the band played their 48th and final show there on October 3.

The Indra Club was subsequently turned back into an exotic dancing showplace, and the Beatles were moved to a larger club called the Kaiserkeller, which had a nautical theme and was also owned by Koschmider. The Beatles would play 56 consecutive

The Beatles and Horst Fascher

nights at the Kaiserkeller, October 5 through November 29, 1960.

On occasion, when the band was feeling low and discouraged, it was John who would help improve morale with the following call and response:

Lennon: "Where are we going boys?"
The band: "To the top, Johnny!"
Lennon: "To the top of what?"
The band: "To the toppermost of the poppermost."

During this period the Beatles alternated sets with fellow Liverpool band Rory Storm and the Hurricanes, one member of which was a drummer who went by the name Ringo Starr.

Former boxer Horst Fascher was the bouncer at the Kaiserkeller and became very good friends with the Beatles. He looked after the youthful and naive band in the rough red-light district of Germany, which was frequented by many servicemen, organized criminals, and prostitutes. Fascher had a reputation as a friendly and genial bouncer who was good to his friends but excellent at stopping trouble as it arose.

Fascher left midway through the Beatles' residency at the Kaiserkeller when he was persuaded to manage the Top Ten Club, a new Hamburg venue opened in late October '60 by German entrepreneur Peter Eckhorn.

The first band to perform at the Top Ten Club was the Jets, which featured English singer and guitarist Tony Sheridan. When it was Rory Storm and the Hurricanes' turn to play at the Kaiserkeller, the Beatles would often take the opportunity to visit their friend Fascher at the Top Ten Club. Fascher was associated with Sheridan, who had played at the Kaiserkeller before going to the rival club and playing there through 1963.

After earning a reputation as a capable and talented unit, the Beatles, or whatever name they were using at the time, were occasionally recruited as a backing band for solo singers. ◆

CHAPTER 4:
THE BEAT BROTHERS

IN JUNE 1961, DURING THEIR SECOND VISIT TO GERMANY, THE BEATLES WERE ASKED BY COMPOSER/ORCHESTRA LEADER/ POLYDOR PRODUCER BERT KAEMPFERT TO ACT AS THE BACKING BAND FOR SHERIDAN.

THE BAND MEMBERS HAD MET Sheridan during their first visit although not yet performed with him. It is reported the Beatles performed as Sheridan's backing band on a few occasions. Their recording session with Sheridan likely took place June 22, 1961, but there are conflicting reports on the exact date as well as the release dates for the material coming out of that session.

Recordings took place at the Friedrich Ebert Halle, a public hall used for school performances as well as occasional jazz and skiffle shows. Rock and roll was a scarce occurrence but the good sound quality of the room made for an excellent temporary recording space. Session notes are sparse, but it is known that on this day the quintet recorded "My Bonnie," "The Saints," "Cry for a Shadow," and "Why."

With inconsistent and greatly unsubstantiated beginnings, "My Bonnie" seems like an appropriate song to record on this uncertain date. The specific origins of the Scottish folk song, commonly titled "My Bonnie Lies Over the Ocean," are unknown, but the song perhaps dates back as far as 1746.

Charles Edward Stuart, grandson of King James II of England, was in a brief exile after his father, James III, was murdered during his attempt to reclaim the throne back from Great Britain. This movement was known as the Jacobite Cause. Stuart was known during his lifetime as Bonnie Prince Charlie, and he became a bit of a romantic figure, hiding and hopefully one day returning to save the land.

It's speculated that while being hunted for several months Charles disguised himself as a shipwrecked sailor simply called Mr. Sinclair or a woman named Betty Burke, tales of which are said to be greatly exaggerated.

How he got the nickname Bonnie also is widely speculated. The term bonnie means a good looking and attractive person, and the Prince fit the bill as an educated man of privilege with great influence and a handsome appearance.

While waiting for the Prince to return to power, his hopeful followers, or Jacobites, would sing the song "Bring back my Bonnie to me."

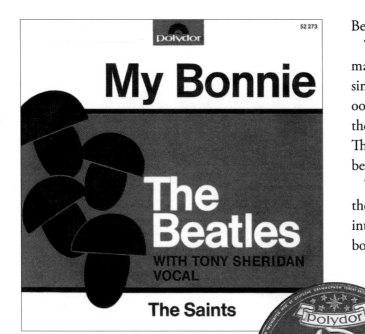

"My Bonnie" survived through oral tradition as it was sung by several generations without being formally written. It is likely that words were changed and verses were added. The tune became very familiar in port towns, of course frequented by sea merchants and sailors. Eventually "Bonnie" made its way to America where the sheet music was published in 1881 by American songwriter Charles E. Pratt under twin pseudonyms H.J. Fuller and J.T. Wood.

"My Bonnie" had been recorded by several artists, including a group of children and more notably Ray Charles, who did a soul/gospel version in 1959, which Sheridan and the Beatles likely enjoyed.

As the term Bonnie can be gender-neutral but also is a woman's name, it was a popular song in pubs all over the world. That popularity reached Hamburg where it was part of the acts of both Sheridan and the Beatles.

On their 1961 recording of the song, Sheridan handles the guitar solo with Harrison playing lead throughout the rest and John playing a rhythm guitar. Paul plays the bass, which he was quickly becoming more than just a little proficient at, while

Best's drumming was adequate but not remarkable.

The arrangement features an intro with the singer maintaining a slow and somber pace. Background singers (John, Paul and George) harmonize adding ooh's and aahs until the pace quickly increases and the song is sung in a rather contemporary style. The rendition has the sound and feel of what was becoming known as the "Mersey sound."

Two versions of the song were released, one with the intro sung in English, and another with the same intro in German. The rest of the tune is in English on both versions.

"My Bonnie" was released as a single on the Polydor label in October 1961, credited to Tony Sheridan and the Beat Brothers in Germany, where it reached No. 4. It should be noted that Beat Brothers was a more easily pronounced foreign phrase for an audience who wouldn't understand the misspelling of Beetle. In England "My Bonnie" was a single credited to Tony Sheridan and the Beatles.

It failed to chart, however it did play a pivotal role in the destiny of the band.

On the B-side of "My Bonnie" was a recording of another traditional song with uncertain origins. "The Saints," more commonly knowns as "When the Saints Go Marching In," dates back to America around the early 1900s. Its roots are traced to similar gospel songs from 1896 and 1908, the latter titled "When the Saints March in for Crowning."

In 1923 the Paramount Jubilee Singers performed the first known recorded version of the song. It later became a hit for Louis Armstrong in 1938.

Very likely the version that Sheridan and the Beat Brothers were modeling their performance after was the Fats Domino recording, released as the B-side to "Telling Lies" in January 1959. It wasn't a hit for Fats, but the eager Beatles and their circle no doubt had his version as part of their collections.

The recording sounds well-rehearsed as the

musicians play fluently together on this familiar tune, which gradually softens before the "big finish." The master tapes have long since been erased, and the session notes don't dictate the number of takes required to complete the song.

"Saints" was released as the B-side to "My Bonnie" in April 1962 in the U.K. where the Beatles, who were occasionally mistaken as a German import, were starting to draw attention.

"Why (Can't You Love Me Again)" was an original song that Sheridan penned with English songwriter Bill Crompton and recorded during the Friedrich Ebert Halle sessions which were likely held June 22-23, 1961.

Crompton had success in England in the early '60s, writing "The House of Bamboo," a Calypso release from Earl Grant, "The Heart of a Teenage Girl" by English pop singer Craig Douglas, and "Man of Mystery," an instrumental hit for the Shadows, all in 1960.

Along with the three singing Beatles, Sheridan executed a fine doo-wop performance, with the large room recording the acoustics of the minimally-orchestrated arrangement. Best's performance is barely audible with a notable flub approximately 1:27 into the song. For the rest of the band this was elementary level

material, even for the novice but quickly improving McCartney on bass.

Sheridan sings but does not play the guitar on the track, which was released in July 1963 on a Sheridan EP titled *My Bonnie*. The EP included the title track, "Why (Can't You Love Me Again)," "The Saints," and a Beatle instrumental called "Cry for a Shadow," recorded during one of the two Friedrich Ebert Halle recordings.

"Cry for a Shadow" was an instrumental credited to Harrison/Lennon, the only known acknowledgement of this songwriting combination. It was originally known as the "Beatle Bop." The song is said to be the Beatles taking a poke at the Shadows, who were Cliff Richard's backing band, and an instrumental group that the Beatles thought very little of as performers.

Cliff Richard is a British pop singer who influenced the band in a minor way, primarily in terms of fashion and style rather than music. A teenage Richard, whose birth name was Harry Webb, joined a band called the Drifters, not to be confused with the American doo-wop/R&B act of the same name. Bandmates encouraged him to change his name in honor of his musical hero Little Richard, while the name Cliff was selected to be synonymous with "rock."

With the Drifters, Richard would release the single "Move It" in 1958, written by Ian Samuel, the guitarist at the time. It was initially to be the A-side to a cover of "Schoolboy Crush" (originally done by Bobby Helms) but the choice was reversed when the energy of the band's original material was heard.

"Move It" was considered by Lennon, as well as musical journalists, to be the first rock and roll record from England worth listening to, and it is widely regarded as the first rock and roll song to originate outside the United States.

The song itself is a Presley-esque rocker that serves as a tutorial

on how to rock, using terminology and phrases about "rhythm getting to your heart and soul," "move it and groove it," and an early declaration that rock will never die. The young and impressionable Beatles were certainly enthralled.

After "Move It," the Drifters had success with "High Class Baby," "Mean Streak," "Never Mind," and "Living Doll," which was their first No. 1 single.

When the American Drifters forced the English ones to change their name, Cliff's backups (which had sustained multiple lineup changes) became the Shadows. They continued to have great success with "Traveling Light," "A Voice in the Wilderness," "Fall in Love with You," "Please Don't Tease," "Nine Times Out of Ten," "I Love You," "Gee Whiz it's You," "A Girl Like You," "When the Girl in Your Arms is the Girl in Your Heart," "The Young Ones" (from the 1961 film of the same name), "I'm Looking Out the Window," "Do You Wanna Dance," "Summer Holiday," "Lucky Lips," "It's All in the Game," "The Twelfth of Never," and "The Minute You're Gone," several of which hit No. 1, either in the U.K. or elsewhere.

Cliff Richard and the Shadows toured the United States in 1960 with relatively positive results but never were able to "break through" as superstars as they had in the U.K. This was largely due to the general lack of interest by the record company.

As with many acts that influenced the Beatles, Cliff Richard and the Shadows had limited success as Beatlemania and the rest of the British Invasion bands rose to the top of the charts more consistently.

The Shadows were Hank Marvin and Bruce Welch on guitar and vocals and drummer Brian Bennett, with several rotating bass players and keyboardists. They were not "just" the backup band for Richard but were their own independent unit primarily "hired" by Richard.

The Shadows struck in June 1960 with the instrumental "Apache" following by hits "Geronimo," "Man of Mystery/The Stranger," "FBI," "The Frightened City," "Kon-Tiki," "Wonderful Land," "Dance On!" "Foot Tapper," "Atlantis," and "Shindig."

In 1964 "Theme for Young Lovers" and "The Rise and Fall of Flingle Bunt" were both hits in England. The Shadows' success continued although they were held to the middle of the charts by bands like the Beatles and other British Invasion groups who secured most of the top spots on every list around.

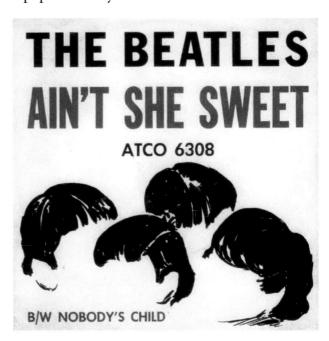

The Shadows disbanded by 1968, reuniting in the late '70s and enjoying renewed interest in their sound. They charted with covers of "Don't Cry for Me Argentina" and "Riders in the Sky" as well as the theme for the Academy Award winning film "The Deer Hunter."

As the Beatles were becoming highly regarded in their own right, they certainly learned from the Shadows. However the Beatles may have seen themselves as superior to the Shadows, considering them (but not all instrumental bands) a bit boring.

During their long performances at any of their assorted extended residencies, the Quarrymen/Beatles would have to get creative to fill the time without repeating too many songs. There are many claims of the band frequently using the Shadows' hit "Apache."

Although no recordings of the Beatles' live performance of "Apache" or any other instrumentals have ever surfaced, there are several

other instrumentals said to have been used in their appearances.

This list includes "Harry Lime," (the song they played at exotic dance club) which was popular as the "Third Man" theme, a 1949 artsy noir movie. Anton Karas wrote and performed the theme for that film accompanied by a zither, a string instrument that is either played by hand, with a bow, or plucked with a plectrum. How the Beatles recreated and arranged this instrumental hit with guitars and bass is highly intriguing, yet sadly unrecorded.

"Three Thirty Blues" is another instrumental the Beatles were said to have performed. It was the B-side to "Yep!" by Duane Eddy, which was a Top 20 hit when released in March 1959. The young Beatles would perform other songs of Eddy's throughout their career, never releasing anything officially.

When selecting instrumental tracks the band sometimes attempted to find ones that were obscure, but they weren't afraid of hits either. "Diamond" by Jet Harris and Tony Meehan is said to have been part of their act, although the song wasn't released until January 1963, and it's unlikely that the Beatles were still covering songs of that nature at that point in their careers.

"Hot as Sun," "Winston's Walk," and "Looking Glass" were all original instrumentals from the band's very early period, as was "Catswalk" also titled "Cat Call."

"Cry for a Shadow" was the Beatles' only released instrumental until late 1967.

While not classified as vocals, there are some recorded whoos and howls, presumably from Lennon and McCartney, and possibly Harrison. George plays a focused and well-crafted lead guitar, with John on rhythm guitar and Paul on bass, again displaying a prowess for the instrument almost instantly.

A third session would take place June 26, which was later in the same week as the Friedrich Ebert Halle sessions, this time at Studio Rahlstedt in the main city of Hamburg. This day would see the recording of "Ain't She Sweet," "Take Out Some Insurance on Me, Baby," and "Nobody's Child," which was also the B-side to the Sheridan recording of "Sweet Georgia Brown," recorded in May 1962.

Similar to the previous day's sessions, notes were inconsistent and it is not known which songs were recorded in which order.

"Ain't She Sweet" was written by Milton Ager and Jack Yellen, first published in 1927. Ager, a native of Chicago, had success as a songwriter throughout what is known as "The Roaring '20s" with hits like "I'm Nobody's Baby" in 1920, "Hard Hearted Hannah (The Vamp of Savannah)" and "Big Bad Bill is Sweet William Now" in 1924, and "Happy Days are Here Again" in 1929.

He composed "Ain't She Sweet" in 1927 for his daughter Shana, who would grow up to be a journalist for *Time* magazine and a correspondent for television's "60 Minutes," using her married name Shana Alexander.

The lyrics were written by American song and screenwriter Yellen, who also composed myriad film scores throughout the '30s. Some of Yellen's more well-known songs date back as far as "Are You from Dixie ('Cause I'm from Dixie Too)" in 1915, "Mama Goes Where Papa Goes" from 1923, and "Are You Havin' Any Fun?" from 1939, collaborating with Ager frequently along the way.

"Ain't She Sweet" was first recorded by Ben Bernie and His Orchestra, featuring Scrappy Lambert and Billy Hillpot in 1927.

The song was recorded consistently after its initial release, becoming an American standard (a standard being a song that was so common it was "standard" for every band to know it). As an example, "Ain't She Sweet" was recorded that same year by Gene Austin, Johnny Marvin, and Annette Hanshaw, as the song became instantly recognizable across the United States.

Along with "'Til There Was You," "September in the Rain," and "Falling in Love Again," these were the types of songs that the Beatles felt were a bit unusual for a rock band to perform. They may not have been considered "cool," but the genre is what helped the band stand out from the competition and ultimately achieve success.

Gene Vincent recorded "Ain't She Sweet" in 1956 with a performance that was slower and more subdued than his typical style. While not as aggressive as some of his other records, Vincent's version displayed depth, which was a quality the Beatles always looked for in both songs they enjoyed listening to and music they created.

The Quarrymen quickly added "Ain't She Sweet" to their act, slowly increasing the tempo and making it more upbeat or "rockin'" as they progressed as a band. Much of this influence came from the vocal German audiences who, according to Lennon, wanted a march, so the band hardened the sound as they continued to perform the song.

Why they selected an old American standard when they had their chance to record an original has always been a source of great speculation.

The Quarrymen may not have known they would have an occasion to record a song without Sheridan and thus had little time to rehearse an original. Further, they may have been unsure of the song's

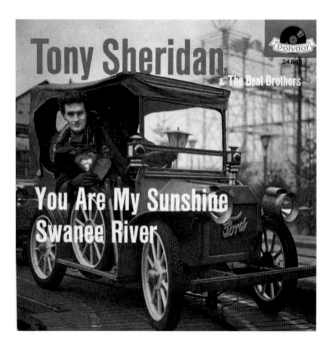

eventual fate, not wanting an original song to be "just a B-side" for another artist.

A lack of confidence is another possible factor for the young songwriters, who may have thought their original songs from this era that were not fully realized and not yet good enough to record.

In addition to the those possible explanations, the band was quite aware of their audience, and knew "Ain't She Sweet" was well-received by German fans. They hoped the song would create record sales, regardless of where it was released.

Ultimately "Ain't She Sweet" stayed unreleased until May 1964, when Polydor decided to get the most out of Beatlemania by releasing the song after leaving it in the vaults for almost three years. The Beatles felt they had far surpassed songs of this nature quickly and were rather dismissive of it upon the 1964 release.

Due to the lack of notes, the order in which the songs were recorded is unknown. The efficient band might have gotten through the songs so quickly that they found themselves with extra studio time, but details are very sparse.

It is also unknown how long these sessions lasted, however the band still had time to play at the Top Ten Club all three nights of the June recording sessions.

"Take Out Some Insurance On Me, Baby" was a 1959 song for American bluesman Jimmy Reed that Sheridan covered and recorded during the 1961 Hamburg sessions. The official title of the song is "If You Love Me Baby" written by Charles "Hoss" Singleton and Waldenese Hall.

Hall was the co-writer of the song and appears to have only two writing credits to his name. One is a 1959 B-side for American soul singer Jimmy Jones called the "Search is Over." The other is a Cliff Richard and the Shadows song called "Nine Times Out of Ten" which was featured in the 1961 musical film "The Young Ones."

On the other extreme is Singleton, an American songwriter who co-wrote more than 1,000 songs, most notably "Moon Over Naples" in 1965, an instrumental that was also recorded with lyrics as "Spanish Eyes,"

TONY SHERIDAN WITH THE BEATLES

MY BONNIE
CRY FOR A SHADOW
THE SAINTS · WHY

and "Strangers in the Night," initially an instrumental called "Beddy Bye," composed by Bert Kaempfert and recorded with lyrics added by Singleton for Frank Sinatra in 1966.

Other artists who Singleton wrote for include Ruth Brown and Her Rhythmakers, Moose Jackson and His Buffalo Bearcats, Rose Marie McCoy, Bobby Prince, Ella Fitzgerald, the Five Keys, Nat King Cole, Nappy Brown, Eartha Kitt, the Crewcuts, Les Paul and Mary Ford, Shirley and Lee, Elvis Presley, Little Willie John, the "5" Royales, Pat Boone, Tennessee Ernie Ford, Tommy Sands, Fats Domino, Brenda Lee, Gene Vincent, Ricky Nelson, Clyde McPhatter, Peggy Lee, Ernest Tubb and His Texas Troubadours, B.B. King, and literally hundreds of others.

It's not known when the Beatles became familiar with "Take Out Some Insurance On Me, Baby." They may have heard the record by Jones, or perhaps saw Sheridan perform it live. It is also possible they learned the song just prior to recording it, since it is a relatively simple tune that the experienced musicians could pick up quickly and finish recording with efficiency.

Reports are inconsistent and incomplete regarding when or if the Beatles ever performed the song live,

however there is a rather good chance Sheridan may have joined them for a song or two on occasion.

On the record George takes the lead guitar and Sheridan sings in his "Elvis style," Paul plays basic bass, and Best contributes minimal drums. John may be playing rhythm guitar on the track as well as sources vary. A drummer named Bernard "Pretty" Purdie (also known as the world's most recorded drummer) reportedly overdubbed additional tracks at a later, unknown date.

"Take Out Some Insurance On Me, Baby" was released as the B-side to "Ain't She Sweet" in May 1964 on the Polydor label. It came out again on July 1, 1964 as the B-side to "Sweet Georgia Brown" on the ATCO label.

"Nobody's Child" was one of the three songs recorded on June 24, the third and final day of sessions for Sheridan and the Beatles. It would also be released as a B-side to "Sweet Georgia Brown," which was recorded in May 1962.

Originally recorded by American country artist Hank Snow, the song was written by Cy Coben and Mel Foree. The song wasn't a hit when released in 1949 on the RCA label, although Snow would prominently feature in his live act.

In 1956 Donegan recorded it for his debut album *Lonnie Donegan Showcase* and the Beatles as well as Sheridan were no doubt fans of the album before they all merged together.

Foree was a songwriter and promoter who had a very long and successful career in Nashville. Coben was a New Jersey native who became a successful songwriter specializing primarily in novelty songs, writing "(When You See) Those Flying Saucers" for the Buchanan Brothers in 1947, and "The Old Piano Roll Blues" in 1950, which was done by Hoagy Carmichael and Cass Daley, Lawrence Cook, Cliff Steward and the San Francisco Boys, Eddie Cantor, Lisa Kirk and the Sammy Kaye Orchestra, Jan Garber and His Orchestra, the Jubalaires, and as a duet by Al Jolson and the Andrew Sisters, all in 1950.

On stage with Tony Sheridan

He also wrote a string of hits with a humorous slant for Eddy Arnold, as well as dozens of other artists including Vaughn Monroe, Carl Smith, the Ames Brothers, and the Hilltoppers.

While songs of Coben's were bright and generally humorous, "Nobody's Child" involves the singer visiting an orphanage for especially disadvantaged children, who cry out to him that they have no parents and are unwanted, a very serious topic for a song of any grade or category.

It's uncertain who was selecting the songs recorded during the sessions with Sheridan, and a song of such a serious nature was an unusual choice.

Sheridan plays guitar and sings while McCartney plays the bass and Best plays drums on the sparse arrangement, which was very likely quickly rehearsed and recorded. The recordings "sat around" until January 1964 when "Nobody's Child" was released as the B-side to "Sweet Georgia Brown," which was released in separate regions with different B-sides.

These three sessions were produced by Kaempfert, who also produced another session the following year which occurred as part of a contract deal. When Epstein began managing the group in late '61 he immediately attempted to get the band a record contract. He discovered that they had already signed a contract with Kaempfert, who agreed to dismiss the band from their commitment in exchange for one more session when they returned to Hamburg.

On May 24, 1961 the band would return to Studio Rahlstedt in Hamburg to record two more songs, only one of which survived, "Sweet Georgia Brown."

"Sweet Georgia Brown" was written by Ben Bernie, Maceo Pinkard, and Kenneth Casey in 1925.

Bernie was born in New Jersey and became a radio and vaudeville performer, violinist, and bandleader, known for his witty and animated stage banter and called "the old Maestro." Bernie met Dr. George Thaddeus Brown, a member of Georgia's state House of Representatives, who shared the tale of August 11, 1911. Brown's daughter was born on August 6 and five days later the General Assembly declared that she should be named after the state. (Georgia claimed her, Georgia named her). As the tale goes, keeping in mind there is great speculation, Bernie mentioned this to Casey, who created the fictional Georgia Brown.

Casey, a star who appeared in several silent films, wrote the lyrics and shared them with Pinkard, an American songwriter and music publisher. Pinkard composed the tune of the song, or fit the lyrics together with a previously-written song.

Pinkard was also a child prodigy, touring the country as a classical music conductor at the age 17. He later moved to New York where he became a successful songwriter throughout the '20s, writing songs such as "Gimme a Little Kiss, Will Ya Huh?" "I'll Be a Friend (With Pleasure)," "Is That Religion?" "Liza," and "Them There Eyes," which would later become an important song for American soul singer Billie Holiday when

she performed it at the Monterey Jazz Festival in 1958.

Pinkard's greatest success came with "Sweet Georgia Brown," first recorded by Ben Bernie and His Hotel Roosevelt Orchestra in 1925 as an instrumental, and by Ethel Waters with vocals.

The most well-known version is the 1949 recording by "Brother Bones," who enthusiastically whistled while playing "the bones," comprised of two animal bones strategically placed between fingers and tapped together. The release is credited to "Brother Bones and his Shadows," of course not to be confused with the English band of the same name. The song was later adapted as the theme song for basketball novelty performers the Harlem Globetrotters.

Over the next four decades "Sweet Georgia Brown" would be recorded hundreds of times both with and without lyrics, most notably by the California Ramblers, Louis Armstrong, Ella Fitzgerald, Ray Charles, and Harry James. A song that was tailor-made for improvisation and expansion, with the lyrics slightly evolving over time, "Sweet Georgia Brown" quickly became a standard in America.

The Beatles were likely familiar with the Coasters' version of "Sweet Georgia Brown" from 1957, and it was possibly (yet unlikely) part of their live act. McCartney was most certainly aware of the song and arranged the version they recorded. Pianist Roy Young, who occasionally performed with the Beatles at the Star Club, also appears on the recording. More likely each of them were familiar enough with it to record what would become a backing track for the song on May 24, 1962, their fourth and final Hamburg session.

On that day they recorded the backing track and possibly some background vocals for Sheridan, who would add the lead vocals on June 7, possibly with a different set of background singers.

As Beatlemania began to increase, Sheridan would re-record the vocals with some slightly altered lyrics to reflect the times, including Georgia getting records and Carolina having Dinah, but not Georgia Brown. There was also the line "in Liverpool she even dared to criticize the Beatles' hair with their whole fan club standing there."

Sheridan's version with the Beatles was released in January 1964 and was a bit of a hit, most likely due to the buzz of the Beatles.

Also recorded this day was "Swanee River," but unfortunately the masters containing the Beatles' performance either destroyed, erased, recorded over, thrown out, or lost.

Sheridan would re-record the song with another band, although frequently the Beatles or the Beat Brothers get credit for playing on Sheridan version. They are also credited on "What'd I Say," "Let's Dance," "Ruby Baby," "Ready Teddy," "Ya Ya (Part 1 and 2)," and "Kansas City."

There are rumors that versions of "Some Other Guy," "Kansas City/Hey Hey Hey Hey," and "Rock and Roll Music" were recorded as well, however these alleged tapes have never been heard of beyond memories.

While ultimately a small amount of actual Beatle music and no original lyrics would come out of these sessions, it gave the band a clear idea of how a studio should work, and they learned that the performers aren't necessarily in charge.

This experience and growing professionalism would help the Beatles significantly when they would deal with the more sophisticated EMI label. This small bit of output would also greatly affect their fate as part of the story of how Epstein became aware of the band. ◆

CHAPTER 5:
ENTER BRIAN EPSTEIN

THE STORY OF HOW EPSTEIN CAME TO KNOW ABOUT THE BEATLES HAS SEVERAL VERSIONS.

BRIAN EPSTEIN WAS BORN in Liverpool in 1934 and lived there most of his life. He dabbled in the arts, briefly playing the violin and taking theater lessons. Ultimately he found his best place as a salesman for his family business, successfully running the music department of the Liverpool NEMS Music store.

One theory is that after noticing the name around town and seeing an issue of *Mersey Beat*, Epstein asked magazine editor Billy Harry who these Beatles were, and Harry invited him to see them in person at the Cavern Club. Another version of the story involves Epstein asking his personal assistant Alistair Taylor about the "My Bonnie" single, and yet another rendition of the saga revolves around Raymond Jones.

Epstein tells of Jones coming into his store as a customer and asking for a copy of the single, which led to Epstein's interest in the band.

Taylor tells a similar tale, but in his version it was he himself who ordered the single, and using Jones' name (an actual real-life customer) to order, paying for the deposit in the hopes that Epstein would notice.

Bill Harry claims he had been "dogging" Epstein

for some time about the Beatles, which was the band that he pushed most aggressively in his magazine. McCartney corroborates this version as well.

Epstein and Taylor headed to the Cavern Club to see a lunchtime performance by the band on November 9, 1961. While there, Bob Wooler announced that the "famous" Mr. Epstein was in attendance and after the show the band met the would-be manager, recognizing him from the record store they frequented.

Regardless of how Epstein actually wound up in the presence of the Beatles, he immediately decided he wanted to manage them. He formally proposed the partnership December 3 after asking their first "manager" Allan Williams if all his ties were indeed completely cut. Williams advised him "not to touch the band with a fucking barge pole."

Epstein clearly did not take Williams' advice. The new manager began "looking out" for the band as soon as they gave him verbal, then written permission. Epstein "polished them up" and developed their image and stage persona, and Epstein instantly became an integral part of the Beatles organization.

Peter Brown was a salesman at the record section

of Lewis' department store in Liverpool until he was lured away by Epstein to come work at NEMS.

As the Beatles' success grew Brown was an important part of their management team, knowing their daily secretive whereabouts and touring with them. He left NEMS and worked directly for the Beatles after Epstein's death in 1967.

A confidant and close friend to Epstein, Brown was a valuable, dependable, and trusted employee, helping him out of several secretive and potentially damaging situations. Brown continued as part of the organization throughout the decade, serving as a board member for Apple Records, also traveling with the band to Rishikesh, India in 1968.

It was Brown who invited American photographer Linda Eastman to the press release party for Sgt. Pepper. After seeing her again at the Bag O' Nails Club, Brown introduced McCartney to his bride-to-be. In 1968 Brown was the witness to Paul and Linda's wedding and was John and Yoko's best man in 1969, earning him a mention in "The Ballad of John and Yoko."

After his unceremonious dismissal from Apple Records, Brown went to work for the Robert Stigwood Organization (RSO Records) as chief executive officer. Brown lost all contact with the

Beatles and later wrote a largely refuted book about being a Beatle insider.

Bob Wooler was a Liverpool native who began managing a band called the Kingstrums, a local skiffle band which disbanded in 1958.

It was suggested by Williams that Wooler take over as the Beatles' manager. He declined, but became instrumental in introducing the Beatles to Epstein.

After his initial experience in the music world, Wooler continued to help promote and assist bands as the compère/host/DJ at the Cavern Club. His opinion of the music scene was considered very valuable by many.

Jürgen Vollmer was a student at Hamburg's Institute of fashion and was close friends with a fellow design student named Astrid Kirchherr. The two were good friends with another style-conscious young German man, Klaus Voorman, who was also an artist.

Vollmer, Voorman, and Kirchherr all shared a similar interest in music, art and fashion with Fascher, and the they were close friends.

Klaus Voorman was one of the "exies" who were friendly fans of the young Beatles. Voorman always did his best to wear the most current and trendiest clothing, and was especially a fan of Sutcliffe, from whom he got fashion tips.

Voorman was raised in Berlin, Germany in a family that valued music, culture, literature, tradition, and art. Although he was very interested in music, Voorman decided to study commercial graphic art at the Meisterschule für Gestaltung, and also worked regularly as professional graphic artist. While in Hamburg, Voorman first met Astrid Kirchherr.

When the Beatles were playing in town, Voorman was always certain to spend ample time with his fellow thinking companions. Later in the '60s Voorman would move to London and continue his association with the Beatles.

Astrid Kirchherr was a German artist and photographer who befriended the young Beatles, becoming romantically linked to Sutcliffe. Kirchherr

Klaus Voormann with Astrid and Stu

grew up in wartime Berlin, fleeing to the Baltic Sea for safety. She witnessed great destruction as a child.

While enrolled at the Meisterschule für Mode, Textil, Graphik und Werbung in Hamburg (loosely translated to art and fashion school) for fashion design she displayed a major talent for black and white photography. She became an assistant to Reinhard Wolf, giving her relatively unlimited access to film and developing time.

Astrid and Voorman were dating for a short while and after an argument Voorman wound up on the Reeperbahn, a main road in the St. Pauli district of Hamburg. After wandering into the Kaiserkeller, located in a dangerous part of town where illicit behavior was the norm, he witnessed a Beatles performance and quickly encouraged Vollmer and Kirchherr to join him to hear this brand new style of music that was called rock and roll.

The three fashionable Germans quickly became fascinated by this exciting new music. They would attend the Beatles shows nightly, frequently sitting as close as possible and studying the band's every move.

Lennon was relatively unimpressed with the trio, referring to them as the "exies" as in existentialism. Sutcliffe, however, was drawn to them, thinking they were indeed true bohemians with lives dedicated to art. Sutcliffe was awestruck that three attended the Meisterschule für Mode, an art college located in Hamburg, and he quickly became romantically linked to Kirchherr, who remained close platonic friends with Voorman.

Kirchherr asked to photograph the band at several locations around town, the Beatles were happy to pose for her.

Although there are conflicting versions of the Moptop origin story, Kirchherr frequently gets credit for inventing the famous Beatles haircut, with long bangs in the front and longer than usual length (for men of that era) in the back. This haircut is frequently called a Moptop, however Kirchherr denies creating the style, saying that many young German boys

Brian Epstein

followed this fashion during the early '60s.

It was Voorman's hair style at the time, and first Kirchherr cut Sutcliffe's hair, then Harrison's. John and Paul got their hair "Moptopped" while visiting Paris with Voorman himself styling their locks. Kirchherr also said that because of Best's very curly hair, his "wouldn't work."

Lou Walters, who was the bass player in the Hurricanes, recorded at Akustik Studio in Hamburg on October 15, 1960 singing "Summertime." The band behind him consisted of John, Paul, George, and Ringo. Also during this eventful first visit to Germany, the four who would eventually become the Beatles performed together as a studio backup band.

"Summertime" was written by George Gershwin in 1934 for the opera Porgy and Bess. The lyrics were written by DuBose Heyward, author of the novel "Porgy" on which the musical was based.

Nine copies of "Summertime" were cut onto an acetate record this day, although none are known to have survived. During the session Walters also

Paul singing lead at the Casbah Club and George, Paul, and John at the Star Club (inset)

The Beatles were already growing weary of the conditions at the Kaiserkeller and were looking to advance to a more prestigious venue so they certainly "made a show" when trying out for this new club. They ended up with a verbal agreement with Eckhorn to perform at the Top Ten.

Fascher spoke very highly of the group and encouraged Eckhorn to hire them as the resident band, telling tales of their stage presence and success. The band had previously visited the Top Ten to see Fascher and watch the Jets perform, perhaps even performing a few songs with them on occasion.

If they did indeed perform at the Top Ten after auditioning for Eckhorn, as several memories and sources suggest, it would have been during their breaks or early in the day because they were booked daily at the Kaiserkeller from October 4 through November 30, 1960. When Koschmider heard of the Top Ten appearances, along with the fact that George was only 17 and not legally permitted to perform, he terminated the band's contract, although they continued to perform there through the month of November.

Harrison was deported back to Liverpool on November 20 after the authorities discovered his age. The night before his long and lonely journey home, George stayed up very late teaching John his guitar parts so that the band could carry on without him.

While continuing to play as a quartet, John, Paul, Pete, and Stuart were upset at the loss of one of their gang, soldiering on because of their passion for performing.

As their time at the Kaiserkeller was ending, the Beatles were slowly moving their belongings to the attic apartment of the Top Ten Club. Best and McCartney were the last to leave as Lennon and Sutcliffe had already moved out, either staying at the new club or with Kirchherr. Sources differ on this minor matter.

recorded "Fever" and "September Song" along with Johnny Byrne and Ty Brian of the Hurricanes on guitar and Ringo on the drums.

Sutcliffe was present but did not play during this session, which was in a space very similar to the Phillips Studio in Liverpool, yet a bit more sophisticated. He likely sat out due to a lack of confidence in his playing, or perhaps Sutcliffe was starting to lose interest in being a Beatle.

The Beatles did express interest in recording a bit of their own on this day, even though they would have done so without Best, who did not attend. They were unable to finish in time, however, and had to go to their nightly performance at the Kaiserkeller.

Koschmider's Kaiserkeller was in direct competition with the Top Ten Club, owned by Eckhorn who had heard the word on the street about this exciting band from Liverpool and offered them an audition.

Meanwhile, although reports vary on the specifics of the incident, the two band members who stayed behind at Kaiserkeller allegedly set a small fire. McCartney said it was a condom that they nailed to the brick wall and set on fire as a little "ha ha" on their way out of the club as they rose to bigger and better things. Other accounts say it was a rag or a large tapestry.

Although the "blaze" quickly burned itself out, Koschmider was already angry about losing the "hottest band in town" to his competition and called the police, accusing them of attempting to burn the cinema down. McCartney and Best were arrested, spent the night in a Hamburg jail, and were deported the following day. They were flown back to London, arriving on December 1, 1960.

Sutcliffe decided to stay in Hamburg, officially announcing he would leave the band in January. He spent much of his time with his inspiring group of German friends, and Lennon spent a week or so alone in Hamburg, playing with an unknown band to earn money for his trip home.

Upon returning to Liverpool, a frustrated Lennon contemplated giving up on music. He did not contact the other members for a few days following his return home on December 10.

Not knowing the future of the band, McCartney even took a "normal steady job" at a coil winding factory, but left it behind quickly to perform again with the Beatles.

On December 17, 1960 the Beatles performed at Mona Best's Casbah for the first time since October 1959. With Sutcliffe still in Hamburg, John, Paul, George, and Pete recruited Chas Newby, a guitarist from the disbanded Black Jacks, to play bass.

The Casbah billed the show as a band "direct from Hamburg" so the crowd expected a German band and was a bit disappointed to see familiar faces.

Months of consistent hard work paid off, and the Beatles demonstrated a more confident delivery in this performance. Their improvement stemmed from their successful series of day-to-day shows in spite of the poor ending of their first visit to Germany.

Liverpool's music scene was continuing to earn a reputation as the best in the land, and as the now more professional Beatles performed for the crowded underground Casbah Club, Beatlemania was just beginning.

The on-the-job rehearsals in Hamburg fine-tuned the band's performance, including their proficient bass player with the addition of Newby. It became apparent that Sutcliffe was not progressing fast enough. McCartney's criticism of Sutcliffe's playing had been met with dismissal from Lennon previously, but now John was also beginning to notice his close friend's limitations.

Paul may have also switched with Newby from time to time, with Paul handling the bass duties, possibly for Newby to rest or take over on guitar.

The Beatles would frequently play and socialize at the Casbah Club until it closed on June 24, 1962. The Beatles were the last group to perform.

On Christmas Eve 1960 John, Paul, George, Pete, and Chas performed at the Grosvenor Ballroom in Wallasey, sharing a bill with Derry and the Seniors. In the week that followed, the band finished off an exciting and tumultuous year on a very high note. They played a "welcome home" show organized by promoter Brian Kelly, who gave the Beatles a second chance after they let him down by failing to show at a performance with King Size Taylor.

Wooler convinced Kelly to book the band at Litherland Town Hall in North Liverpool on December 27. Also on the bill were the Del Renas, the Searchers, and the Deltones.

Wooler was the in-house disc jockey at the ill-fated Liverpool location of the Top Ten Club (owned by Allan Williams) until a mysterious fire forced the location to close leaving Wooler jobless. He would ultimately become the in-house DJ at the Cavern Club and would introduce the Beatles to Epstein.

There would be more changes the following year, but the band was slowly beginning to solidify. ◆

SONGS PRODUCED BY GEORGE MARTIN

GEORGE MARTIN (1926-2016) WAS A MUSIC PRODUCER, ARRANGER, AND PERFORMER WHO WOULD PROVE TO BE ABSOLUTELY PIVOTAL TO THE BEATLES' HARMONIOUS MUSICAL TRAJECTORY.

Born in the Highbury district of London, Martin grew up with a fascination for music after briefly taking lessons as a child when his family acquired a piano.

As a teen Martin was very moved by the BBC Orchestra when he witnessed them performing live. Despite his obvious talent coupled with his adolescent fantasies of being the next Rachmaninov, Martin did not plan to pursue a career in the music business and instead worked as a construction purveyor and a clerk in the U.K.'s War Office.

After serving in a non-combat role for the Royal Air Force, Martin used his veterans' education grant to enroll in the Guildhall School of Music and Drama, where he continued his study of piano. He also learned how to play the oboe from Margaret Eliot, who was the mother of Jane Asher.

Martin graduated from Guildhall, then briefly worked for the classical music department of the BBC. He was later hired by EMI as an assistant to Oscar Preuss, who was then head of one of their subsidiary labels, Parlophone.

Martin immediately proved a valuable ear to have around, producing Sidney Torch and His Orchestra's "Coronation Scot" and "Barwick Green," also known as the "Archer's Theme."

He also produced a single that came about in an unconventional way. Jack Parnell's "White Suit Samba" was from the 1951 film of the same name starring Alec Guinness as Sidney Stratton, an inventor/scientist who creates a stain- and wear-resistant fabric. During the scenes in the laboratory the sound effects of the science technology (described as "guggle glub guggle") were designed by sound editor Mary Habberfield, although she went uncredited for many years. These extremely clever sounds, achieved with tubas and bassoons, were set to music by Parnell (who would go on to be the head of the music department of "The Muppet Show" in the 1970s)

and movie scriptwriter T.E.B. Clarke. The result of the blend of sound effects and musical score was released as a single, produced by Martin.

Being able to think of music as something more than just traditional instruments making traditional sounds was one the qualities that would help the Beatles and Martin work so wonderfully together.

In 1952 Martin produced the "Bluebell Polka" for Jimmy Shand, a Scottish accordionist. It was by no means a complicated performance, but even at this early stage Martin was very conscious of recording the permanent record.

Another Martin-produced polka was "The Scottish Polka" for Scottish-born duo Mickie Ainsworth & Jimmy Blue. Once again this was not a complex recording, but it was carefully produced as Martin set up the mics in the studio for accordions in an attempt to hear the instruments more distinctly, which wasn't always the case.

Also in 1952 was "Ae Fond Kiss" by Scottish singer Kenneth McKellar, who trained as an opera tenor only to pursue a career recording folk and comedy records.

"Melody on the Move," prominently featuring harmonica virtuoso Tommy Reilly with the Vic Hammett Quartet, was another record from 1952 produced by Martin. The producer had an openness to all styles and types of music as well as a desire to continue learning and improving. The Beatles would develop a similar work ethic as they formed their own band.

Peter Ustinov

Peter Ustinov along with Anthony Hopkins had a minor hit in 1952 with "Mock Mozart" which was reluctantly released by the label personnel, who considered it too odd to market. Much of this Martin-produced song is nonsense and very "goon-like" (although that term may not have been coined as of yet) with lots of recorded silliness.

"Mock Mozart" was a minor hit, which led to Martin beginning to get more freedom in what and how he would record. He continued to progress steadily, picking up skills and gaining a reputation as an amiable and desirable producer..

Martin also produced for the Kenny Baker Quartet, part of the Super Rhythm Style series on the Parlophone label. Releases included "Hayfoot, Strawfoot," a Baker trumpet performance that was considered "new jazz" as opposed to "trad" or traditional jazz. Baker was already an established and highly regarded performer and session player who would continue working with Martin throughout the '50s and into the '60s with several other combos.

Martin became familiar with another type of jazz

altogether after producing for Graeme Bell and His Australian Jazz Band, a Dixieland jazz combo who recorded for Parlophone. Bell was a classically trained pianist and a major figure in the Australian jazz world. The Sydney-based jazz band briefly toured with Big Bill Broonzy, resulting in the *Big Bill Broonzy in Concert* LP in 1951.

"High Society" was recorded while Bell's band was in England, releasing four singles for the Parlophone label. While unconfirmed, it is highly likely that the singles were produced by Martin, possibly all from one lengthy session.

Martin's ability to make "clean" recordings and get artists to give their best as they preserved their performance were important traits. He was also able to help arrange and assist these bands to make their records a bit more marketable, in the case of Bell that meant utilizing his classical as well as Dixieland abilities.

The Luton Girls Choir dates back to 1936 when church choir master Arthur Davies formed an all-girl ensemble, fearing that the vocal style was falling out of favor, hiring girls primarily in their teens and early twenties. As this group of young ladies represented England for several decades, of course rotating members, they recorded for many occasions and crossed paths with Martin as they recorded for Parlophone throughout the '50s.

When England hosted the Olympics in 1948 the Luton Girls Choir would perform at the opening ceremonies, and that same year they would appear of the Royal Command Performance.

Along with the band of Irish guards the Luton girls performed "Princess Elizabeth of England" in 1951, produced by Martin for Parlophone. Once again he proved his worth by being able to capture large performances, in this case a full vocal ensemble, with a clean recording. This is a skill that not all producers and engineers possessed in the early '50s.

Similar to the Luton girls was the Glasgow Phoenix Choir, formed in 1951 from the "ashes" of the Glasgow Orpheus Choir, which had been in existence since 1901.

Beginning in 1962 the large vocal choir recorded a

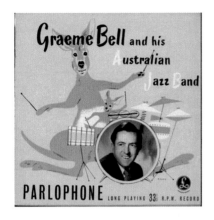

series of folk, Celtic, classical, and "world" music (as it would eventually be called) with full-length LPs *Songs We Love* in 1962, *Will Ye No Come Back Again?* in 1963, and *The Road to the Isles* in 1964. All were presumably produced or supervised by Martin, once again achieving distinct and clear recordings of large groups of performers in rooms that weren't intended to be studios such as churches and theaters designed for live presentations.

Freddy Randall was an English jazz trumpeter who led his band through a series of recordings for Parlophone between 1953 and 1963, many of which were likely produced by Martin. These include "Sensation Rag," "Won't You Come Home Bill Bailey," "Way Down Yonder in New Orleans," "At the Jazz Band Ball," "Ain't Gonna Give Nobody None O' This Jelly Roll," "Clarinet Marmalade," "Original Dixieland One-Step" "Hotter Than That," "Georgia Cake Walk," "Sugar Foot Strut," "Dark Knight Blues," "My Tiny Band Is Chosen," "Memphis Blues," "Ostrich Walk," "Sheik of Araby," "Professor Jazz," "The Anvil Chorus," and "Elizabeth." Randall also worked with Johnny Dankworth on his "Experiments with Mice," another Martin-produced record.

Joe Daniels was an English jazz drummer who formed the Hot Shots (with Billy Mason) and recorded for Parlophone as early as 1935. Daniels recorded a six-song EP in 1957 for Parlophone with Martin (likely) producing called *Juke Box Jazz*.

As the bandleader Daniels was the focal point of the live shows, and Martin made it his goal to keep him in that role on the recording, using unusual techniques for his sessions.

In 1957 Martin would record Joe Daniels and His Band with the Butlin Campers live at the Butlin holiday camp, releasing "Oi! Oi! Oi!" and the "Bottle Beatin' Blues." Martin would also oversee several sessions which yielded singles for the Joe Daniels Jazz Band beginning in 1953.

Max Geldray was a jazz harmonica player, known to the Beatles as the guy who played the "Goon Show" music. He was in fact the man who played the interludes for BBC radio's "Crazy People" later to be renamed "The Goon Show."

"Crazy Rhythms" was a 1928 swing show tune that Geldray recorded with the Ray Ellington Quartet in 1961. Martin produced the song which would also double as the play-out music for the Goons.

In 1959 Martin produced the *Goon with the Wind* EP featuring instrumental versions of "Once in Love with Amy," "It's Only a Paper Moon," "Our Love is Here to Stay," "Cherie," and "Duke's Joke."

John Scott was a multi-instrumentalist specializing in flute who was also well-versed on the violin, clarinet, harp, saxophone, and vibraphone. "They Say" b/w "How About That" was his debut single released in 1960 followed by

"Hi-Flutin' Boogie" and "Peace Pipe" later in the year, all produced by Martin.

Due to his ability to arrange music Scott was hired by EMI, becoming the first outside musician to be invited to perform on a Beatles track in 1965, also becoming a well-regarded session musician and film score composer.

Roberto Inglez was a Scottish-born bandleader and composer who became a Latin bandleader on the Parlophone label. Along with assorted bands, Inglez recorded a series of records for Parlophone as early as 1942 with "Jamaican Rumba" b/w "Tico Tico," followed by "The Green Cockatoo" b/w "Chiquita Banana (The Banana Song)" in 1946, "Brazil Samba" b/w "Rio De Janeiro Samba" in 1947, and "Caribbean Caprice" b/w "Copacabana" in 1948.

In 1949 Inglez recorded "The Harry Lime Theme" and beginning in 1950 he would release about 10 singles on Parlophone per year. These were occasionally produced by Martin, who may have served as a performer as well on several of the recordings.

Martin produced/recorded a live album from the Savoy Hotel in London (year unknown) which explored several different styles of Latin music including bolero, calypso, rhumba, and samba, all within a single evening performance. This was another example of how Martin continued to develop his skills by being exposed to many different styles of music, which would prove valuable throughout his career.

Vic Hammett was a virtuoso Wurlitzer organ player who Martin produced for on all or most of his Parlophone recordings. These included "Melody on the Move," "Bop! Goes the Weasel" (with the Sonny Terry Trio), "Firefly" "Stormy Weather," "Begin the Beguine," "Blue Moon," "Down Under," "Yokohama Holiday," "Blow Man Blow," and "No Dice."

The Southlanders were a British and Jamaican vocal group who released their debut single on the Parlophone label in 1955, which was a cover of the Penguin's 1954 "Earth Angel (Will You Be Mine)" b/w "The Crazy Otto Rag," both produced by Martin. They would move to Decca Records shortly after scoring with "Choo-Choo-Choo-Choo Cha-Cha-Cha" b/w "The Mole in a Hole" in 1958.

When Preuss retired in 1955, Martin became the head of Parlophone, which primarily released EMI's less important acts and dealt primarily in comedy and novelty recordings. While Martin had success with several humorous songs, and he took a very serious approach to recording them in a highly technical and professional manner. Martin was just 30 years old when he took the position, one generally reserved for more seasoned veterans. He continued to record a wide range of music including more comedy records, Broadway show tunes, traditional Irish and regional music, as well as pop bands.

In his first year as head of the label Martin produced a Top 10 record for female pop vocalist Eve Boswell with

"Pickin' a Chicken" which reached No. 9 on the British Hit Parade. The song was based on a South African tune with words added by Paddy Roberts, another unusual combination of elements merged together by Martin.

Also in '55 Martin produced "Arrivederci Darling" by Edna Savage, an English rewording of an Italian song originally titled "Arrivederci Roma."

The following year was an extremely productive one for Martin, now confidently taking charge of his label and continuing to create interesting music with many different types of roots.

An example of the niche artists produced by Martin was Eamonn Andrews, an Irish-born sportscaster, radio and television personality who had "The Shifting Whispering Sands," a two-part spoken word recording with the Ron Goodwin Orchestra accompanying.

Prior to switching strictly to the music publishing side of the business, Dick James had a brief career as a singer. He had several releases on Parlophone, as well as the lead vocal on the theme produced by Martin for "Robin Hood," a '50s British television series.

The Ivor and Basil Kirchin Band, a father-son combo, had a skiffle record

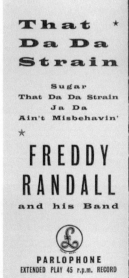

called the "Rock-a-Beatin' Boogie," which was a new type of music that Martin was able to successfully record despite being still unfamiliar with the style. Once again Martin encouraged participants to perform at their absolute best for their record, which he often reminded them would "be around for a while."

It's uncertain if Martin was familiar with the previously recorded versions of the "Rock-A-Beatin' Boogie" from the Esquires (1952), the jump blues take on the song from the Treniers (1954) or the version by the song's composer Billy Haley with the Comets in 1955.

English jazz pop singer Cleo Laine recorded a four-song EP titled *The April Age* which had songs about the fourth month, "I'll Remember April," "April Age," "April in Paris," and "I Dedicate April," all of which Martin performed on, playing either saxophone or clarinet.

In '56 Martin also produced the aforementioned "Experiments with Mice" for Johnny Dankworth and His Orchestra, a spoken word jazz recording of the story of three mice who lived in a recording studio. The mice were named after Billy May, Benny Goodman, and Glenn Miller, and the song tells of their visit with the farmer's son, a drummer, and a couple of "Irish cats" Finnegan and Mulligan.

In the narrative, Stan Kenton, who had never seen such a thing in his life as three blind mice, wrote some music for the occasion, called the "Theme for a Trio of Sightless Rodents," which frightened the mice away.

As each of the characters in the song gets mentioned they have specific themes, all based on the very simple tune "Three Blind Mice." An interesting ingredient occurs when the orchestra plays the theme for the mouse named after May, with a trumpet lead and a clarinet-based Three Blind Mice theme, all in a slow and romantic Miller-style song.

The Beatles would have been impressed with a song containing as many different styles of music as "Experiments with Mice" had, but is unknown if they were familiar with the record prior to meeting its producer.

"Smiley" was a 1956 film set in Australia with a theme sung by Shirley Abicair, an Australian musician and actress who also worked with comedian George Martin, a completely different George Martin.

"Nellie the Elephant" was a novelty track from 1956 sung by Mandy Miller, a child singer and actress who recorded the song at age 12. The previous year she released "(How Much Is) That Doggie in the Window?" (originally done by Patti Page in late 1952) also produced by Martin and his staff of engineers and recording perfectionists.

"Nellie" was written by Ralph Butler, who had success as a light-hearted novelty songwriter for four decades beginning in the '20s. The Martin-produced recording features an orchestra conducted by Phil Cardew and an arrangement by Ron Goodwin, whom Martin had worked with in the past. The song follows the story of Nellie the intelligent circus elephant who escapes (packs her trunk) from the circus heading to Hindustan, and was never seen again.

In 1957 as the skiffle craze was continuing to gain momentum, Martin was further exposed to the newer sounding music as he oversaw the recording of the Vipers Skiffle Group (later known as the Vipers) performing "Don't You Rock Me Daddy-O," a retelling of Uncle Dave Macon and His Fruit Jar Drinkers' 1927 standard "Sail Away Ladies."

Martin's work with the Vipers, who were untrained although highly skilled and very enthusiastic, proved a valuable experience when it came time to work with bands of the Beatles' caliber.

The Beatles were familiar with "Rock Me Daddy-O" although likely the version they knew was by Lonnie Donegan, who had also recorded the song during 1957. It's extremely likely that the Beatles were familiar with the Vipers' recording of "Maggie May," a Liverpool folk song about a thieving prostitute.

Jim Dale was an English singer and actor who recorded a series of hit singles produced under the direction of Martin and his staff. In 1957 he had "Be My Girl" and in 1958 it was "Just Born (To Be Your Baby)," "Crazy Dream," and "Sugartime," all consistently well-produced and successful to varying degrees, adding to the confidence the label put in Martin and the freedom he was allowed.

Martin had developed his own methods and standards for records he was affiliated with, and he was able to effectively help create serious or straightforward records.

Frequently in the industry the same care and concern wasn't given to songs of a humorous or novelty nature, however Martin would treat each of his sessions the same, and his brand of excellence was unmistakable to the ear.

Ian Wallace was an English opera singer who had several animal-themed recordings including "The

ALONE
(WHY MUST I BE ALONE)

Words by SELMA CRAFT   Music by

Featured & Recorded by
THE SOUTHLANDERS

DUCHESS MUSIC LTD., 25, Denmark Street, LONDON, W.C.2   2/-

Hippopotamus Song" in 1957, written for his one-man stage act by songwriting team Flanders and Swann.

The contrast between the childlike subject matter (about a Hippo wallowing in mud, mud, glorious mud) and the trained and talented opera singer delivering a dedicated and serious performance (in spite of the unique events) made for yet another impressive production from Martin, who was becoming in demand for his very specific expertise.

In '58 Martin produced a version of the song "Splish Splash," originally performed by Bobby Darin, who also co-wrote the song with "Murray the K" Kaufman. The Beatles would become friends with "Murray the K" during their first visit to the United States.

English comedian Charlie Drake capitalized quickly by re-recording the song only a month or two after the original was released. Drake would continue to record his novelty records throughout the decade for the Parlophone label, many produced by Martin himself, including "Volare," "Itchy Twitchy Feeling," "Tom Thumb's Tune," and "Goggle Eye Ghee," in 1958, "Sea Cruise," b/w "Starkle Starkle Little Twink" in 1959, and "Naughty," "Old Mr. Shadow," "Mr. Custer," and "Glow Worm" in 1960.

In 1961 Drake would have his biggest hit with "My Boomerang Won't Come Back" the B-side to "She's My Girl," also produced by Martin. In "Boomerang" Drake tells the story, in his very thick cockney English accent, of the Aboriginal pow wow in the bad, bad lands of Australia, and Mac is causing trouble all because his boomerang won't come back. Mac is banished and sent away to a land of kangaroos, where ultimately he is visited by a witch doctor who tells him in order for the boomerang to return "first you got to throw it." Mac hits a doctor, and then a flying doctor, which is an Australian medical airplane.

The sound effects, as well as the musical

accompaniment on the song, have a uniquely Australian feel, imitated for a novelty audience. Martin recreated a didjeridu as well as adding the plane crash noises near the end of the song, both examples of skills that would help him in his production with the Beatles.

The song also was the cause of some controversy as it was banned by the BBC for its themes and language choices, as a "pow wow" would refer more to a Native American, and the chanting sounds are very African, as opposed to Aboriginal.

There are also lines about "practicing 'til I was black in the face" and being "a big disgrace to the Aborigine race" which were less than appropriate even by early 1960 English standards.

Although the record was very popular in terms of sales, it wasn't charting due to its radio ban. A re-recorded version was released which had the line "black

in the face" changed to "blue in the face." That was the version that wound up becoming a U.K. hit, peaking at No. 14 on the British charts.

The song was a hit in the United States as well, with the updated lyrics, slightly re-edited and released on the United Artists label. This was possibly the first time a record label would reimagine a Martin-produced song.

Drake would continue to have minimal success, and his recording career tapered off as the mainstream youth of England became more interested in skiffle music and less in comedy records.

In 1961 Martin composed "Double Scotch (Dance of the Spirits)" as the B-side to the theme to the film "Murder She Says," both for Ron Goodwin and His Orchestra. Goodwin was a music publisher who became a very successful composer of musical scores as well as an EMI employee. He would arrange, direct, and conduct sessions produced by Martin, and also released music with his own orchestra.

Goodwin would also accompany Peter Sellers and Sophia Loren on the "Goodness Gracious Me" single from 1960 which would inspire the four-song EP featuring selections from the full-length LP *Peter and Sophia*, all meticulously produced by Martin.

Film Favourites was a collection of Goodwin's orchestra performing scores and themes including music from "Limelight" and "Modern Times" (both written by Charlie Chaplin), "Shane (Call of the Far-Away Hills)," "Where is Your Heart" (also known as the theme from "Moulin Rouge"), "It May Be You" (From "Love Lottery"), "When I Fall in Love" from "One Minute to Zero," and "The Melba Waltz" from "Dream Time."

Goodwin's orchestra would also back Glen Mason on "Don't Forbid Me" b/w "Amore" and Eamonn Andrews on the aforementioned "Shifting Whispering Sands," both in 1956. "Red Cloak" b/w "Elizabethan Serenade," "I'll Find You" b/w "Swinging Sweethearts" (also known as "Skiffling Strings") were released in 1957, followed by a series of Martin produced/supervised recordings throughout the decade and into the early '60s.

Goodwin would go to work for MGM's British Studios in 1959, composing the scores for hundreds of films during the '60s and '70s, occasionally crossing paths with Martin throughout their highly successful careers.

Rolf Harris was primarily considered a comedy or novelty performer, however on his full-length *Sun Arise* album (produced by Martin) the title track is a rather straightforward tale of the calmness and overwhelming beauty of the sunrise. The remainder of the very successful 1963 LP included Harris and his thick yet charming Australian accent performing his comedy originals including "The Big Black Hat," "Living It Up," "Hair Oil on My Ears," "Ground Hog," and "Someone's Pinched My Winkles."

"I've Been Everywhere" was a song originated in Australia in 1959 by composer Geoff Mack, who listed Australian towns delivered in an extremely fast and poetic tempo. Hank Snow was a Canadian country singer who reworked the lyrics to represent North America, primarily the United States. In '63 Harris would do the same, only with English towns, the patient and determined Martin's productions skills must have been very useful in this situation.

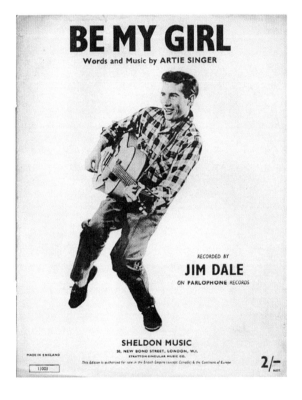

Martin would have several composer credits, including "Sitting on a Bench" for Dudley Moore, as well as "The Niagara Theme" for Alyn Ainsworth and His Orchestra, both in 1962.

Lance Percival was an English comic and singer who had "Dancing in the Streets Tonight" in 1963. Martin shares writing credit along with Barry Took, yet another English comic.

The B-side to Billy J. Kramer with the Dakotas' "I'll Keep You Satisfied," was "I Know," written by Lennon/McCartney and given away, credited to Martin along with Bob Wooler and released in '63.

As Martin attempted to nurture and encourage the Beatles and their development, he simultaneously did this with Kramer, both as a solo artist and with the Dakotas. Martin produced their Parlophone output, as he would for the Fourmost and Cilla Black.

Martin arranged the Frankie Howerd recording of *A Funny Thing Happened on the Way to the Forum*, and he co-wrote "Riviera Cayf" with Myles Rudge and Lance Percival, the singer of the song.

Singer Ritva Mustonen and guitarist Heikki Laurila were two Finnish performers who recorded "Taikamatto," which was penned by Martin, with foreign language lyrics added by Veikko Vallas (Sauvo Puhtila) in '63

An instrumental version of the song called "Magic Carpet" appeared on the A-side of the Dakotas' (without Kramer) 1963 single, with "Humdinger as its B-side.

Martin would have a wide range of success with versatile performer Peter Sellers, who was born into an entertainment family and from his infancy was part of show business. Singing, acting, and being funny came naturally to him, as did his ability to immerse himself into a character as a serious dramatic actor as well.

The Goons were a comedy troupe with Sellers, Spike Milligan, and Harry Secombe whose radio show as well as films and television work would be very influential on the developing sense of humor of the individual

Beatles.

Martin would also have an integral part in an 11-minute experimental "The Running Jumping & Standing Still Film" which was co-directed by Richard Lester, and featured eccentric English artistic performer Bruce Lacey. In these performances Sellers would frequently play several different well-defined characters, occasionally using "trick photography" which would allow him to interact with himself.

Martin would continue to be considered among the best in the field and in 1957 would begin producing for Sellers. *The Best of Sellers* was his debut album released in 1958, and set a new standard of excellence for full-length comedy records.

Combining intelligent humor that was well-written and masterfully performed by Sellers was an unusual challenge for the producer, who had to capture all the different personalities that his performer was portraying, frequently simultaneously. Martin was able to successfully fulfill this task on the LP, utilizing his production skills and talents in a musical, theatrical, and technical way, which led to large record sales.

The Best of Sellers featured the song "The Trumpet Volunteer," which consists of Sellers interviewing

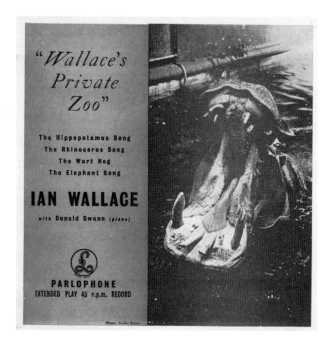

himself as a rock star who wants to "classen it up" so he adds a trumpet to his song. It was a rather ridiculous premise for the time but still a unique production performed within the confines of an interview.

"Auntie Rotter" is a spoken-word recording which features an accompanying piano and Sellers as several members of the Rotter family. "I'm So Ashamed" is a pop song about a singer lamenting not being on the charts anymore (a whole three weeks), and "We Need the Money" is a spoken-word skit in which Sellers interviews himself again, portraying a well-to-do member of royalty, as well as several other members of the press.

Other tracks on the album feature much of the same, comedy mixed with music, both at a very high level of quality and sophistication. Sellers' subsequent full-length as well as single releases would maintain this high standard.

As the Beatles were first introduced to Martin they no doubt did their own research on his credentials, and were likely intrigued and impressed with his affiliations. Sellers was certainly at the top of that list.

Martin produced *Songs For Swingin' Sellers* in 1959, which shared a similar format as his debut LP, including a part 1 and part 2 for "The Contemporary Scene" and "Putting on the Smile," which was a sendup of the current folk boom in England.

Also produced by Martin in 1959 was "New Saturday Jump" for jazz trumpeter and bandleader Humphrey Lyttelton, who had a previous hit in 1956 with "Bad Penny Blues" that Paul McCartney would draw inspiration from nearly a decade later.

Lyttelton was presenter on the BBC's "Best of Jazz" program for more than 40 years and released a series of records on the Parlophone label, occasionally produced by Martin himself.

English television host Bruce Forsyth had "I'm in Charge" in 1959, with Martin once again using Goodwin's arranging. Forsyth sings of how wonderful things would be if he was in charge, once again with the orchestral accompaniment, background vocals, and the general structure of the song well-balanced in a light but serious arrangement.

In 1960 Martin would produce an album for Sellers along with Sophia Loren, who the actor was madly in love with, leaving his family due to his unreciprocated affection for her.

The album *Peter and Sophia* was recorded with hopes that the song "Goodness Gracious Me" would be included in the film "The Millionairess" from the same year. Instead the single became a novelty hit, with the album being a minor hit.

With a combination of straight and sincerely performed duets, along with comedy routines and songs, the album was a well-crafted "performance" with both entertainers having their individual space on the album as well as a fair portion showing off their unique chemistry.

This model of an album was extremely similar to those Martin would produce with the Beatles, having strong songs and performances at the beginning of each side, closing both with a song that is hard to follow. These exact applications would be used on several Martin-produced albums until becoming very common and standard within the rock and roll industry.

Spike Milligan was a comic, Parlophone recording artist and "Goon" member who would release several solo LPs produced by Martin, some musical, some primarily poetry or spoken word. *Milligan Preserved* (1961) featured Milligan on "Q5 Piano Tune" which was comprised of unusual sound effects, a nonsense language, and piano, likely played by Martin himself. The song served as the theme for Milligan's "Q" television series.

Tape manipulation was also used to speed up Milligan's already high pitched voice, again singing nothing intelligible.

The album also included "I'm Walking Out with a Mountain," which is about a man who is going steady with a girl who is, in fact, a mountain. One long section of the song features him singing about all the girls from his past, the names are obscured by sound effects, again placed into the song with perfect precision by Martin. Other highlights from the album, which was widely-regarded as groundbreaking in the world of comedy, include "The Sewers of the Strand," "Another Lot," "Have They Gone," "Australia," "Hit Parade," and "Fun Fun Fun."

"Word Power" is an interview by voice actor Valentine Dyall as Milligan portrays a "retired redundant" who is a word expert, yet cannot remember any of the definitions. "Cougher Royal" is an interview with the man who invented coughing, using Dyall again.

"The Sewers of the Strand" tells the romantic tale of a couple falling in love near the sewers, a generally disgusting image. The combination of Martin's well done production and Milligan's purposefully off-key singing of a sweet-seeming song about a foul setting

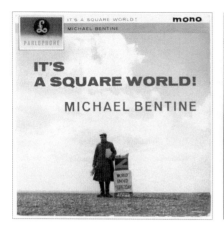

was well-balanced and highly successful. This was a skill that Martin would use frequently with the Beatles, especially as their ideas became more unusual.

In 1962 Martin would produce "Bridge on the River Wye," a script written by Milligan that was previously performed on "The Goon Show" as "The African Incident." Based on the 1957 film "The Bridge Over the River Kwai," the single was simply to have same title, until shortly before its release when EMI was threatened with legal action. Martin had the tedious job of editing of the "K" every time the word "Kwai" was spoken, a meticulous task that was carried out phenomenally well.

The record bore the label: "For best results, play this record in a circular fashion."

"Milligan's Wake" was a surrealistic comedy broadcast in the U.K. in 1964 which Martin compiled into the two-sided *Best of Milligan's Wake* LP. Martin does not receive credit as it was released on the PYE label and he was contractually obligated to EMI.

Martin may have (very likely) produced the 1964 LP *How to Win an Election (Or Not Lose by Much)* for Sellers, Milligan, and Secombe.

Michael Bentine was also a "Goon" who released the Martin-produced 1962 *It's a Square World* comedy album which, much like the work of his cohorts in Goonery, was political, current, and newsworthy in nature.

"Square World" was Bentine's television show from 1960-64, which depicted events using miniature scale models. It would also report "news from the eight corners of the world" (which is how the world becomes square). The album shares the news reporting concept as he plays several characters and also performs the commercial breaks.

"The Horse Show" depicts a highbrow equestrian show gone wrong complete with sound effects, and "Football Results" portrays a bored sports announcer occasionally going mad.

Other tracks from the album include the "Tower of London," "Geneva Conference," Dingleweed," and a Moscow television commercial.

Stuart Eltham, an EMI engineer and the keeper of the sound effects library, recorded this and several of the other albums produced by Martin. Eltham's work would prove to be very important for the Beatles in their future.

Harry Secombe also had a string of albums and singles for the Phillips label (a subsidiary of the Dutch Philips Electronics company, not the Sun Records-related label of Memphis). These releases were primarily serious and well-done recordings of his classical interpretations of traditional religious songs, producer unlisted.

British comedy duo Flanders and Swann had "At the Drop of a Hat," a politically and socially charged musical comedy review, and in 1960 Martin oversaw

their live recordings of several of the performances which yielded two LPs worth of material. This foray into recording live comedy performances added to the diverse skill set Martin was collecting.

Michael Flanders and Donald Swann would also record "A Transport of Delight" single and several albums with cooperation from Martin and his staff. "Transport of Delight" was the lead track from the *Drop of a Hat* LP which explains the duo's "smart" humor as they sing of their love for buses. "Songs for Our Time" was medley of "compositions" that the duo wrote consisting of "Philological Waltz," "Satellite Moon," and "A Happy Song."

Also on the album was "A Gnu," "The Reluctant Cannibal," "Kokoraki - A Greek Song," "Madeira, M' Dear?" and their own version of "Hippopotamus," also sung by Ian Wallace.

Martin produced a single for Matt Monro in 1960 called "Portrait of My Love," which reached No. 3 on the U.K. record charts. Martin would continue to produce most of Monro's subsequent work, remaining dedicated to developing acts as they became more familiar with recording.

Monro first crossed paths with Martin after being hired to sing a demo of Frank Sinatra-style song called "You Keep Me Swinging" for Sellers, who was to re-record his own take on the song. Sellers decided to simply use the Monro version of the song to kick off the

record, crediting Fred Flange, a completely fictional name invented by Sellers.

After word got out who the real singer was and what great reviews he got from his performance on the Sellers album, Monro was signed to the Parlophone label. He released a string of records to varying success until this middle of the decade when his record sales began to decline. A main reason Monro stood out was his selection of material, which were not standards from Tin Pan Alley in America, but instead he searched for new composers who were writing promising new music.

Some of Monro's other standout tracks include "My Kind of Girl" in 1961, and "Softly As I Leave You" in 1962, all Top 10 hits in the U.K. As the decade continued Monro's records would have minimal success but were always well regarded by the record company and the critics, allowing he and Martin to continue to consistently record singles as well as albums. He remained successful a bit longer than many of the acts that were overshadowed by the British invasion.

Peter Cook, Dudley Moore, Alan Bennett, and Jonathan Miller were a troupe of musical comics who collectively performed as "Beyond the Fringe," a British stage review that began in 1960, becoming extremely influential in the field of satirical English comedies. For their record Martin recorded and edited a performance, and the first album was released on Parlophone in

1961. Again this raised the standard not just for the quality of a recording, but for the impressiveness of the performance itself in the field of record making.

Occasionally Martin's comedy world would collide with his more serious work as it did with Nadia Gray who co-starred with Sellers in the 1961 comedy "Mr. Topaze."

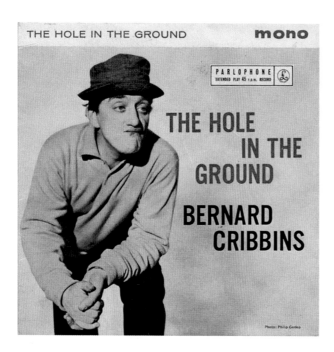

"I Like Money" was the theme to the movie which Gray sang very comically with her very thick Romanian accent and breathy voice. The sincere recording and performance coupled with the humorous tone of the song work wonderfully together, a consistent mark of Martin's work.

Johnnie Spence and His Orchestra recorded the "Dr. Kildare Theme" in 1962 for the American television series, the B-side was "The Midnight Theme." Spence would also have "Adventures in Paradise" b/w "The Balcony" in 1960, "Wheels" and "First Romance" in 1961, and "Baby Elephant Walk" b/w "Sugar Beat" in 1962, all Martin products.

Martin produced "Strictly for the Birds" for Dudley Moore in '61, a relatively serious performance featuring a nonsense scat-style vocal from Moore, who plays piano

on the song with his trio performing.

Jazz music had a reputation as being stuffy or highbrow in England, but within the early '60s there would be a renewed interest for a younger audience. The style frequently called "trad jazz" (traditional jazz) as well as records that had jazz elements and a sense of humor were certainly a part of this resurgence.

In 1961 there was "You're Driving Me Crazy" from the Temperance Seven, a jazz group specializing in recording tracks from the 1920s. They steadily recorded and released for Parlophone until 1964 when the market became dominated by current pop music.

Some Temperance Seven records which may have had minimal if any participation from Martin include "Pasadena" b/w "Sugar," "Hard Hearted Hannah" b/w "Chili Bom Bom," and "The Charleston" b/w "Black Bottom" all in 1961, "Sahara" b/w "Everybody Loves My Baby," "Runnin' Wild" b/w "The Mooche," and "Shake" b/w "Bye Bye Baby" in 1962, as well as "From Russia with Love" in 1963, which was originally produced by Martin for Monro for the James Bond film of the same name, also in '63.

Bernard Cribbins was an English comic actor and singer who had come to the attention of Martin in 1960 after Martin saw him perform in a review called "And Another Thing." He performed "Folk Song" which intrigued Martin enough to record it for Cribbins' first release.

Parlophone released the full-length album *A Combination of Cribbins* in 1962, which was a rather successful year for the novelty performer.

Martin produced "A Hole in the Ground" for Cribbins, which features a big discussion all about a hole in the ground, which ultimately winds up with a man being buried, an uncommon theme for a Top 10 hit.

"Right Said Fred" was Cribbins' follow up, also a Top 10 hit which tells the tale of a group of men moving a large object (presumably a piano), having lots of difficulties, and going to great lengths to get it up the stairs. Throughout the song there are well-timed punctuations of sound effects, springs, grunts, climbing stairs, tools clanking, and other strategically-placed bubbles and buzzes, all very well balanced in terms of storytelling and theatrics.

"The Gossip Calypso" was Cribbins' third single of '62. It tells of the "he said/she said" of suburbia, within the confines of a reasonable facsimile of Cuban calypso music.

His next release "The Bird on the Second Floor" (1963) failed to chart, and Cribbins largely bowed out of the recording business, sensing his act had run its course. He the recorded sporadically, possibly with Martin taking only a small part in the sessions as his attentions were drawn to several more high profile acts.

Cambridge Circus (formerly A Clump of Plinths) was a comedy revue that ran in 1963 featuring future Monty Python member John Cleese. Cambridge Circus released an album of their performance recorded and edited by Martin.

The Alberts were another comedy act who, along with Bruce Lacey (from the "Running, Jumping & Standing Still" film), were a part of "An Evening of British Rubbish" review recorded by Martin.

"Morse Code Melody" was recorded in May 1962, another in the long series of well-crafted novelty records which were musically stable, yet included "mistakes" and other planned breakdowns. This was similar to some of the Beatles recordings, a prime example being the count-in to "I Saw Her Standing There."

Many of these records produced by Martin were very likely heard by the Beatles, who were no doubt impressed with his resume when they crossed paths in 1962.

"That Was The Week That Was" was a satirical English television show hosted by David Frost. The show featured the song of the same title sung by Millicent Martin (no relation to George) that would depict the weekly news with the phrase "That was the week that was, it's over, let it go ..." and be "updated" each week. Staff writers included Cleese, Graham Chapman, and Peter Cook, and greatly targeted the current political climate of the day in monologues, humorous debates, and a weekly calypso number sung by Lance Percival, also consistently current.

Millicent Martin also performed "In the Summer of His Years" during the "Week That Was" tribute to President John Kennedy, as they abandoned the comedy for their November 23, 1963 broadcast, choosing instead to reflectively and respectfully honor him.

In 1963 a soundtrack of show highlights was released, supervised by Martin. The following year the show was canceled in spite of its success due to the general election that was going on in England simultaneously.

While the Beatles were always a top priority for Martin and his label, he also continued to produce for many other acts throughout the next two years, including, but by no means limited to, Terry Scott ("My Brother b/w "Don't Light the Fire 'Til After Santa's Gone"), Joan Sims ("Hurry Up Gran" b/w "Oh Not Again Ken" and "Spring Song" b/w "Men") all in 1963.

Shirley Bassey had a hit with a Martin-produced cover of "I (Who Have Nothing)" in 1963, a hit for Ben E. King earlier in the year. Originally an Italian song called "Uno Dei Tanti" ("One of Many"), Jerry Lieber and Mike Stoller rewrote it as "I (Who Have Nothing)" and produced it for King.

In 1964 Martin also produced the theme for the James Bond film "Goldfinger."

Martin was also involved in many, if not all of the sessions involving Lennon/McCartney songs for Billy J. Kramer with the Dakotas, the Fourmost and Cilla Black.

Gerry and the Pacemakers were a Liverpool act which would have success on the Parlophone label as well as with Martin. He produced "How Do You Do It?" for them after the Beatles rejected it as their debut single. He also produced "Don't Let the Sun Catch You Crying" and "I Like It" in 1964.

Under the direction of Martin, Gerry and the

Maddalena Fagandini

Pacemakers recorded several singles and full-length LPs, always garnering considerably less attention than the Beatles.

The Pacemakers' follow up to "How Do You Do It?" was "I Like It," also produced by Martin, as was "You'll Never Walk Alone" which he also arranged.

The Pacemakers would continue to record throughout their career under Martin's advisement. They attempted to be a band with multiple levels (rock with an intense beat as well as sweet, mellow standards) as the Beatles had done, but the Pacemakers were not as successful in this endeavor and the Beatles surpassed them relatively quickly.

Some of the selections for the Pacemakers' album tracks may have been songs that they and the Beatles both simultaneously covered before becoming recording artists. Both acts were generally careful not to record songs that the other had already done, some examples of possibilities include "A Shot of Rhythm and Blues," "Where Have You Been All My Life," and "Summertime," which were all recorded by the

Pacemakers. "Slow Down" was a rare exception.

The Pacemakers also recorded a version of "Hello Little Girl" which was left unreleased in favor of the Fourmost's version, also produced by Martin.

Martin produced Cilla Black's very successful version of "You're My World" in early '64, which was an English translation of the 1963 Italian language record "Il Mio Mondo" co-written by Umberto Bindi along with Gino Paoli and translated to English by American songwriter Carl Sigman.

Black sang lead and the Breakaways supplied background vocals along with Black's road manager and future husband Bobby Willis. Johnny Pearson and His Orchestra, who had also played on her previous single "Anyone Who Had a Heart," also play on this track.

Very early on in his partnership with the Beatles, Martin recognized their talent as performers quite capable of writing and playing their own songs and giving unused compositions to others. He also realized the potential of having their songs recorded by other artists, who were not in the same category.

Ella Fitzgerald was an American jazz singer who in 1964 released Hello Dolly, a studio album with her out in front of an orchestra performing standards from many different walks of music, most interestingly covering "Can't Buy Me Love." Martin is credited on occasion as the producer on this recording, although it's not known if he had anything to do with it at all.

This put a Lennon/McCartney song alongside the likes of Richard Rodgers ("The Sweetest Sounds") and Cole Porter ("Miss Otis Regrets") as well as standards "How High the Moon," "Hello Dolly," "Volare," and "People," a hit for Barbra Streisand in 1964 after she performed it in the play *Funny Girl*.

As a highly skilled producer who had excellent instinct and experience, as well as the general run of several studios at all times, Martin was able bring out something excellent from not just the Beatles, but seemingly in each performer he was assigned.

Alma Cogan was a child singer who grew up recording. Martin produced her single "I Knew Right

Away" b/w "It's You" in 1964 with McCartney playing the tambourine on both sides.

While his pop sensibilities were piqued during his pre-Beatles era, Martin's classical and orchestral work was highly regarded as well, for many of the same reasons that his "pop" recordings were so well respected.

The London Baroque Ensemble performed segments of the Brandenburg Concerto with Martin producing in 1952. "Time Beat" b/w "Waltz in Orbit" was an unusual and experimental recording from 1962, less than a month before he was first introduced to the Beatles.

"Time Beat" was a reworking of an interval signal (a distinctive and unique musical phrase that identifies a station or network) that was created by Maddalena Fagandini (who would design sound effects for "Dr. Who"). Martin added a tape loop and instruments to the already pre-recorded track.

"Waltz in Orbit" featured sound effects from Fagandini's BBC Radiophonic Workshop as well as tape manipulation. Ray Cathode (as in a cathode ray amplifier tube) was the pseudonym of Martin and Fagandini.

As the Beatles would grow as musicians, as well as untitled producers, Martin was absolutely treasured by them as they mutually respected one another's talents and trusted his judgment.

In early '64, just as the height of Beatlemania was spilling across the ocean, Martin began recording with the Action, an act he was hoping to groom into another of "his bands." The Action had minimal success and were dropped from the label by 1967, after scoring some minor hits in 1965.

Off the Beatle Track was a late 1964 release by George Martin and His Orchestra, with 11 Lennon/McCartney songs, as well as "Don't Bother Me" (Harrison's sole recorded composition at that time) performed as instrumentals by a pop orchestra.

Martin would continue to reinterpret his Beatles catalog in subsequent years with other artists, in both traditional and unconventional fashion, learning with them as well as teaching them. ▨

CHAPTER 6:
THE 1960 REHEARSAL TAPES

ON TWO OCCASIONS IN EARLY 1960, MCCARTNEY WAS ABLE TO BORROW A HOME TAPE RECORDER TO CAPTURE THE SOUNDS OF JOHN AND STU REHEARSING WITH HIM. IT IS UNLIKELY THAT HARRISON WAS PRESENT ON THIS FIRST SESSION, SAID TO BE AT MCCARTNEY'S HOUSE AT 20 FORTHLIN ROAD IN LIVERPOOL, POSSIBLY IN APRIL. THE SPECIFIC DATE AND LOCATION REMAIN UNSUBSTANTIATED.

PAUL RECALLS RECORDING these tapes with the three squeezed into the bathroom of his home, where the sound was best. He also tells of his brother Michael occasionally adding a bit of percussion by hitting a suitcase during what Paul remembers as "Easter break." This would put the date of the first tape roughly at April 17, which was Easter Sunday 1960, although the official date is unknown.

The trio rehearsed aimlessly for a long stretch, likely with the sole purpose of letting Sutcliffe hear himself so that he could improve as a musician.

Lengthy instrumental performances fill the bulk of the tape, all played at a slow pace. The recording reveals a barely capable Sutcliffe on bass, clearly holding back the two more experienced and natural talents of Lennon and McCartney.

On the record is also an instrumental that was a bit more evolved and complete. "Cayenne" was a Shadows/surf-inspired instrumental said to have been written solely by McCartney, who claims singular credit on the track. George is credited as playing on the 1960 track, although while he was indeed a band member at this time, his participation is very unlikely.

The song "Looking Glass" was bootlegged for many years, apparently after Sutcliffe took this first tape home with him. It wound up with Astrid, who was rumored to lend it to German musician Frank Dostal in the late '70s. Dostal made a copy for himself, which ultimately became copied and re-edited for the bootleg market.

On the official release the instrumental is faded out at 1:14, whereas previous bootlegs were almost twice as long. This was likely caused by copies of the tapes being "looped" so as to extend the length of the song.

Similar unofficial recordings reveal many of the aimless instrumental "jams" with titles such as "I Don't Know," "I Don't Need No Cigarette, Boy," "Come on People," or simply "Untitled Instrumental Number 1-6."

The original tapes were given back to Harrison by Kirchherr in 1994 to serve as the masters on the band's "new" release.

One of these relatively aimless instrumental recordings features a highly speculative voice singing a hard-to-decipher song. It's very difficult to tell, however the voice sounds much like McCartney either singing a standard, a traditional song, or an original composition, made up on the spot or premeditated.

There is also a barely audible vocal on a song that might be titled "Well Darling" if it would have evolved past this point. "Well Darling" was said to have been recorded on a Grundig reel-to-reel home recorder. McCartney curiously describes it as "the one with the little green eye on it" which is likely him referring to the four leaf clover logo on the machine.

While minimal, there are some enlightening moments on the poor quality tape, specifically involving the interplay between John and Paul.

The recording, while extremely rough, contains an early attempt at songwriting collaboration between Lennon and McCartney, occasionally harmonizing on words that seem familiar to them. It is likely they spent a great deal of time doing songs that they

invented as they played, and on this occasion there just happened to be tape running.

It's interesting to ponder how many other tunes of theirs were lost just after being played.

While singing together loosely on this brief recording, it does sound as if the two harmonize on a line "Meanwhile what do you think? I think you stink like a sink, boy!" which is said to be a playground rhyme that the two Liverpudlian guitarists knew.

The band was much more prolific by the time McCartney would borrow the recorder again. The young songwriters even recorded several original compositions which they had been working on slowly.

Once again the date of these home recordings is unknown, although it is estimated to be May or June 1960. One scenario is that the band got together at McCartney's home on Paul's 18th birthday (June 18) to record more rehearsals, this time seeming a bit more focused and cohesive.

The order in which the songs were recorded, and over what span of time, is unknown. It is possible that several rehearsals were recorded over a span of days, weeks, or months. The main participants seem to be John and Paul, with occasional snippets of George and Stu running through a series of songs.

"Hallelujah I Love Her So" was written by Ray Charles

in 1956 and was his first single for Atlantic Records. The song would appear on his self-titled debut LP the following year. The impressionable young band members were awestruck with Charles and enjoyed the way he put his whole package together. His music was tougher than the average "sappy" pop of the day, yet he could still be sensitive and was an all-around performer who had showmanship.

They were also drawn to the gospel roots of "Hallelujah I Love Her So" although they probably didn't yet know the term. Charles would frequently adapt religious hymns to fit a more commercial rock and roll feel.

Even in the formative days of the band the young musicians knew what they liked and who they would model themselves after.

Another influential figure who brought inspiration to the band was a guitar player from Oklahoma City who also covered "Hallelujah I Love Her So," Eddie Cochran.

The band was impressed with Cochran's ability to write and record his own songs, and also re-interpret others' music as his own. He even changed the lyrics to replace Charles' "daddy" with his own name, as in "Eddie's all alone." McCartney would also sing "Eddie is all alone" instead of including his own name. This points out that the band wasn't yet as confident as they would eventually become with experience.

In "Hallelujah" the singer boasts about his fantastic love interest who brings him coffee in his favorite cup, is dependable at a moment's notice, and of course gives him kisses him and holds him tight, all common themes but put into short series of words cleverly placed together. "Hallelujah" is a prime example of the type of song John and Paul hoped to write one day.

The song became a part of their act shortly after they got their hands on the Cochran version, released in December 1959. Not only was there a recording of the band performing this song in 1960, but there is a second unofficial recording from New Year's

Eve 1962 at the Star Club in Hamburg with Horst Fascher singing with the band.

It doesn't appear that the Beatles did "Hallelujah" past that December 1962 performance. They may have possibly stopped doing it much sooner, reviving it in order to give Fascher a chance to join in on the fun.

In 1995 an edited and sped up version of this recording was released on the *Beatles Anthology 1* album. Two other recordings from this era were included, "Cayenne" and another alleged to be an early Lennon/McCartney song.

"You'll Be Mine" is said to have been a McCartney composition inspired by Elvis, and sung by Paul as an opera singer, over-exaggerating greatly. John adds a part that has him speaking like one of the Ink Spots, an all-black American vocal doo-wop group that was universally accepted during a segregated era.

Paul sings the simple lyrics such as "you'll be mine, 'til you die, and the stars always shine" in his over-the-top style while John, and possibly George, half-heartedly harmonize in the background. As a novice songwriter, Paul was already emerging with a style that would follow him throughout his career. Even at this extremely early stage of Paul's progression he was a aware of nature as a theme.

Similarly, John joins in with a spoken word segment about someone "burning" or "bringing" (possibly "brunt" which would be a made-up Lennon word) "that toast the other morning" and including a phrase about "your national health eyeball" displaying his love for odd and unusual phrases built from relatively common words. He finishes the section with "I love you, like I have never done before," curious lyrics from a young Lennon.

Even at an early stage of their collaboration, the two worked well together, quickly allowing the other to contribute or offer opinions on how to complete a song.

As John takes over the lead vocal with his spoken word segment, we can hear the two singers repositioning to get closer to the recorder. It is likely that as they sang into a home unit more often, they experimented to find the ideal place to stand in order to get the best recording. They were acutely aware of how things

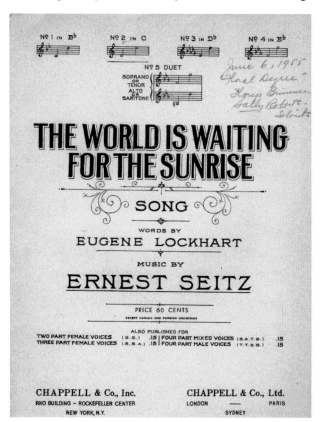

should sound, even at this point in their progression.

Sadly, this also probably means that they recorded over performances as they rehearsed and re-recorded.

Sutcliffe and Harrison may or may not have performed on this specific track, as the recordings weren't necessarily completed in one "session" and the attendees may have changed from song to song.

A careful ear seems to reveal only two performers on the song, however sources frequently credit four Beatles, possibly while inside McCartney's bathroom where it was said to sound best. John and Paul may have done some recording as a duo in the lavatory, and other recordings may be at a different location in the house, likely the main living space or parlor.

Lennon and McCartney performed as the Nerk Twins in April 1960. Little is known of this engagement other than the memories of McCartney, who recalls their opening number on one of these occasions.

"The World is Waiting for a Sunrise" dates back to approximately 1894 when Canadian concert pianist and composer Ernest Seitz wrote the tune around age 12. He was rather embarrassed about it so he kept it under wraps until 1919 when he published it under the pseudonym Raymond Roberts, as the classically educated pianist looked down upon the mass scale of popular music and did not want to be associated with it.

"The World is Waiting for a Sunrise" was recorded by tenor singer John Steel circa 1922. An instrumental version was done by the Victor Salon Orchestra in 1924.

Stan Laurel performed the song (while playing a bed frame like a harp) in the 1939 Laurel and Hardy film "The Flying Deuces." The comic duo portrayed condemned prisoners awaiting execution in the early morning, making the song especially satirical.

Other notable recordings of the song include versions by the Benny Goodman Quartet (1943), Canadian "King of Swing" Bert Niosi (1946), Cuban bandleader Machito (around 1948), Django

Blind Lemon Jefferson

Reinhardt (1949), Duke Ellington with Al Hibler on lead vocal (1950), and an unusual novelty version recorded by comedian Stan Freberg (1952).

Seitz co-wrote the song with Canadian playwright and stage/screen actor Gene Lockhart, who appeared in over 50 films between 1922 and his death in 1957. Lockhart's movies include the silent "Smilin' Through" (1922), "Something to Sing About" (1937), "Mission to Moscow" (1943), "The Inspector General" (1949), "The Big Hangover" (1950), "Bonzo Goes to College" (1952), and "Carousel" (1956).

The version of "The World is Waiting for a Sunrise" most familiar to John and Paul was the 1951 Les Paul and Mary Ford performance (utilizing double-tracked vocals as well as multiple guitars overdubbed on top of one another) which was more upbeat and faster than many of the other ballad-tempo versions they had heard.

In April 1960 John and Paul hitchhiked to Caversham, Berkshire to spend a week visiting Paul's cousin Bett Robbins and her husband Mike, who ran a pub called Fox and Hounds. John and Paul spent the Easter week tending bar and were allowed to perform in the taproom on the weekend, April 23-24.

Bett and Mike were former performers, recently leaving their jobs as "Butlin's Redcoats," which was the term for entertainers at one of the many U.K.-based holiday camps.

The young and eager Lennon and McCartney respected the opinions of their hosts, and were enthusiastic to learn as much as they could about the industry. They soaked up information and asked lots of questions of their older relatives, who likely recognized their talent and encouraged them.

Paul also credits Mike for teaching him a lot about putting on a show.

While John and Paul were reparing to perform as the "Nerk Twins" Mike Robbins asked them what song they were going to open with, they answered with "Be Bop a Lu La" which Robbins told them was too slow. He explained that it was best to open with something fast and energetic, suggesting the upbeat "The World is Waiting for a Sunrise," referring to the Paul/Ford version. It is interesting to note that Robbins as well as George Martin would encourage the band to open with something strong and engaging.

Likely within a month or so the song was performed again and recorded in the McCartney home, this time with a more traditional approach and much slower tempo than energized Paul/Ford version.

McCartney sings lead and there is a well-crafted guitar solo included, either played by Paul himself, or Harrison, who may or may not be included at all on these tapes. Lennon plays a second guitar and Sutcliffe adds his minimal bass on this novice song.

Another widely-heard song the Beatles recorded when they possessed the Grundig was one that they would make an official release almost four years later.

"Matchbox" dates back to 1924. That year, Ma Rainey recorded a song called "Lost Wandering Blues" on which she sings "Lord, I'm standing here wondering, will a matchbox hold my clothes."

Three years later in 1927 Blind Lemon Jefferson did "The Matchbox Blues" where he slightly altered the lyrics to "I'm sittin' here wonderin' would a matchbox hold my clothes." Although he would record the song several more times throughout his career, it was never a substantial hit.

In 1957 while at the Sun Records studio in Memphis, Carl Perkins was searching for a song to use as the B-side to "Your True Love." Perkins' father Buck suggested "Matchbox Blues," possibly recalling the 1949 version as recorded by the Shelton Brothers, who sing "I'm standing here thinking will a matchbox hold my clothes."

Carl claims to have been unfamiliar with the song when his father suggested it. He joined session piano player Jerry Lee Lewis as well as siblings Clayton (bass) and Jay Perkins (acoustic guitar) to pick out a tune and make up some on-the-spot lyrics that had little in common with the Rainey, Jefferson or Shelton Brothers versions other than the first line where Perkins sings "well I'm sitting wondering with a matchbox holding my clothes."

It is believed that Perkins came up with the rest of his lyrics spontaneously as they rehearsed and recorded.

When the single made its way to England, the Quarrymen quickly added it to their act, with John initially taking the lead vocal duties. There are also reports of drummer Best taking lead as he would step to front of the stage and McCartney would take over on drums, and when Best was not in attendance the vocals went to Lennon.

Around this period Richard Starkey would sing lead on "Matchbox" while performing with Rory Storm

and the Hurricanes at their Butlin's summer camp residency in 1960.

During the summer 1960 session(s), possibly done on McCartney's birthday, the band recorded a crude version of the song with John on lead vocals and guitar and the novice Sutcliffe on bass, still slowly learning the instrument. Paul presumably plays the guitar solo. Again George may or may not have been present for any of these recordings although he is frequently credited on these unofficial performances.

"Matchbox" stayed in the Beatles' repertoire well into the era of Beatlemania. It was performed live for the last time on May 1, 1964 for the BBC's "From Us to You."

A month later, June 1, 1964, Perkins visited the studio when the Beatles recorded "Matchbox." Reportedly the Beatles and Perkins had an impromptu jam session, but unfortunately it was not recorded.

Another rockabilly song recorded on these tapes, occasionally listed as the Hans-Walther Braun Tapes, was a Gene Vincent song from November 1959.

"Wild Cat" was co-written by Aaron Schroeder and Wally Gold and released by Gene Vincent and the Blue Caps on the Capitol label in late 1959. The record made its way to England in early 1960 and quickly became a favorite of the Beatles, or whatever name they were going by at the time.

The audio quality is very poor but the passion of the performance is apparent. On two slightly different versions we hear Paul singing a proud lead vocal, and both John and Paul likely gave Stu some private lessons in the hopes of improving his playing.

Schroeder was a New York born songwriter, producer and publisher who would co-write more than 1,000 songs throughout his career. He was also a successful talent scout for a publishing company. He would have his most success writing for Elvis Presley with "Any Way You Want Me (That's How I Will Be)" and "First in Line" in 1956, "Young and Beautiful," "Santa Bring My Baby Back (To Me)," "Don't Leave Me Now" and "Got A Lot O' Livin' to Do," all in 1957, "Young Dreams," "Dixieland

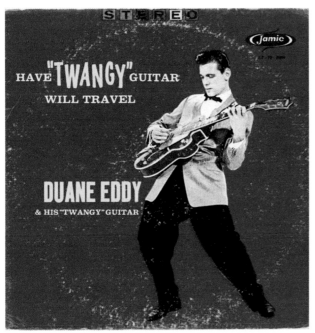

Rock," and "I Got Stung" in 1958, and "A Big Hunk O' Love" in 1959.

A small sampling of Schroeder's compositions for others include "If I Knew You Were Comin' I'd Have Baked a Cake," written for Eileen Barton and the New Yorkers in 1950, "Now Don't That Prove I Love You" for the Five Keys in 1956, "Rock Boll Weevil" for Pat Boone in 1958, "French Foreign Legion" for Frank Sinatra in 1959, "Because They're Young" in 1960 from the Duane Eddy album *$1,000,000.00 Worth of Twang*, "Rubber Ball" in 1961 for Bobby Vee, and hundreds of others throughout the decade.

Another song that was written by Schroeder was "Glad All Over" which would be recorded by Perkins in 1957 and performed by the Beatles on many occasions, several of which were recorded.

Gold was a similar songwriter who had a string of hits, some of which were also co-written with Schroeder. Gold's compositions include "Summer Vacation" and "Repeat After Me" for the Four Esquires, a Boston-based vocal group he formed. He also wrote or co-wrote "Sweet Bird of Youth" for Nat King Cole and "Fools Hall of Fame" (co-written with Schroeder) for Pat Boone in 1959, "Person to Person" for American jazz singer Mildred Anderson and "It's Now Or Never" in 1960 (also co-written with Schroeder), and "In Your Arms" also for Elvis in 1961.

Gold would go on to be a contributor to "It's My Party" with lyrics written by Seymour Gottlieb, inspired by the real life events of his daughter Judy's sweet 16 party. It was first recorded by Helen Shapiro in early '63, and was again shortly after by Leslie Gore, whose version became a No. 1 hit in America. "It's My Party" was produced by Quincy Jones, who was quickly getting a reputation as an effective arranger in the early 1960s.

In "Wild Cat" we hear the singer telling a woman not to try and tame the wild cat, and not to put a cage around him. He will hug and kiss but then must be set free, and refers to the woman in the song as a "crazy little kitten."

Not only did the young Beatles enjoy the toughness of the lyrics, but they enjoyed Vincent's aggressive intensity. Along with his "tough sound" Vincent was willing to have a soft side as well, covering show tunes such as "Over the Rainbow," "Summertime," and "Ac-cen-tu-ate the Positive," and he was an important inspiration for the Beatles.

As adolescents in a traditionally male-dominated society, it was important for young English boys to be "manly" in whatever craft they chose. The Beatles were no exception, receiving validation from their idols, as in Buddy Holly making it "acceptable" for John to wear glasses in public.

In the post-war era, as a younger generation began to think more openly, acts like Holly and Vincent made it more acceptable for a rock band to play what might be considered their parents' music. The Beatles would gain confidence knowing they weren't alone in their love for all types of music, which was a quality they would retain throughout their careers.

Also during this period the Beatles performed two Duane Eddy instrumentals.

"Movin' n' Groovin'" was Eddy's debut single from his album *Have 'Twangy' Guitar Will Travel*. While it didn't become a huge hit, the song was noticed by a select audience, including the young Beatles who would continue to observe Eddy's career closely.

Eddy's sound was unique due to his technique using the guitar's bass strings to play the lead, creating a low, reverberating sound. Referring to it as a "twangy" sound, Eddy along with his producer Lee Hazlewood wrote and recorded the instrumental in November 1957.

Hazlewood was a disc jockey in Arizona when he

crossed paths with the young singing duo Jimmy and Duane, comprised of Eddy and Jimmy Delbridge, who would later record as Jimmy Dell.

After their "Soda Fountain Girl" single in 1955, the duo would join Buddy Long's Western Melody Boys, an Arizona country and western band.

Utilizing the "twangy" sound, Hazlewood and Eddy would record their co-written instrumental in an Arizona studio that had no echo chamber (an enclosed room to help the sound reverberate). To resolve the issue Hazlewood purchased a 2,000 gallon water tank for Eddy to perform in to help emphasize his unique guitar sound.

The song's intro liberally borrows from Chuck Berry's "Brown Eyed Handsome Man" which the Beatles loved immediately. Once again the "tough" sound that Eddy created, as well as his slick, cool look attracted the young Beatles, who would listen to his records repetitively in an attempt to recreate the sound as closely as they could.

On the Beatles' recording of "Movin'" it's difficult to tell exactly who is playing on the track, frequently credited to John, Paul, George, and Stu, even though George was inaudible or perhaps not present at all.

Harrison was inspired by Eddy, but perhaps given only a couple of selections as they had limited tape space, and the recorder was eventually going to have to be returned. George's possible role as the "junior Beatle" was already emerging.

Regardless of the players, the performance is well above adequate, even with the low fidelity of the recording.

Paul and George were both improving rapidly as guitar players and it was George who "fancied himself" a bit of a guitar specialist or "slinger." It's quite likely he indeed was playing lead on the two Eddy tracks recorded.

"Ramrod" was also an instrumental from Eddy's *Have 'Twangy' Guitar Will Travel* LP in 1958. It is not known if the band was familiar with Eddy's music from the singles or the full-length album.

During these early days the young band members were thoughtful of who among them had which records so they could trade and not duplicate records in their combined collection. Full-length LPs were considerably more expensive than singles, and they didn't want to "risk" spending their entire budget on a long player if they only cared for a few of the songs. This would change when Epstein joined the fold and the band would have greater access to records.

Eddy's *Have 'Twangy' Guitar, Will Travel* would have been a wise purchase as they were all fans of instrumental guitar rock. The album was comprised of instrumentals primarily co-written by Eddy and Hazlewood, however "Ramrod" was written by Al Casey, who plays bass, guitar, and piano on the album.

Hazlewood wrote and produced a song called "The Fool" that was a hit for Sanford Clark in 1956 featuring Casey's guitar, which also had a "twangy" quality about it.

Casey was another "guitar slinger" who Hazlewood produced for regularly. He co-wrote Cochran's "40 Miles of Bad Road." This "twangy" instrumental was released in 1959 as a single as well as on the *$1,000,000 Worth of Twang* LP.

The more evolved songwriting Beatles would not venture into the "guitar hero" instrumental genre often, but in their early formative days they certainly did. The band displayed a familiarity with this material and completed it with confidence, although precision was still something they needed to improve upon.

Knowing that recording and then listening to their performances was essential to improving as a band, the young Beatles no doubt were self-critical of their shortcomings, as well as mindful of what they felt they were doing right.

The Beatles continued to perfect their craft of "copying" their idols, while adding something of their own to each song. This desire to write music was nothing new, as John and Paul had aspirations of writing their own material even before they met.

One of the songs that John wrote at an extremely early age was performed while the band had the tape recorder in their possession. Another original song that they would rehearse during this period was an early McCartney composition.

"I'll Follow the Sun" was ultimately recorded by the band for their 1964 *With The Beatles* album after Paul recollected the song from his memory to finish up and get it ready to record. As discussed, McCartney had a great love for using nature themes in his songs, and the idea of following the sun exemplifies this for the promising songwriter. The sad but hopeful tone also defines a young McCartney's style, a tone which combines optimism with realism.

As with all of the performances during this short era, the lineup is difficult to determine. This recording might possibly be the trio of Paul, John, and George, with Paul's brother Mike McCartney helping out with his "suitcase" percussion, as referred to by Paul.

These elementary songs written prior to the Beatles' record deal were frequently worked on for a bit, possibly written down, and then forgotten about (or thrown out), although some were revived in later years to record.

One of the band's more persistent tunes was one

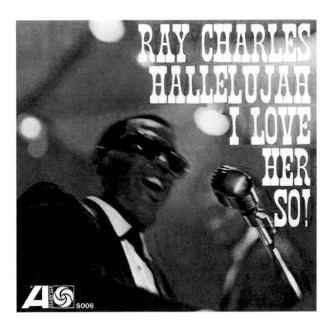

they finally released about 10 years after its initial recording.

"One After 909" was one of the first songs Lennon wrote, originally conceptualized when he was about 17 years old (which may predate his writing of "Hello Little Girl").

Lennon states that he came up with it on his own although McCartney seems to recall it being a collaborative effort. It may be a case where one writer had the song all but complete, then the other assisted with a word or phrase. If so, this could possibly be the first case of a Lennon/McCartney collaboration.

The inspiration came from Lennon's romantic notion of the United States, through Lonnie Donegan and other skiffle artists who covered much American music including some on the subject of trains. Songs like the "Midnight Special," "The Rock Island Line," and "Freight Train," along with songs of heartache and sorrow such as "Heartbreak Hotel," "Crying, Waiting, Hoping," and "Bye, Bye Love" motivated the young writer to combine the two topics.

In rather early Lennon fashion the song has a unique twist, the singer is racing to the train to prove to the girl that he indeed loves her by meeting her on the train, however when he arrives he finds that he has the wrong location.

Even as a novice writer John had an excellent ability to tell a story with very few words, including the pay off or "joke" at the end that he went to the wrong train. Another witty feature of the song is that John never explains, in the song or in the real world, if 909 is the number of the train, or the time. Apparently at one point in time the song was written as "9:09" but the colon was removed by Lennon to add a bit of mystery.

Rumors circulate that they did "One After 909" at Percy Phillips Studios when they recorded "In Spite of All the Danger" and "That'll Be the Day." An acetate was said to exist at least for a short period of time, but if that was the case it quickly disappeared, never to turn up again. Other sources say George, Paul, and

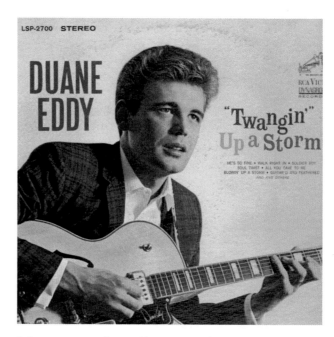

John went to the studio on another occasion to cut Lennon's original train song.

There are two versions of the song on the tapes which sound like John and Paul singing as a duo, along with one or two guitars, player(s) unknown. The bass and percussion are absent. Once again Lennon and McCartney harmonize very well together as they continue to sharpen their skills as performers.

The song would have a unique history with the Beatles as it was not officially recorded and released until almost ten years after its composition. Not all early attempts at songwriting would have such a fortunate fate.

"You Must Write Everyday" appears to be an original from this early era as well, another attempt at an original composition from John and Paul. McCartney sings the title and some other undecipherable lyrics as the band, possibly a four-piece but still without a drummer or any percussion, stumbles through the rudimentary song.

This is how they likely wrote songs at the time: Playing basic progressions repeatedly, starting lyrics with a possible title, and making it up as they went along, occasionally filling in more words to make the composition a full song. They frequently took time to include a guitar solo.

Some of the first Lennon/McCartney collaborations originated in this training-like style, including another from the early 1960 tapes.

"Some Days" also includes the aforementioned traits: Some (but few) decipherable lyrics sung by Paul, a guitar solo, and an elementary chord progression. As is typical with these early recordings, several elements are hard to identify, and the song was likely made up on the spot, or shortly prior to recording.

The lyrics, when understandable, are as simple as the band would ever get, "some days we are happy, and others are sad," and "some days we remember, some days we forget." Paul sings the unremarkable lyrics with a young and enthusiastic delivery, while the guitar solo, likely played by George, is bit sloppy but shows signs of a dedicated band working hard to become better.

The guitar work from John and Paul, and possibly George during these recordings displayed that they clearly spent time learning how to play and perform along with others.

Meanwhile Sutcliffe was struggling to keep up with the band. Theses tapes would all eventually end up in his possession, likely for him to listen and play along in hopes that he would begin to improve. McCartney said "it was better to have a bass player who couldn't play than to not have a bass player at all".

The band quickly moved past the types of tunes and phrases heard in "Some Days," "Well Darling," and "You Must Write Everyday," as all were never heard of again during the Beatles' career.

Before the Grundig was returned (reportedly to Paul's neighbor Charlie Hodgson) the young musicians copied whatever they had recorded onto three fresh reels. The originals were presumably taped over by the recorder's owner, but this is not substantiated.

The first of the fresh reels, mostly instrumental recordings, went with Sutcliffe, then wound up with Astrid Kirchherr, who gave the original tapes to Harrison in 1994 for use in the *Beatles Anthology* release.

Prior to the official release, much of this was widely bootlegged after Kirchherr loaned the reel to Frank Dostal, who compiled the audio along with the second reel from these "sessions."

The second of the three reels was given to Hans Walther Braun, a friend who the band members met in Germany. One theory is that he also lent his copy to Dostal sometime between 1966 and 1979. Dostal was said to have compiled the two reels before making copies for himself, Kirchherr, and "Icke" Braun.

It is believed that Braun's copy still exists, safely under lock and key. Kirchherr's copy was given to Harrison, but the whereabouts of Dostal's copy are unknown.

Details vary widely on specifically how the material was leaked onto the bootleg market.

The mysterious third original reel, which apparently is owned by McCartney, is rumored to have early versions of "When I'm 64," "There's a Place," and another song known only as "Winston's Walk." As the tale goes, the tape was discovered by Hodgson's nephew Peter in the attic of his home. Peter either sold it directly to McCartney, or it was purchased anonymously by McCartney at an auction. Details also vary widely on this tape as well.

It is remarkable that audio documentation from this era exists at all, and the quality is extremely raw. Even with modern technology and digital techniques to improve recordings, the quality was boosted only slightly on songs that were ultimately released from this era.

"Hallelujah I Love Her So," "You'll Be Mine," and Cayenne" were the only three songs from this era that made the cut. They were all edited extensively, with only about three and half minutes of actual audio eventually seeing the light of day.

The band would quickly advance, although Sutcliffe would be "left behind," and these tapes document this era wonderfully, revealing the earliest stages of a band that would grow in unimaginable ways. ◆

CHAPTER 7:
BACK TO GERMANY

AS THE NEW YEAR APPROACHED, THE BEATLES WERE NOW STRICTLY THE BEATLES, SPELLED/MISSPELLED WITH THE "A." MANY OTHER CHANGES, FIRSTS, AND SIGNIFICANT EVENTS OCCURRED RAPIDLY FOR THE BAND IN 1961.

THE FIRST CHANGE came early on with the departure of Newby on bass after only four shows, as he decided to return to college instead of following the Beatles back to Germany.

Sutcliffe would return to Liverpool and play occasional shows with the band, but was beginning to lose interest in being a Beatle. With Sutcliffe indefinite as a band member, it was around this time that Paul became the band's bass player, likely as early as January 5, 1961.

Another possibility is that John, George, and Paul all took a stab at the bass, with Paul emerging as the best. Paul perhaps stepped up when the others didn't want to stop playing guitar, as each was quite proficient.

Throughout January the band performed around Liverpool at the Aintree Institute, Latham Hall, Hambleton Hall, and Alexandra Hall, sharing the bill with such bands as Derry and the Seniors and Faron and the Tempest Tornadoes. They also played Litherland Town Hall in Liverpool throughout the year, attracting consistently large and excited crowds.

Brian Kelly of Beekay Promotions was helping the hard-working band find consistent work, along with Dave Forshaw, an eager 17-year-old who was putting on various events around Liverpool.

By the second month of 1961 as the Beatles started getting more gigs, sometime two or three a night, they decided a driver was needed to transport them and their equipment. At Best's suggestion they hired his friend Neil Aspinall, a student at the Liverpool Institute where he was friends with George and Paul as well.

Aspinall's family lived in Liverpool but he was born in North Wales after his family was evacuated from their home during WWII air raids. Aspinall's family returned to Liverpool when he was an infant. He was enrolled at the Liverpool Institute at age 12, where he would be in the same English and art classes as McCartney.

Aspinall also became friends with Harrison, and the two smoked their first cigarettes together

(Woodbines. a popular brand of the era) along with Lennon and McCartney.

While studying to be an accountant Aspinall accepted a part-time position with the Beatles in early 1961. He left his job as an accountant trainee later in the year as he was making more money as the band's road manager and personal assistant.

As the band gained larger fame Aspinall's role became considerably more important. He was given greater responsibility in planning the band's travel arrangements, and he handled some of their more exotic whims in future years.

In 1968 Aspinall married Suzy Ornstein with Magic Alex Mardas as his best man, and McCartney, Starr, and wife Maureen were also in attendance. The couple would remain married until Aspinall's death in 2008.

Although he was not a musician, Aspinall appears on several Beatle tracks, even being asked for his opinion on songs on occasion. In later years Aspinall would play a pivotal part in running Apple Records, serving as the representative for them in various court proceedings throughout the '70s and remaining part of the Beatles organization throughout his life.

On February 9, 1961 (exactly three years before their breakthrough appearance on "The Ed Sullivan Show") the Beatles played for the first time at the Cavern Club in Liverpool.

Ultimately they would play approximately 155 lunchtime performances (generally noon until 2 p.m.) at the Cavern, located on Mathew Street in an area known as Liverpool's City Centre. They also performed at least 125 evening performances, along with a wide range of different bands and musicians.

On Valentine's Day while playing their second show of the days at Litherland Town Hall, Paul performed with a red satin heart on his jacket while doing "Wooden Heart," an Elvis song from the brand new film "G.I. Blues."

The heart was to be raffled off and the winner would get a kiss from Paul. When the victorious girl's name was called fans mobbed the band, knocking John to the ground and interrupting the show until the bouncers were able to rescue the band and restore order.

Early events where Paul would "outshine" John were unsettling for Lennon. He was thrilled that his band was gaining success and notoriety, but certainly jealous of the attention that McCartney was receiving over him.

Shortly after the band was signed to EMI it was questioned if they should call the band "John Lennon and the Beatles" or "Paul McCartney and the Beatles." Ultimately of course the decision was made not to define a leader of the band..

February 21 proved to be an exciting day, beginning with a lunchtime performance at the Cavern Club with Sutcliffe performing and his fiancé watching from the crowd. After the Cavern Club they traveled to the Casanova Club, and after that it was Town Hall on Litherland. This was the first time of many they would perform three shows at three venues in one evening, likely being driven around Liverpool by Aspinall.

At the beginning of March the Beatles began

performing more regularly at the Cavern, playing on Mondays, Wednesdays, and Fridays with Derry and the Seniors and the Big Three playing the other afternoons.

Along with Gerry and the Pacemakers, Rory Storm and the Hurricanes, the Big Three, Kingsize Taylor and the Dominoes, and Derry and the Seniors, the Beatles played at the Liverpool Jazz Society on March 6, the first of five appearances there within the month.

The following year, the Jazz Society became the Storyville Jazz Club and the Beatles would play there as well during March. The club, located on Temple Street in Liverpool, would eventually revert back to its original name, the Iron Door Club, where the Silver Beatles performed on May 15, 1960 along with Cass and the Cassanovas.

The "Mersey Beat" sound was becoming much more popular than jazz, which was often referred to as trad jazz (shortened from traditional). Local clubs that would previously not permit rock and roll acts to perform there slowly loosened their self-imposed rules and catered a bit more to what was popular, and therefore successful at drawing crowds.

On March 11, 1961, likely going on well after midnight, the Beatles performed at the "Rock Around the Clock All Night Rock Ball" which was advertised to take place from 8 p.m. until 8 a.m. the following morning. Also on that bill were headliners Gerry and the Pacemakers with supporting acts including the Remo Four, Rory Storm and the Hurricanes, Kingsize Taylor and the Dominoes, the Big Three, Derry and the Seniors, Ray and the Del-Renas, Dale Roberts and the Jaywalkers, Johnny Rocco and the Jets, and Faron and the Tempest Tornadoes. It's very likely that the Beatles went on second to last, possibly as late, or early, as 4 a.m.

Sutcliffe was still an active player during most of the Liverpool dates in early '61. In mid-March he traveled to Hamburg to spend some time with his fiancé as well as to sort out some legal arrangements

involving the band.

On March 15, likely with Paul on bass, the Beatles played an afternoon event at the Jazz Society, sharing the bill with Gerry and the Pacemakers as well as Rory Storm and the Wild Ones, a band which included Ringo on the drums, and McCartney on piano.

St. Patrick's Day 1961 saw the Beatles performing at Mossway Hall in Liverpool and then heading to the Jazz Society for a second show of the day. The band didn't get paid for the first show at Mossway, but were allowed "all the Guinness they could want." It is unknown how the Jazz Society show went.

Other highlights of March included headlining a bill that had Gerry and the Pacemakers as a supporting act. Also in the lineup were the familiar faces of Kingsize Taylor and his Dominoes, as well as Simon Cardovo and his Royal Caribbean Steel Band, and Bill Bailey's Calypso Band.

Continuing to play frequently at the Cavern Club, the band started attracting consistently excited and loyal crowds. The first time the Beatles would play a nighttime show at the Cavern was March 21, 1961. Prior to this they only performed for the lunchtime crowd. On this night they performed alongside the Blue Jeans, who would eventually become the Swinging Blue Jeans. Also familiar with the streets of Hamburg, that band would have a hit in 1963 covering "Hippy Hippy Shake," which was originally done by American Chan Romero in 1959. Bob Wooler recalls lending the record to McCartney and his bandmates, who performed it on the first night they played the Cavern.

Present at these early performances was a young regular who would become president of Beatles fan club, Freda Kelly. She described the smell of the

The Beatles with Davy Jones

Cavern, which was a combination of all sorts of horrible things, as a very unique odor that could only be attached to the Beatles performing at this underground venue.

At some point during 1961 the Beatles would have a falling out with Williams over money, deciding that if they were going to be doing their own negotiations and bookings, he didn't deserve payment.

On March 27 the band started their long trip back to Hamburg. Sutcliffe and Kirchherr arranged for their legal return after an unfortunate series of events led to a rather disappointing end to their first visit to the area.

The band's lengthy residency at the Top Ten Club started April 1, and would run nightly until July 1. During this stay the band would play from 7 p.m. until 2 a.m. throughout the week and until 3 a.m. on weekends, with a 15-minute rest period per hour.

In June 1961 Sutcliffe would enroll in the Hamburg College of Art to begin courses to become an art instructor. That same month, likely but unconfirmed to be June 22-23, the Beatles' aforementioned recording sessions with Tony Sheridan took place in Hamburg.

After a very successful second stay in Hamburg, the Beatles returned to Liverpool July 2-3, rewarding themselves with a 12-day rest, performing again on July 13 at St John's Hall in Liverpool.

The first issue of *The Mersey Beat* was published on July 6 by Bill Harry, who would continue to report news of the Liverpool music scene throughout the British Invasion.

After their respite, the extremely hard-working and driven band continued to play their usual Liverpool venues, consistently attracting crowds who were continuously impressed by the exciting leather-clad musicians.

On July 27 at St. John's Hall in Liverpool the Beatles acted as the background band for Cilla White, later known as Cilla Black.

On August 17 the Beatles served as Johnny Gustafson's background band at St. John's Hall. The young musicians were amassing an incredible reputation as professional and dependable. That same evening Gustafson of the Big Three sat in with the Beatles on bass. This freed up McCartney to act as the frontman on several songs, leaving his guitar behind and working the crowd into a frenzy.

John and Paul took a trip to Paris together in late September, causing a couple of shows to be canceled, which was very unlike the generally reliable, professional performers.

While intending to hitchhike all the way the Spain, the duo only got as far as France, primarily by train. They visited with Jürgen Vollmer who they met in Hamburg and had since moved to Paris to study photography. While there Vollmer allegedly cut their hair into the long bangs cut that would come to be known as the trademark Beatle haircut, or the "Moptop."

After spending a week with their Paris Existentialist friends, the duo returned home with a newly increased attitude and level of confidence.

The band played at the Albany Cinema on October 15 for an event benefiting the St. John Ambulance Brigade. It was their first show after John and Paul's trip to Paris to celebrate Lennon's 21st birthday.

Comedian Ken Dodd was topping the bill which

featured the Dusty Road Ramblers, Les Arnold, Joe Cordova, Dunn and Markey, Bob McGrady, Lennie Rens, Shirley Gordon, Bert King, the Eltones, Dennis Horton and Gladys Ambrose, Jackie Owen and the Joe Royal Trio, Edna Bell, Jim Gretty, and Denis Smerdon.

The Beatles played as the first act after intermission, and then hurried to the more familiar Hambleton Hall for an evening performance.

While the venues where they performed were typically filled with screaming girls, there was the occasional "off night." This was the case on October 17 when the band played for "about 60 people" at the David Lewis Club in Liverpool.

The Beatles, Gerry and the Pacemakers, and the Cruisers all shared a bill at Town Hall, Litherland on October 19. It was suggested that the groups should do a set together, so along with Cruisers' Karl Terry the two groups performed as the Beatmakers with John on piano, Paul and George on guitars, and Pete Best sharing drums with Freddie Marsden, older brother of Gerry, who played guitar and sang. Les Chadwick played the bass and Les Maguire, who was the Pacemakers' pianist, played the saxophone.

The Beatmakers would only perform on this one occasion, although there were other opportunities to revive this all-star act.

Although the specific details of what happened remain unclear, an event occurred on October 28 that would prove vital to the success of the Beatles and their fate as a band.

Raymond Jones, a young Liverpool printer's apprentice and record collector, went to his usual record store to search for a new single by a band named the Beatles. North End Music Store (NEMS) was the record store and Jones was looking for "My Bonnie," which was said to be recommended to him by Wooler. The owner of the record store was of course Epstein, who may have never heard of the Beatles before this date, as unlikely as that may seem for anybody living in Liverpool in 1961.

According to some stories, until the record actually arrived at the store, Epstein's assistant Alistair Taylor was convinced that Jones was creating a fake record for them to order. Other accounts state that even though Jones was indeed a real customer, it was Taylor who actually was compelled to order the single.

The group would still occasionally serve as a backing band for solo singers. Davy Jones (not Davy Jones of the Monkees but rather a black American singer living in the U.K.). On November 24, the Beatles backed Jones at the Tower Ballroom, New Brighton, Wallasey. The solo singer is also not to be confused with David Bowie, whose real name is David Jones.

Also in November, the band performed with Earl Preston and the TTs. George unofficially began writing songs with Preston, one reported to be called "Sweet Love."

Some of the more significant events of November 1961 involved Alistair Taylor. Hired by Epstein as a salesman at his NEMS, Taylor later became his personal assistant.

As discussed, stories conflict greatly about the role that Taylor may have had in the discovery of the Beatles. One theory is that he created the name Raymond Jones, or that he just used the name of a regular customer to order the record so that Epstein would start carrying it. Although greatly disputed, it is highly likely it was indeed Jones who ordered the single (rather than Taylor) in an attempt to help the business carry a record that they already should have had in stock. Taylor's role is likely minimal and has been exaggerated.

Taylor briefly left NEMS but returned in 1963 just as the Beatles were beginning to gain widespread notoriety. He became known as "Mr. Fixit" to the Beatles for his ability to solve problems, simple as well as complicated. As the band began to tour the country and then the world, it was Taylor who would help arrange schedules and hotel reservations, also organizing the elaborate escape plans to avoid oceans of fans.

In '66 the Beatles would stop touring and Taylor, as well as Epstein and his staff would have less to do within the organization. Taylor continued to assist the Beatles in any way he could, serving as a real estate hunter for the band.

In late '67 Taylor would also play a role in writing "Hello Goodbye."

After Epstein's death several employees would leave NEMS and work directly for the Beatles. Taylor became the general manager of Apple until he was dismissed along with many of the other employees who were cleared out amidst financial issues in 1969.

In 1968 Taylor appeared, dressed as a one man band, for an ad encouraging artists with talent to submit samples to Apple Records. He can be heard apologizing for not bringing George Martin his bottle of claret (a dark French wine) in "Revolution 9."

After his departure from Apple and his estrangement from the Beatles, Taylor was recruited by Dick James to help promote Elton John, a novice artist at the time. In 1973 Taylor would leave the music business and would run a tea room in Derbyshire with his wife, eventually retiring. Taylor passed away in 2004.

Based on the excitement surrounding this "new band" from Liverpool, which Epstein quickly researched, he and Taylor attended the Beatles' afternoon performance at the Cavern Club on November 9.

Epstein was immediately impressed with their obvious talent and onstage proficiency, but after meeting them he was also greatly impressed by their charm, which was self-confident without being smug. He quickly began attending as many performances as possible.

As the year ended the band continued to work diligently and frequently, playing multiple shows per day on several occasions.

The band again backed Jones on December 8 at the Cavern Club and later that evening for another appearance at the Tower Ballroom.

December 9 brought one of the few unsuccessful shows of the year. For the first time ever the band would be playing south of London at the Palais Ballroom Aldershot, a military town nearly 40 miles from London. After a nine-hour journey from home the Beatles performed for an entire evening as the other band slated to perform, Ivor Jay and the Jaywalkers, failed to show. There may have been two other unknown bands on the bill, as the Beatles performed for only about 18 people.

The following night Rory Storm and the Hurricanes played the Palais Ballroom to slightly more success.

On the way back from their only visit to Aldershot the Beatles stopped to play an impromptu show at the Blue Gardenia Club, run by Brian Cassar, the former lead singer for Cass and the Casanovas. The Blue Gardenia served as a spot for local musicians to congregate at after their evening performances and play with whomever was on the stage. On this evening it was said to be Georgie Fame.

After performing at their first London show the band headed back

Kingsize Taylor and his Dominoes

home, driving all night and arriving in Liverpool late the following morning. Because of their long travels the band showed up quite late at their December 10 engagement at Hambleton Hall where they were met with a very angry Epstein, who was shocked at their easygoing attitude towards fulfilling their commitments.

He would give them one of many "lectures" about how he thought they should be acting as a professional band, both on and off the stage.

Epstein quickly convinced them to allow him to manage them, asking Williams first if he had any legal ties to the band. Williams replied that he did not, and also warned Epstein "not to touch them, for they would only let him down."

Epstein was completely inexperienced in the field of managing pop acts. After boldly avoiding Williams' warning, the novice Epstein quickly took charge of the band, and tried to get them signed to a record deal.

Present at their evening performance on December 13 was Mike Smith, an A&R man for Decca Records. Smith had heard about the Beatles through Tony Barrow, a Liverpool native who had moved to London and also wrote record reviews for the *Liverpool Evening Echo* using the name "Disker."

Epstein had asked Barrow to mention the Beatles in an article, but he declined because they had no recorded music yet. Barrow did however mention the band to the A&R department of Decca, where he was employed as a writer of liner notes. Barrow arranged for the ill-fated Decca auditions and was eventually convinced by Epstein to join his new artist management company NEMS enterprises on a full-time basis for twice the salary.

Barrow has another claim to fame: While still working at the competing record label, Barrow compiled the band's first official press kit in October 1962, coining the term "The Fab Four." While he didn't invent the term "Beatlemania," he certainly used it to help promote his band, which quickly became a very easy task as the entire world was consistently reporting on them. After the Beatles appeared on the "Sunday Night at the London Palladium" television program in October 1963, Barrow declared that he no longer had to contact the press, instead they would be the ones contacting him.

As the band ambitiously toured the world, Barrow was always part of the entourage, organizing the chaotic press conferences wherever the band would happen to be. Barrow would also assist in the promotion of the Fourmost, Cilla Black, Gerry and the Pacemakers, and Billy J. Kramer with the Dakotas.

In mid-December 1961, Dick Rowe was the head of Decca A&R and sent Smith to Liverpool to scope out the unknown band. After dining with Epstein, Smith went to see the band's second performance of the day, the 14th and final time the band would play both the afternoon and the evening shows at the Cavern. While he wasn't amazed by the band itself, he was very impressed with the reaction that they received. Smith must have been impressed enough with the band to agree to offer them a formal audition, and booked it for January 1, 1962 in London.

The four Beatles had their first formal photo session on December 17 at the studio of Liverpool wedding photographer Albert Marrion, whom Epstein met while the photographer was taking pictures for his brother Clive's wedding.

The photo session went very well and the leather-clad Beatles acted relatively professionally after Epstein again lectured them on their behavior. Marrion mentions Lennon occasionally sticking out his tongue and slightly irritating the bald photographer by calling him "Curly."

As 1961 drew to a close, with their new manager firmly in charge, things looked bright for the band. They had continued success in their live shows and were excited to be auditioning for Decca Records on the first day of 1962.

The Beatles performed their last show of the year on December 30 at what was becoming their home base, the Cavern Club. ◆

CHAPTER 8:
THE DECCA RECORDS AUDITION

EPSTEIN TRAVELED TO LONDON AHEAD OF THE BEATLES, STAYING AT A RELATIVE'S HOUSE WHILE THE BEATLES WERE DRIVEN DOWN IN ASPINALL'S VAN ON NEW YEAR'S EVE 1961. A SNOWSTORM SLOWED THEIR PROGRESS CONSIDERABLY.

AFTER SPENDING ABOUT 10 hours crowded in the van with their equipment, the Beatles arrived just before their Monday morning audition was scheduled to begin, meeting Epstein at the London studio.

Smith had stayed out late the previous evening celebrating the New Year (which wasn't a national bank holiday at the time) and was late arriving to the appointment. This greatly annoyed Epstein who considered it unprofessional. The four Beatles, who were already a bit anxious, became even more nervous as the tension mounted when Smith insisted that they use the house amplifiers, declaring the band's equipment unsuitable.

In spite of the band's discomfort, the red light was turned on and they quickly performed 15 songs while being recorded on a two-track mono recorder with no overdubs.

It isn't known who selected the songs that they performed for the audition, but it is widely thought that Epstein picked a range of music he thought would best represent the band's diversity. He wanted to not only present a range of music they could perform, but wanted to make it known that they wrote original compositions.

Of the 15 songs performed, three were Lennon/McCartney originals while the others were selections from their live act. This repertoire included more traditional rock and roll, some show tunes, and some novelty or relatively humorous selections.

While unconfirmed, it's likely that the songs were performed in the order that they were most frequently released on bootleg recordings.

"Like Dreamers Do" would ultimately find its release

when recorded by the Applejacks in June 1964, oddly enough on the Decca label. Paul was the primary writer of the song that dates as far back as 1957, according to his recollections.

The January 1 performance of the song is the only known recording and likely the last time the band would perform it, as they quickly surpassed it in quality. After not being rewarded the Decca contract they may have had second thoughts about "Like Dreamers Do," losing a bit of confidence not in the art of songwriting, but the song itself.

While trying to highlight their wide range, they would also perform songs that would remain in their repertoire past the failed audition.

"Money (That's What I Want)" would get recorded officially for the band's second EMI LP *With The Beatles*. It was a song that the band began doing sometime in 1960 and consistently performed until early 1964.

If in fact this was the second song recorded during the brisk and rushed performance, it's likely that nerves were a factor. The result was a less-than-energetic performance from Lennon, and a hurried performance from the band.

By the time the band would record the song for official release they would have a different drummer, the enthusiastic Ringo Starr, as well as the capable ears of producer Martin, who would instruct the band on recording a far superior version.

"'Til There Was You" shared a similar fate as "Money." Both were recorded for the second album, both had been around for a while in the band's act, and both would improve drastically with a skillful and imaginative drummer and gifted producer.

During the audition, McCartney was unfamiliar with studio microphones and the cracks, pops, and hisses frequently heard in the otherwise adequate performance of "'Til There Was You." Best has occasional tempo issues in his otherwise simple performance which features a

basic but fairly well-executed guitar solo from Harrison.

While by now a seasoned live act, the band had very little experience with a noiseless studio setting, and was a bit out of sorts because of the silence in the studio. The loud clubs they were used to would drown out any errors they may have made, but the silence only seemed to amplify them.

"The Sheik of Araby" was one of the songs selected to perform this day to showcase not only their impressively broad range of music, but also their ability to be considered fun, bordering on novelty.

Joe Brown was an English pop singer who teamed up with a backing band, an assortment of studio musicians he collected and named the Bruvvers. In 1961 Brown released a slightly rocked-up version of

a vaudeville era-song that dates back to 1921, and this spurred the Beatles on to perform the song as well.

Ted Snyder, a midwestern American composer, wrote the music. The lyrics were written by Harry Smith along with Francis Wheeler, co-writer on such songs as "Egyptian Rose" from 1923, "Roam On, My Little Gypsy Sweetheart," "Let a Smile Be Your Umbrella," and "It Was Only a Sun Shower" from 1927, and "What a Wonderful Wedding That Will Be" from 1938.

Inspired by the 1921 silent romance film "The Sheik" starring Rudolph Valentino and Agnes Ayres, the song "The Sheik of Araby" quickly became a Tin Pan Alley-era standard and was recorded by many artists.

A verse of the song appears in F. Scott Fitzgerald's jazz-era classic novel "The Great Gatsby," symbolizing that Daisy Buchanan's love actually "belongs" to Gatsby.

In 1926 for the film sequel to "The Sheik" called "The Son of the Sheik" Snyder wrote "The Night in Araby," which features elements of the original song.

Smith was a successful songwriter and who wrote approximately 300 librettos (musical stage plays) and more than 6,000 songs. His operettas (shorter and lighter in nature and subject matter than operas) include "Fatinitza" from 1879, "Robin Hood" in 1890, "The Wizard of the Nile" in 1895, "The Little Duchess" in 1901, "The Wild Rose" in 1902, "Sweethearts" in 1913, and "Countess Maritza" in 1926.

His full-length musicals include "Miss Dolly Dollars" from 1905, "The Spring Maid" in 1910, "Watch Your Step" from 1914, "Ladies First" in 1918, and "The Circus Princess" from 1927. He also wrote the music for several Ziegfeld Follies and revivals.

"Araby" refers to Arabia, or more specifically the Arabian Peninsula of Western Asia. "Arabi" is also a Louisiana town just south of New Orleans made famous by gamblers in the first half of the 1900s.

The first recorded version of "The Sheik of Araby" was (likely) by Clyde Doerr's Club Royal Orchestra in 1921 with other notable takes on the song by the California Ramblers in 1922, Guido Gialdini (who whistled) in 1923, Woody Herman and His Orchestra, as well as Fats Waller and His Rhythm Kings in 1939, Harry James and His Orchestra and the Benny Goodman Sextet in 1940, Spike Jones and His City Slickers in 1942, as well as literally hundreds of other recordings worldwide, including one the band may have been familiar with, a 1960 recording from Fats Domino.

As the young Beatles were slowly falling into their individual roles, they would each begin to develop specialties. Harrison's quickly became covering the girl

group stuff, as well as the Joe Brown material. That included "The Sheik of Araby" and "A Picture of You," which Brown would record in June 1962 for release in the U.K. on Decca, with the Beatles adding it to their act shortly after.

"The Sheik of Araby" was reportedly a fan favorite when performed live, with George taking the proverbial spotlight. George delivers a commanding lead vocal complete with the rather childish "na ha" from Lennon during the breaks.

As with many of the more immature or less civilized songs, "The Sheik of Araby" was dropped from the rotation shortly after the Decca auditions.

"To Know Her (Him) is to Love Her (Him)" was originally done by the Teddy Bears, a vocal group that boasted Phil Spector as a member, as well as the leader, songwriter, and producer.

With Annette Kleinbard (who would later change her name to Carol Connors) singing lead, the lyrics are about "him," as the original title reflects. The Beatles were drawn to the technique of the background singers who harmonized both with and against the lead vocalist.

John, Paul, and George had rehearsed this song incessantly and delivered a fine harmonic performance on the recording made on audition day. McCartney states it was the first song that they learned three-part harmonies for, which would have likely been shortly after the song's 1958 release.

Other recordings of the song demonstrate that the band performed it a bit faster during the Decca auditions, likely as the result of the pressure and nerves of the day.

John takes the lead vocal duties as Paul and George supply background harmonies with their usual grace and self-assurance. They never outshine the main singer, yet still make their presence known. This was a quality that the three would learn quickly from such records as "To Know Her…" They would continue to use the trademark harmonies through most of their career, with several combinations depending on who is singing lead. This dynamic would change drastically when the advent of multi-tracking became available to the Beatles.

Another element illustrated by the multiple recordings is what a difference a drummer can make, even on what would be considered a relatively simple song. Subsequent performances, including the Star Club in December '62 as well as the BBC recordings, demonstrate how accurate and consistent Starr's playing was, as opposed to Best's noticeably tense and erratic performance.

Unlike several other songs recorded during the audition, "To Know Her is to Love Her" continued to be a part of the band's act, although never recorded officially.

It is possible and quite likely that it was McCartney's suggestion that led to Peter and Gordon recording the song in 1965. They did it as "To Know You is to Love You" (slightly altering the lyrics once again) after the Beatles decided they would only record originals,

possibility is that Epstein suggested they learn the song which would have been fresh in the minds of the decision makers. George confidentially takes over on the lead vocals for the track with John and Paul once again supplying harmonies to enhance the leader, and not compete with him.

Epstein thought a song like this would display that the band was marketable as pop act as well as strictly rock and roll.

The band did tend to favor songs of a more rock nature, so it's likely they considered this type a song a bit soft for them but they understood the value of versatility. Likewise, while they weren't after a "pin-up boy" image, they weren't afraid to use their looks in an attempt to gain fame.

"Memphis" was originally written and recorded by Chuck Berry in 1959 and released as the B-side to "Back in the USA." The record quickly made its way to the port town of Liverpool where the band immediately took it as their own with John singing lead.

therefore eliminating the song as a candidate for an official recording.

"Take Good Care of My Baby" was another song the band would attempt during the Decca auditions, and then quickly abandon.

Carole King wrote the music in the Brill Building and almost handed it off to Cynthia Weil before King's husband and writing partner Gerry Goffin came up with the lyrics. The song tells the tale of a spurned lover offering the winner of the girl's affection a bit of congratulations and a requesting that if he decides he doesn't love her, he could return her.

It is interesting to note that the song has a male-dominated subject involving one man singing to another about the woman in question, as opposed to singing directly to the woman. The band would use this angle from time to time throughout their career.

Bobby Vee recorded the original which was released in August 1961 on the Liberty label in the U.S. where it reached No. 1. London Records released it in the U.K., where it would reach No. 3.

The band must have quickly learned the song and just as rapidly stopped performing it. Another

Berry's writing technique, as well as his guitar prowess was always very intriguing to the band.

Lyrically the song seems to be about a love interest (once again a song that isn't sung directly to the main subject of the song but to another person, this time the long distance operator). The singer is looking to get back in touch with Marie, who is the only one from Memphis who would want to contact the singer, who goes on to reveal that Marie's mother pulled them apart.

It is slightly misleading throughout and the big reveal in the song is that "Marie is only six years old" and therefore not a love interest, but likely a daughter (or stepchild) of the actual love interest.

"Memphis" as well as Berry's lyrics in general, would make the songwriters think on broader scale of not only what a well-crafted rock song could sound like, but also the many ways to tell a story.

Berry had an immense influence on the band, both musically and lyrically, as his frequent mentioning of U.S. geographical locations were highly romanticized by the Beatles, making America even more desirable in the process.

American rock and roll and rockabilly were among the band members' personal favorites as teenagers, and these genres greatly influenced the band. This was another of the attributes used to sell the band when auditioning.

"Sure to Fall (In Love with You)" was originally recorded by Carl Perkins, along with Bill Cantrell and Quinton Claunch in December 1955, but not released until 1957.

The song's first release was on *The Dance Album of Carl Perkins* LP from 1957, although there was test pressing of "Sure to Fall" as a 45 released only to radio stations in the Memphis area. Eventually the song would be released as a single. It's highly likely that band members, specifically George, would consider splurging on a full-length Perkins record well worth it.

Perkins had a similar appeal to the Beatles that Buddy Holly had, not only was his music American country, but he also wrote, sang, and played guitar, which to John, Paul and George was a feat beyond words.

Bill Cantrell was a Texas-born songwriter whose credits include "I've Been Deceived" for Charlie Feathers on the Flip label and "Daydreamin'" for Doug Bragg in 1955, "I'm Serious" for the Hilltoppers in 1957, and "Tootsie" for Carl McVoy in 1958, all co-written with Claunch. Besides his songwriting credits, Cantrell was also a musician and was in a band Claunch formed in 1943 called the Blue Seal Pals. Through his association with disc jockey and Sun records owner Sam Phillips, Claunch played on some very early Sun Records releases for Perkins, Feathers, and Wanda Jackson.

After having great success and becoming a regular act on the Grand Ole Opry, Claunch and Cantrell decided to create the Hi Records label in 1957, which had relative success locally. In 1959 Claunch sold his interest in the label, leaving the music business to focus on building his hardware store.

As touched on earlier, the Beatles developed certain individual roles in the band. Paul sang the sweet show tunes and Little Richard covers, John was the lead on Chuck Berry and Buddy Holly numbers, and George would do the girl group songs and the Perkins numbers. Of course as with all things Beatles, there are exceptions,

and Paul sings lead on the band's take on "Sure to Fall."

While the band no doubt had many chances to rehearse the number on stage, the recording from the Decca audition lacks the confidence that subsequent recordings would possess. Paul's voice shakes with nerves at points and, although relatively consistent, Best's drumming appears to considerably faster, anxiety getting the best of the two performers.

On Perkins' version Carl and his brother Jay sing the lead together. For the Beatles' rendition, Paul takes the lead and John once again supplies flawless harmony vocals through much of the song.

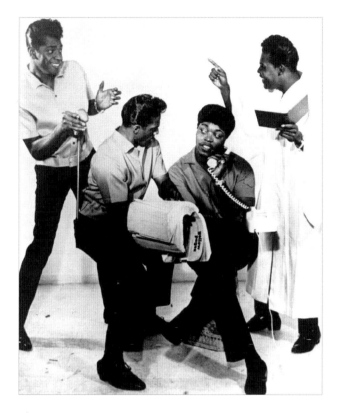

The Coasters

Very similar to Berry's "Memphis," "Sure to Fall" was performed by the Beatles on several other occasions, yet never officially recorded and released by the band. Likely this is because while planning a full-length album, the band and Martin never wanted to have too many songs of one genre, or specific covers from another artist.

For the second album the band was very into soul and rhythm and blues music, but for the fourth LP, which would be the last time they would compile songs written and recorded by others, they were enjoying a resurgence in their love for Perkins and rockabilly. However, they thought a third Perkins-related song on one album would be "too much."

For the BBC the band would perform "Sure to Fall" four times between June 1963 and May 1964, all with Ringo on the drums. Starr slightly developed the song by adding a double-time beat to the bridge, which was an element the original song didn't possess.

Speculation is that this was a song the Hurricanes used to do as well, and that was their arrangement.

The Beatles stopped performing the song after their May 1964 BBC appearance on "From Us to You." While the Beatles undoubtedly enjoyed Perkins' music, the specific reason they did this particular number was that many may have still remembered it as a Beatle song.

"Sure to Fall" was later done by the Fourmost who would record the song on their 1965 release *First and Fourmost*.

Country, rockabilly, hillbilly, or however the band may have labeled Perkins' style, it was yet another entry in the wide variety of music the band had to offer.

"Hello Little Girl" was another song that the band had around for a while when they decided to play it at the Decca auditions. There is a rather crude version of the song recorded in early 1960 during the period where Paul borrowed a reel-to-reel tape recorder from a neighbor for the Quarrymen, or possibly the Beatals depending on what they were currently named.

While the uninteresting lyrics didn't develop much in the time between the initial writing and the auditions, the performance of the song certainly did. With John singing lead and Paul supplying harmony vocals it seems as if the band started to relax a bit and perform up to a more expected level.

In spite of its sophomoric content, a well-crafted and commercially viable original was presented to the powers that be at Decca Records.

The song didn't remain as part of their act for much longer after the failed Decca audition. The Beatles still considered it worthy of their representation, however, as on Feb 12, 1962 they successfully auditioned for BBC producer Peter Pilbeam who specialized in music aimed at the young.

Pilbeam wasn't especially impressed with the band, considering them "an unusual group, not as 'rocky' as most," also curiously referring to them as "country and western with a tendency to play music."

In his assessment to Epstein, Pilbeam said "yes" to Lennon, but "no" to McCartney, each of whom sang two songs during this sadly unrecorded performance.

McCartney's numbers were "'Til There Was You" and "Like Dreamers Do" while John sang "Memphis" and "Hello Little Girl."

Even though he wasn't too sure about the band, Pilbeam booked them for the "Teenager's Turn" radio show for March 1962, their first performance to be broadcast country-wide. It was recorded live on March 7, broadcast shortly after on March 20.

With the band quickly surpassing an original song of such a low quality, they would retire "Hello Little Girl" from their act, recalling it one final time when giving it to the Fourmost in July 1963.

Jerry Leiber (left) and Mike Stoller (right)

Original songs certainly remained a part of the band's repertoire on stage, however novelty-style songs would be dropped rather quickly from live shows.

"Three Cool Cats" was originally recorded by the Coasters in 1958 and released as the B-side to "Charlie Brown." Both were written by songwriting team Jerry Leiber and Mike Stoller, who met in Los Angeles in 1950 when they were both 17 years old.

Leiber grew up in Baltimore, heading west with his family. Jerry Stoller had East Coast roots, from Long Island, New York. Stoller was a piano player and Leiber worked at Norty's record store. The two quickly became friends after discovering their love for the same types of music, primarily African American-created blues and R&B.

While just "doing it for fun," the team instantly began writing songs together, with Stoller supplying the bulk of the melodies and Leiber adding vivid and enjoyable lyrics to the tunes created.

Their first professionally recorded song was "Real Ugly Woman" by Jimmy Witherspoon, and the songwriting unit garnered success very quickly, co-writing "Hard Times" by Charles Brown and "Kansas City" (known then as "K.C. Lovin'") by Wilbert Harrison in 1952, and "Hound Dog" for Willie Mae "Big Mama" Thornton in 1953. "Hound Dog" would go on to become a breakthrough hit for Elvis Presley when he covered it in 1956, and Little Richard would rework "K.C. Lovin'" several times before the Beatles would adopt his version as part of their act.

Leiber and Stoller would form the Spark Records label in 1953 along with their mentor and business partner Lester Sill, who was also was the head of Colpix Records and a co-owner of Philles Records with Phil Spector as well.

They wrote as well as produced the "Loop de Loop Mambo," "Framed," "Wrap it Up," and "Riot in Cell Block No. 9," all in 1954 for the Robins, who would later become the Coasters, another sizable influence on the Beatles.

As a songwriting partnership Leiber and Stoller would co-compose "Love Me," originally recorded by Willy and Ruth in 1954 and re-recorded by Elvis who had a Top 10 hit with it in 1956.

"Searching" and "Youngblood" were hits for the Coasters in 1957 and the eager young band quickly began performing them as part of their act.

For the Robins they would write "Whadaya Want?," "One Kiss," and the aforementioned

"Smokey Joe's Café."

Leiber and Stoller penned more than 100 songs for the Coasters alone. The list includes "Down in Mexico," "One Kiss Led to Another," "What is the Secret of Your Success?" "Along Came Jones," "Poison Ivy," "Shoppin' for Clothes," "Little Egypt," "What About Us," "Girls, Girls, Girls," "Soul Pad," "The Slime," and "D.W. Washburn."

The Coasters would also perform a version of "Besame Mucho," which would be the specific version that the Beatles would rework as their own. Endless versions of songs by this most talented songwriting team have been recorded by an extremely vast group of performers.

Leiber and Stoller's "Charlie Brown" (possibly loosely written about singer Charles Brown or conceivably with comic strip blockhead Charlie Brown in mind) was a huge crossover hit for the Coasters when released. Just as the Beatles would frequently do, they would focus more on the B-side of the record than on the single itself.

The Coasters were formed in late 1955 in Los Angeles after several members of the Robins recorded "Smokey Joe's Café," written and produced by Leiber and Stoller, and released on their Spark label.

While only moderately successful, it was charming and intriguing enough to get the band and songwriting team a contract offer from Atlantic Records, based in New York.

Only two of the band members were willing to move to the label and were replaced as the band was renamed as the Coasters. The new name had multiple meanings, including West Coast, driving aimlessly, a roller coaster, or the fact that they jumped from band to band before landing in the Coasters, who would have several lineup changes.

The first Coasters lineup included Carl Gardner and Billy Nunn, both former members of the Robins, along with Billy Guy and Leon Hughes as well as guitarist Adolph Jacobs who would leave the band in '59. Nunn and Hughes would be replaced by Cornell Gunter and Will "Dub" Jones when they all relocated to New York. All had roots on the California coast.

The "Youngblood"/"Searchin'" record was the Coasters' breakthrough single in 1957, with Gardner, Gunter, Guy, and Jones as the most successful line-up. They had string of hits with "Yakety Yak," "Charlie Brown," "Along Came Jones," "Poison Ivy," "I'm a Hog For You," "Run Red Run," "What About Us," "Besame Mucho," "Shoppin' for Clothes," and "Little Egypt (Ying-Yang.)"

As the decade ended, the Coasters became less successful with frequent lineup changes. Their legacy, however, is far-reaching beyond their influence on the Beatles, as there are countless other songwriters and performers who have cited the Coasters as a model for songwriting as well as stage and recording theatrics. In late 1965 the Beatles would even attempt to write a pair of novelty-style songs with inspiration from the Coasters.

No official recordings were made of the Beatles doing any Coasters songs, but they did perform several throughout their early days, some of which were caught on tape.

"Youngblood" was part of the band's act from the start, but it eventually faded away only to be revived for the BBC's "Pop Go the Beatles" in summer 1963. George took lead on the song which features numerous background vocals from John and Paul, all three have their own individual solo line and all three sing during the chorus.

The story follows a simple and effective tale of a boy falling in love at first sight with a girl with a yellow ribbon in her hair. He follows her home only to be shut down by the girl's father, and the singer pines over her as he tries to sleep. The love interest of course is an attractive yet inexperienced young girl, or a "youngblood," which is an African American slang for a virgin.

With seemingly innocent lyrics and well-hidden sexual jargon along with a playfully dramatic delivery, the young-blooded Beatles were highly inspired by Coasters' records.

"Searchin'" was the B-side to "Youngblood" and the band immediately learned both, possibly before Harrison

joined the band. The tapes reveal the drumming to be considerably different from the Decca Records version from January 1962 or the BBC version from June 1963, due to the inclusion of Starr as a band member.

"Three Cool Cats" shared a similar fate as "Searchin'," as the band included it in their act until performing it during the Decca auditions, then dropped it when they decided the songs were "too silly" for their image. The following year the Beatles revived the song for the BBC radio show "Here We Go" which was recorded but never broadcast.

While "Three Cool Cats" gave the band a chance to act a bit goofy and "do voices," it didn't line up with the harder edge rock and roll image they were attempting to achieve.

A youthful Harrison again confidentially takes lead vocal on the rather whimsical song about a trio of "cool cats," not literally hip felines but stylish young men chasing after three cool chicks, not small birds but sharp young women. The three young men approach the ladies and are quickly dismissed, becoming three fools.

While the song had a rather significant novelty quality it still tells a simple story, with an introduction and explanation of characters, interest, conflict and, unfortunately, a negative resolution. Using common slang and rather vivid imagery, a "picture with words" was created, a quality that the Beatles were always trying to emulate.

The bulk of the song featured the three singers together, with George taking a frequent lead, and Paul and John each reciting a solo line of their own, in rather "goonish" or silly voices, particularly Lennon.

The song was rather humorous and the Beatles felt it may have caused the record label to not take them as seriously as they would have if the band had performed only straight rock and roll. Being taken seriously was important to the band, although it took them as well as Epstein a bit of time to realize that certain songs might be considered more novelty than others.

In spite of the silly nature of "Three Cool Cats," the band calmed down as time wore on and performed a well-played and assertive version of the song.

They would never attempt to record "Three Cool Cats" for an official EMI release, however they would perform it on at least one other occasion for that same unbroadcast "Here We Go" segment for BBC.

Leiber and Stoller would also write "Bazoom (I Need Your Lovin')" for the Charms in 1954, "Ruby Baby" for the the Drifters and "Lucky Lips" for Ruth Brown in 1956, "Jailhouse Rock" for the Elvis movie of the same name in 1957, and "Love Potion No. 9" for the Clovers in 1959. Many of their songs featured suggestive language, not necessarily sexual in nature, but included a fair amount of social and racial implications as well.

When the band was selecting songs to listen to as music fans they were always concerned about not only who was performing the record but also things like record labels, producers, and who composed the song.

In 1960 Leiber and Stoller wrote "Lorelei," which was recorded by Lonnie Donegan. This was a song that the young Beatles were undoubtedly familiar with, likely increasing their awareness of the team via record label credits.

Another Leiber and Stoller was a song that the Beatles would quickly adopt into their act was Richie Barrett's 1962 "Some Other Guy."

With such a wide variety of artists and a large resume of success Leiber and Stoller were also on the large unwritten list of entertainers that the Beatles aimed to be, not necessarily realizing that they were a production team as well as songwriters.

A very small sample of songs penned by the partners include "Tears of Joy" in 1956 for Etta "Miss Peaches" James (also credited as Etta James and the Peaches), "Saved" for Laverne Baker, "Stand by Me" in 1961 (written along with Ben E. King), "The Man Who Robbed the Bank at Santa Fe" for Hank Snow, and "Reverend Mr. Black" for the Kingston Trio (with Billy Edd Wheeler), "On Broadway" (with Cynthia Weil) for the Drifters in 1962, and "Only in America" for Jay and the Americans in 1963.

After Presley's success with "Hound Dog," he would

Consuelo Velazquez

go on to record many songs written by Leiber and Stoller, including three songs written for his films as well as "Santa Claus is Back in Town" for his 1957 Christmas album.

In an odd change of events, the Beatles and other British Invasion bands would continue to dominate the charts but success for some of their indirect mentors would actually diminish. One of Leiber and Stoller's last hits was "Is That All There Is?" recorded by Georgia Brown in May 1967, followed by Dan Daniels and Leslie Uggams the following year before Peggy Lee struck a hit with it in 1969.

On occasion, for completely unknown reasons, the duo's work was credited as Elmo Glick.

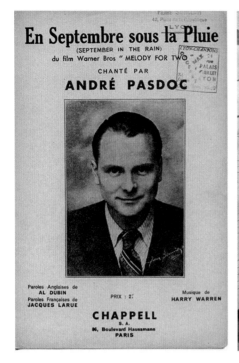

Other songs performed for the audition included "Crying, Waiting, Hoping," a Buddy Holly song that the band would perform frequently, drawing attention to their ability to deliver three-part harmony as well as interpret compositions written by others.

"Love of the Loved" was ultimately given to Cilla Black to record in '63, but had a history with the band long before that. One of the earliest, if not the very first song Paul ever wrote, it dates back to 1960 or earlier. The song evolved as the band gained experience through frequent and lengthy rehearsals as well as extended performances requiring a deep repertoire to fill an entire evening of music without repeating themselves.

Serving as another example of an original composition the band had to offer, Paul carries out a performance that presents the band's versatility and professionalism. Well-rehearsed and well-executed, the band calmed down as the Decca session wore on, although apparently not enough to be able to impress the powers that be.

While McCartney's songwriting skills developed over time, he possessed a very natural quality in his performances even from an early date. His exuberance

for the song shines through rather brightly on this early original.

Another song that Paul took a commanding lead vocal on was a show tune that he was raised with, once again possibly selected on the spot and assigned by Epstein. "September in the Rain" originally appeared in the 1937 film "Melody for Two," sung by James Melton, a movie musical actor and radio personality from the '30s.

The song was written by Harry Warren and Al Dubin, who were frequent collaborators, co-writing "Too Many Tears" in 1932, "You're Getting to Be a Habit With Me" in 1933, "I Only Have Eyes for You" in 1934, "Lullaby of Broadway" in 1935, "I'll Sing You a Thousand Love Songs" in 1936, and "Remember Me?" prior to "September in the Rain" the following year.

Warren was the musician of the team and would also co-create other notable songs, "Jeepers Creepers" and "You Must Have Been a Beautiful Baby" with Johnny Mercer in 1938 and "Chattanooga Choo Choo" with Mack Gordon in 1941.

Dubin wrote music for Broadway plays as well as film and would collaborate with others on standards such as "42nd Street," "Shuffle Off to Buffalo," and "You're Getting to Be a Habit with Me" all from the "42nd Street" film, as well as music for a series of films called "The Gold Diggers."

Each of the individual Beatles were likely familiar with "September in the Rain," and probably knew several versions of this standard.

Harry James and His Orchestra recorded "September in the Rain" in 1945, and it was also recorded by German pianist Andre Previn in 1946, the George Shearing Quintet in 1949, Herman Chittison and Paul Weston and His Orchestra in 1950, Dave Brubeck's Octet in 1951 and literally dozens of others throughout the decade, both with and without lyrics.

It is uncertain which artist's version was known to the band, the likely candidates being American vocalist Al Hibler, who did "September in the Rain" in 1956, an African American vocalist known as "The Divine One" Sarah Vaughan and her trio from 1957, and jazz vocalist and pianist Dinah Washington from 1961. These three records likely could have been available to the young band members, who quickly learned it and kept it as part of their act.

Paul delivers a confident solo vocal performance of the uptempo take "September in the Rain," which is generally played at a slower pace on most other recordings. John and George also give steadier performances on this number than on some of the other audition songs; seemingly they were a bit intimidated by the atmosphere and had slight troubles concentrating on playing and singing simultaneously.

The Beatles wouldn't record the song officially, likely dropping it from their act after the January 1 auditions. Cilla Black would perform the song on "The Ed Sullivan Show" in 1965, possibly from a suggestion by the Beatles from their discarded song memory.

"Besame Mucho" is another song that the band had a lengthy history with but ultimately never officially released during their active recording years.

The song itself had been around since 1940, recorded by such diverse artists as Phil Hanna with Harry Sosnik and His Orchestra in 1943, Jimmy Dorsey and His Orchestra in 1944, Wingy Manone and His Orchestra in 1946, Josephine Baker in 1951, Mantovani and His Orchestra as well as the Edmond Hall Swing Sextet in 1953, Xavier Cugat and His Orchestra as well as Eydie Gorme and Steve Lawrence in 1955, Perez Prado and His Orchestra in 1956, the Art Pepper Quartet in 1957, Morton

Gould and His Orchestra as well as Richard Berry in 1958, The Mary Kaye Trio, the Three Sounds, Connie Francis, and Trio San José in 1959, and Ray Conniff, His Orchestra and Chorus released a version in 1960.

It is very possible and rather likely that the individual Beatles may have all been familiar with at least one or more of these renditions of the song.

In March 1960 when the Coasters released their version, McCartney purchased it, adding to his "very diverse little record collection." The single featured the song in two parts, one per side, and Paul was especially intrigued by the change of key, from a minor to a major, a relatively new concept for the novice musician. Paul began to learn the song, but did not share it with his bandmates until the following year when they added it to their act. It would stay around for a while, ultimately being recorded on several occasions.

Due to the association with the Coasters, the song was more legitimized than it had been in the past, and the band considered it more acceptable to perform.

If the order in which the songs were frequently bootlegged is indeed the order in which they were performed, it is possible that the band had calmed down and Mike Smith was impressed with "Besame Mucho," and wanted to hear more similar material. That would indeed lead to the final song from the session.

"Searchin'" was released by the Coasters in March 1957 as the B-side of "Youngblood," both written specifically for the Coasters by Leiber and Stoller in a successful attempt to help the Black band cross over to a more mainstream audience, while not alienating their current admirers.

Paul tells a story of going to see a friend of Colin Hanton's to "relieve" him of the "Searchin'" 45 (steal it from him) and later performing the song frequently at the Cavern Club.

As was their habit, the band members would flip

the record over and learn the B-side, then also add "Youngblood" to their act, recording it for the BBC in June 1963.

The Beatles were adoringly drawn to all things American, so the impressionable young musicians all individually enjoyed "Searchin'" which makes frequent mentions of several American detectives, and tells a story of love in a most unusual manner. The first part of the song details traveling to rivers and mountains to find the girl, although we are not ever sure why or if she needs to be searched for, but the singer relates that she will be searched for any which way, and guarantees to bring her in.

A Northwest Mountie is mentioned, which is more of a Canadian entity, but the band thought the entire continent was one giant land of dreams called the USA. "Blueberry Hill" is also mentioned which by another of the band's favorites, Fats Domino, and they were also always impressed with songs that mentioned other songs.

The list of popular fictional detectives mentioned in the song is lengthy:

Sam Spade was the detective in the novel the Maltese Falcon created in 1930 by Dashiell Hammett, Spade was portrayed in film in by Ricardo Cortez in the 1931 version of the film, and in 1941 by Humphrey Bogart.

Sgt. Friday was the fictional Los Angeles police detective in "Dragnet," a radio drama adapted into a television show. Friday was portrayed by Jack Webb, who was also the show's creator.

Charlie Chan was created by Earl Derr Biggers in 1919, who fashioned his character after reading about Honolulu detective Chang Apana, introducing the character in the 1925 "House Without a Key" novel.

Boston Blackie was initially a jewel thief and safe cracker created by Jack Boyle in 1914, then was turned into a reformed criminal who would solve crimes to clear his name, portrayed by Chester Morris in film and for radio.

Sherlock Holmes, a British private detective created by Sir Arthur Conan Doyle and portrayed in film by Basil Rathbone.

Bulldog Drummond was literature, film, and radio character created by H. C. McNeile in 1920. Drummond is a wealthy British gentleman adventurer who would seek excitement after being bored once the fighting of the Great War commenced.

As the Beatles performed the song on many occasions, there is only one known recording of "Searchin'," and it is from the Decca auditions.

It's uncertain if Paul knew the lyrics and changed them gradually over time or never knew them in the first place and just added his own words when needed. He mentions "Simon Spade" which was likely just the way he misheard it and always sang it.

Paul also mentions a detective that wasn't in the original version. "Peter Gunn" was an American television series in the late 1950s and had a theme song that was composed by Henry Mancini. Trumpeter Ray Anthony had a hit with "The Peter Gunn Theme" in June 1959 and other than knowing the song was the theme song about a show with a detective, the Beatles knew Peter Gunn would fit in, a well-placed bit of artistic license from McCartney.

There is a high energy performance from all four Beatles, who may have sensed this was their last chance at impressing the label, and a very well-performed solo from George.

We also don't know if this was just the arrangement that the band used, or if under the pressure of the situation Paul made a mistake in the performance, as the Beatles' version differs greatly from the Coasters' version. The first verse of the original is missed completely, and there is no mention of swimming or climbing or rivers or mountains or Blueberry Hill. This might be artistic licensing or nerves, or even overconfidence from the band, who by the time they performed this track had settled in but were still sloppy as compared to other recordings from the pre-EMI era.

While the band thought highly of the song at the beginning of '62, it was soon left off their list, considered a little too goofy, or "hammy" and didn't fit especially well with the image of serious musicians. Being taken seriously was very important to the Beatles.

Smith apparently told them they did a great job, which may have just been a kind gesture to a band that he didn't think auditioned especially well, and he was likely just ushering them out quickly to prepare for the next auditioning band scheduled.

At the time the band and Epstein thought the audition went very well. The band and their manager celebrated in London with a dinner before returning to Liverpool, where they expected to hear good news that never came.

Later in the day London-based Brian Poole and the Tremeloes auditioned for the label in the same room, apparently with more success, as they were ultimately rewarded the one contract that Smith was elected to present. Smith recalled that it ultimately came down to the fact that the Poole and his band were local Londoners and they simply performed better on that occasion.

Brian Poole and the Tremeloes did achieve a bit of success on the label in the U.K. between '63 and '65, but clearly the decision makers would regret their choice.

Shortly after February 1, the Beatles received official news that they were turned down for a contract, in spite of Epstein traveling back to London to meet with the head of Decca's A&R department Dick Rowe and sales manager Sidney Arthur Beecher-Stevens in an attempt to persuade them otherwise.

Epstein was told that the band sounded too much like the Shadows and this is where Rowe uttered the infamous quote "guitar bands are on the way out."

It is also widely rumored that Epstein pledged to purchase 3,000 copies of any Beatles record released at his store, which would be an instant and guaranteed economic success for any label. Rowe denies knowing about this borderline unethical practice at the time.

While dejected and disappointed, the band did get a bit of an awakening as to the level of professionalism required to move up to that next level of fame.

Epstein also now had a high quality performance on a reel-to-reel tape to help sell the band to other labels. It was suggested to him that he get the tape pressed onto a record for easier instant access and so he wouldn't have to haul around the fragile single copy of the reels.

Jim Foy was cutting the engineer who cut the disc for Epstein. Foy was impressed with what he heard, calling music publisher Sid Coleman in to take a listen. Coleman was impressed with the originals and offered a publishing contract right then and there, but Epstein declined, saying that a record deal was his main concern at that point.

Wanting to help the band and therefore help himself, Coleman contacted George Martin, an associate of his who was the A&R man at an EMI subsidiary known as Parlophone Records. Martin heard the Decca recording and was interested enough to arrange a meeting between him and the young band from Liverpool, which would ultimately lead to a landing of a record deal.

Once the band was officially signed, the Decca demos were considered useless, with the band not realizing how fascinating this look into the Beatles' progression would be. With several copies of these recordings in the hands of people other than the Beatles or Epstein, copies were quickly made and traded around Liverpool, London, and by the late '70s, the world.

The rushed and hurried sessions resulted in the band falling a bit short in their attempt to move on to the next level. However in perfect hindsight, the Beatles would have taken a very different path had they been swept up by Decca, as opposed to the teaming of the Beatles and Martin, who would be an integral part of the music of the band, as well as the addition of Ringo Starr. ◆

CHAPTER 9:
DOWN BUT NOT DEFEATED

FOR A BRIEF TIME THE BEATLES WOULD PERFORM ALONGSIDE JAZZ BANDS AT THE CAVERN, BUT AS THE SCREAMING GIRL CROWD TOOK OVER AS THE HIGHEST PERCENTAGE OF ATTENDEES, THE CLUB WOULD BECOME STRICTLY A ROCK VENUE.

AFTER SPENDING THE FIRST DAY of 1962 in London the band traveled back to Liverpool to perform both the lunch and evening shows at the Cavern Club on January 3.

With a slight increase in confidence the band continued to maintain their busy schedule, frequently performing twice or more daily. They hit the Casbah Club often as well as their usual haunts including the Tower Ballroom in New Brighton, Wallasey, and the Aintree Institute in Liverpool.

On January 12 the band played the lunchtime and evening shows at the Cavern, and then filled in at the Tower Ballroom in New Brighton after Screaming Lord Sutch and the Savages didn't show up for their scheduled performance.

Epstein would arrange for the band to perform at the more upscale Kingsway Club in Southport.

In an attempt to improve the band's image he would also arrange for newspaper press prior to the performances.

The band would perform in Manchester at the Oasis Club on February 2, which would be their first organized out-of-town performance. This may explain the typewritten set list that allegedly exists for this date, with sources that are unconfirmed yet widely reported. There is a photograph of the setlist which appears to be legitimate.

"Hippy Hippy Shake" was written by Chan Romero when he was only 17, originally recorded by him for the Del-fi label in 1959. Romero was managed by Don Redfield, a Billings, Montana disc jockey, who sent a tape of Romero to Bob Keane. Keane managed Ritchie Valens until the plane crash that took the life of Buddy Holly and the Big Bopper took Valens as well.

Keane managed Romero, hoping he would be the "new" Valens as both were rock and roll Latinos, although Valens was pure Mexican while Romero's heritage includes Mexican, Spanish, Apache, and Cherokee Indian, and also apparently a bit of Irish.

Romero not only idolized Valens, but recorded in the same studio as him. After being introduced to the Valens family by Keane, Romero would stay with them while he was in California, sleeping in the room that belonged to Ritchie himself.

Romero's success never did surpass that of his fallen idol, however his "Hippy Hippy Shake" certainly earned its place as rock and roll cornerstone for the Beatles. They performed the song frequently as part of their act along with songs from other rock and roll heroes.

Italian heartthrob "Little Tony" Ciacci covered "Hippy Hippy Shake" later the same year with his background band the Brothers. Ciacci's version became a modest hit in both the U.K. and Italy. The Beatles quickly added it to their act, and shortly after that the Swinging Blue Jeans and likely several other local bands would do it as well.

There is a recording of the song from the Beatles' New Year's Eve 1962 performance, and throughout 1963 the Beatles would sporadically perform the song for the BBC, first in March for "Saturday Club" and three times for "Pop Go the Beatles."

By the time the band stopped performing the song, the Swinging Blue Jeans had recorded their own version, which was a hit for them in December 1963.

As soon as the Beatles began to rise in fame, there were many local bands that would start to emulate their four-member lineup and multiple singers.

The Swinging Blue Jeans were a Liverpool band who gradually, and then at a more rapid pace, discovered and fell in love with rock and roll and moved away from their jazz roots (adding "Swinging" to their original name). They would have hits with "Hippy Hippy Shake," "Good Golly Miss Molly," originally recorded by Little Richard in 1956, and "You're No Good," which was first done by Dee Dee Warwick (sister to Dionne) in 1963. Coincidentally, their last success came in 1966 with a cover of a Burt Bacharach and Hal David song from 1962 called "Don't Make Me Over" which was Dionne Warwick's debut single.

After the Beatles and some of the more "top level" bands of the British Invasion continued to maintain success, the Blues Jeans were left a bit behind.

"Sweet Little Sixteen" was originally done by Chuck Berry in 1957, and it became a standard of the Beatles' act rather quickly.

"The Sheik of Araby" and "September in the Rain" were both recorded during the Decca auditions and remained in the band's act at least for a short while

WHAT A CRAZY WORLD
(WE'RE LIVING IN)
Words and Music by ALAN KLEIN

Featured, Televised & Recorded by
JOE BROWN
on PICCADILLY 7N 35024

2/6

PAN-MUSIK LTD.
21 DENMARK STREET.   LONDON, W.C.2

Selling Agents
PETER MAURICE MUSIC CO. LTD
21 DENMARK STREET, LONDON. W.C 2

after, until they were both left behind.

"Dizzy Miss Lizzy" was originally written and recorded by Larry Williams in 1958, and eventually was officially recorded by the Beatles for the *Help!* album in 1965.

"Take Good Care of My Baby" and "'Til There Was You" were both recorded for the Decca auditions, yet had different fates for the band. They performed "Take Good Care of My Baby" for a short time after the auditions, but continued to performed "'Til There Was You" consistently, recording it for their *With The Beatles* LP.

"Memphis" was another song the band kept around in the their repertoire for a fair amount of time without ever officially recording it, as they did with "Like Dreamers Do," "Money (That's What I Want)," "Young Blood," "Hello Little Girl," "To Know Her is to Love Her," "Roll Over Beethoven," "Ooh! My Soul," "Searchin'" and "The Love of the Loved," which all had various fortunes with the band.

"The Honeymoon Song" was a McCartney-led song featured in the 1959 movie "Luna de Miel," which was later changed to "Honeymoon." The song was composed by Greek songwriter Mikis Theodorakis, with lyrics being translated to English and rewritten by William Sanson. Paul heard the song and saw Marino Marini perform it in the 1959 film as well as on television, taking special note of the guitarist's volume pedal.

While the other Beatles may have considered the song a bit too delicate for their rock and roll ideals (even calling it "soppy" as McCartney conveys), they understood the effect of Paul's romantic love ballads, proving once again that they were more than just a rock band.

Most of the songs would wind up being recorded at one point, but there are three mysterious titles listed as well.

"Dance/Twist in the Streets" is a curious selection as there doesn't appear to be a song with that name, which likely means there was some sort of confusion involved in the translation of information.

We know it is NOT "Dancing in the Streets," which wouldn't be a hit for Martha and the Vandellas until 1964, and "Twist in the Streets" doesn't appear to be a song that was ever recorded by others or mentioned by a Beatle.

It was possible that it was just "The Twist," which was around since 1959 but not a large hit until Chubby Checker took it to No. 1 in 1960. It could be a variation of the twist, possibly the "Pepper Twist" from Joey Dee and the Starlighters in 1961.

The mystery song could also possibly be "Twisting the Night Away," which was written and recorded by Sam Cooke in late December 1961, released in January 1962, and became an instant hit in both American and England.

If the song was brand new that could possibly explain the unfamiliarity to whoever was keeping track of the setlist for the performance.

"Dream" was also listed as being part of the performance on this night. There are several possible songs this could have been. It is likely that it was "Dream Baby (How Long Must I Dream)," which was released in early '62. The Beatles Immediately learned it, also performing it for the BBC's "Teenager's Turn/Here We Go" the following month.

Another possibility is the song "Dream (When You're Feeling Blue)" which was a hit in the 1940s for the Pied Pipers and became a standard that was covered by Frank Sinatra, Ray Anthony, and Johnny Preston, all of which may have been familiar to the band.

The mystery song may also be the Everly Brothers "(All I Have to Do Is) Dream" which was never recorded by the Beatles, but very likely was included or at least attempted by the band on occasion.

The Everly Brothers were an American singing duo whose close harmonies were a great inspiration for the singing Beatles, also giving the band exposure to American country music.

The duo recorded "Bye Bye Love," written by husband and wife songwriting team Felice and

Joe Brown and the Bruvvers

Boudleaux Bryant after dozens of other artists turned it down. It became their first million seller, hitting on the country, pop, as well as the R&B charts.

The three singing Beatles would immediately attempt to imitate the Everlys, listening very closely, immediately noting all of the specific lifts and enunciations of their harmonies. They also noted that Phil and Don had similar yet unique accents. John, Paul, and George would experiment greatly in their attempt to recreate the style of music that the Everlys presented for them.

As was the case with other music they emulated during this era, the Beatles never attempted to record any Everly songs for official release, performing one for the BBC in July 1963, reviving an "oldie" for the occasion.

"So How Come (No One Loves Me)" written by the Bryants for the Everly Brothers in 1960, was also on the February 2 set list.

The couple would pen more than two dozen songs for the Everly Brothers, including "Wake Up Little Suzie" in 1957, and "All I Have to Do is Dream" (which was written by Boudleaux to his wife Felice) in 1958, as well as the aforementioned "Bye Bye Love."

As the Everly Brothers were one of the Beatles' greatest influences, the band members no doubt also recognized the Bryant/Bryant credit on "Problems," "Poor Jenny," "Radio and TV," "Take a Message to Mary," "Bird Dog," "Devoted to You," "Nashville Blues," "Love Hurts," "Always it's You," "Donna, Donna," and "A Change of Heart."

It's very likely that the band did "So How Come (No One Loves Me)" along with other Everly Brothers' tracks in their act from the time they first started performing together.

Vocal duties typically would have been shared by

mono DFE 8500

DECCA

A PICTURE
of JOE
BROWN

A letter of love
Comes the day
Stick around
People gotta talk

George who would enjoy Brown's country rock style of music. Beginning in 1959 Brown would release "People Gotta Talk" b/w "Comes the Day," followed by "The Darktown Strutters Ball" b/w "Swagger" the following year, and in 1961 he would have "Crazy Mixed Up Kid" b/w "Stick Around," "Shine" b/w "The Switch" and "Good Luck and Goodbye" b/w "I'm Henery the Eighth" (note the intentional misspelling of Henry).

In 1962 Brown had "A Picture of You," which was quickly learned and performed by the Beatles. As influenced as the band was by Brown, they would quickly lose interest in him as they gained their own notoriety in the U.K., and Brown's fame would decline.

This setlist serves as what is very likely a prime example of what type of shows the Beatles were putting on in early '62, slightly before original compositions would begin to slowly take over.

On February 5, with Best getting sick and unable to perform, the Beatles recruited Ringo to fill in for both the afternoon and evening shows at the Cavern.

They had become friends with Starr when the Beatles and the Hurricanes both had residencies at the same time in Hamburg, Germany. Starr may have performed with them on special occasions while the two bands were sharing stage space, but nothing was documented prior to the early February occasion.

Starr had a rare day off as a Hurricane on February 5, and was able to fill in with the band during the lunchtime performance at the Cavern Club, and later at the Kingsway Club in Southport.

On February 12 the Beatles traveled to Manchester to audition for the BBC, a meeting that was arranged by their very ambitious manager Epstein.

Even though the band had heard bad news about their future at Decca Records, they continued to work hard and play as many shows as they could.

The Beatles performed on February 23 at the Cavern Club during their typical noon to 2 p.m.

John and Paul, but it was George along with John who harmonized on "So How Come No One (Loves Me)," which was the only Everly Brothers song to be recorded by the Beatles, although not for an official album.

There are a couple of elements of this particular song that the Beatles found especially interesting. They were intrigued by the tight and accurate harmonies, the fact that the song was a question, and the mentioning of unusual rock and roll terms like the "ugly duckling" and "little black sheep." While only using a few words, the song told a full story.

"Crazy World We Live In" was listed, more accurately titled "What a Crazy World We're Living In," which was a Joe Brown single from early '62 and likely a record that the band members picked up from NEMS.

Brown is an English entertainer who was a great early influence on the Beatles, particularly

WHAT A CRAZY WORLD
WE'RE LIVING IN
(Alan Klein)
PAN-MUSIK

PICCADILLY

7N.35024

JOE BROWN
and the Bruvvers
Recorded during his act at
Granada, Woolwich

show, then at the Tower Ballroom in New Brighton, Wallasey at 9 p.m. and again at 10:45 p.m. Between their two sets they quickly traveled to Technical College Hall Birkenhead to perform a 30 minute set.

The following day the band traveled to the YMCA in Hoylake, Wirral, where they were booed off the stage by the rowdy crowd who wasn't enjoying the band's banter between songs.

After that they traveled back home to Liverpool where they took the stage at the Cavern Club just after midnight to top the bill at an all night long show.

The band performed their radio broadcast debut on March 7, 1962 for "Teenager's Turn/Here We Go!" They traveled to the Playhouse Theater in Manchester, where they rehearsed in the afternoon, then performed after 8 p.m. that evening, wearing matching suits for the first time ever.

A seemingly simple wardrobe change would drastically change the way the band was perceived by many, resulting in them being taken considerably more seriously.

Still a bit self-conscious about their original material after the defeating experience with Decca, the band chose to perform three cover versions.

Chuck Berry's "Memphis" would never be officially recorded by the band, although it was frequently performed. "Please Mr. Postman" would remain in their act as well making it onto an official album.

The first song they performed for this edition of "Teenager's Turn" would never advance past this date.

"Dream Baby (How Long Must I Dream?)" was released by Roy Orbison in early '62, making it a current hit for him at the same time the band was performing it on the BBC.

The song was written by Cindy Walker, who had Top 10 hits spanning five decades. Her first published song was "Cherokee Maiden" for Bob Wills and his Texas Playboys in 1941, the same year she would write "Lone Star" for Bing Crosby. She wrote "Over and Over Again" for Gene Autry in 1946, also writing "Blue Canadian Rockies" for Autry for his 1950 film of the same name. After two continuous decades of success Walker continued to evolve as a songwriter, composing songs that fit the artist they were intended for very well.

She didn't have much confidence in "Dream Baby," which she gave to Orbison. He provided a dynamic and powerful performance which helped make the song his fifth Top 10 hit in early 1962. The following year Orbison and the Beatles would become friends as they toured together.

After that BBC broadcast on March 8, the Beatles continued to work very consistently.

During the evening of March 22, the band performed with Peppy and the New York Twisters, who brought the twist craze along with them. The Beatles allegedly wrote a song called the "Pinwheel

Twist" on the spot, only performing it or attempting it on very few occasions.

At the Hesswall Jazz club on March 24 the band was said to have premiered their new suits for the world, although conflicting reports say this happened several weeks earlier.

The band clearly ended one era and started another on April 5, 1962.

When listening to recordings of the band in their pre-EMI days, there is a level of confidence that is always displayed. However, it seems that only as they entered "the suit era" did they begin to be taken more seriously, as they continued to take themselves more seriously as well. Professionalism is a contribution of Epstein's that cannot be understated.

Epstein had rented out the Cavern for a private Beatles Fan Club performance where the band played a set of music while wearing their leather jackets. Then while the supporting act, the Four Jays (who would become the Fourmost) played, the Beatles got into their brand new Beno Dorn suits, a look that the band would keep for several years, although it evolved slightly.

The Cavern Club

Once again the "Peppermint Twist" was performed this evening, with Paul sitting behind the drums, George possibly switching to bass for this one simple song, and Pete Best taking center stage to demonstrate the twist with his future wife/ then girlfriend Kathy.

Also during this informal Cavern club performance, the members of the Four Jays merged with the Beatles on stage as did owner Ray McFall, who joined the Beatles for a pair of Elvis tunes, "I Can't Help Falling in Love with You" and "Love Me Tender."

On April 6 promoter Sam Leach held a Beatles Farewell Ball at the Tower Ballroom, New Brighton, Wallasey just before the band was set to head off to Germany for their third extended visit, which was agreed upon shortly before Epstein joined the organization.

After a few more final goodbye shows around Liverpool, the band prepared for their third and final visit to Germany. ◆

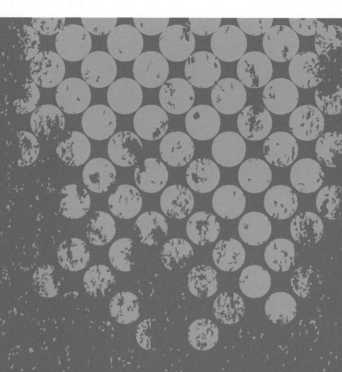

CHAPTER 10:
RETURN TO GERMANY

SAD NEWS WAS AHEAD FOR THE BAND AS THEY ARRIVED IN HAMBURG ON APRIL 11 FOR THEIR RESIDENCY AT THE STAR CLUB.

ASTRID KIRCHHERR MET LENNON, McCartney, and Best at the airport where she informed them of the devastating death of friend and former bandmate Stuart Sutcliffe. Harrison and Epstein flew there the next day where they were informed of the tragic events upon their arrival.

Sutcliffe had been experiencing severe headaches for several months, causing him to have to resign from his art teacher position. At the insistence of the Kirchherr family, who suspected a brain tumor, he visited two separate doctors who found nothing out of the ordinary. By March his pain was nearly constant, causing him to experience occasional blindness and terrible mood swings.

On April 10, 1962 Sutcliffe collapsed and an ambulance was called. Astrid was contacted and hurried home to accompany him in the ambulance, where Stuart tragically died in his fiancé's arms while heading for help.

This was news that all of the Beatles took very badly, but they knew for them to succeed in the music business they needed to remain tough, and continue to perform as scheduled.

Despite the devastating loss of their colleague and friend, the band began a lengthy residency at the Star Club on Friday, April 13, performing every night except for April 20 (Good Friday) for seven full weeks. Epstein remained in Hamburg for their first few shows, returning home after that.

On April 19 Stuart Sutcliffe was buried in Huyton, Merseyside. The Beatles were unable to attend. Cynthia Powell (later Lennon) was present, as was George's mother Louise and Allan Williams. Astrid Kirchherr and Klaus Voormann attended from Germany.

When Epstein first joined forces with the Beatles he immediately started trying to get them signed to a record contract, although they were technically previously signed with Bert Kaempfert, who produced the sessions with Tony Sheridan in 1961.

Kaempfert agreed to free the Beatles of their obligations if they would agree to record one more session with Sheridan which took place on May 24, 1962 at Studio Rahlstedt in Hamburg.

A piano player named Roy Young, who had occasionally joined the Beatles on stage at the Star Club, performed on at least one of the two songs recorded on this day. Sheridan was unable to attend on this occasion; his vocals were added on June 7, and then slightly altered the following year.

"Sweet Georgia Brown" was arranged by McCartney,

John Lennon and Cynthia Powell (sitting) with two unknown friends from Liverpool

longer exist. The song was re-recorded with a different set of musicians, possibly the same singers that are heard on "Sweet Georgia Brown" although those background vocals may possibly be John, Paul, and George.

Later that night the Beatles performed as scheduled at the Star Club as part of their residency. During this first residency which ran through May 31, the Beatles would refine their act, eliminating what they felt didn't work, always trying to add new numbers into their set. After that booking was complete, they would return to the club twice more before the year was over.

After their failed Decca auditions they were discouraged, but also confident that the extremely eager and determined Epstein would continue to do his best to sell the band, and get them bigger and more prestigious shows, as well as the ultimate prize of a record contract.

They also started questioning specifics about the lineup of the band, curious if perhaps their drummer was a weak link and holding them back. They recalled how exciting it was when they performed with Ringo as their drummer.

It is unknown if the band wore their new matching suits which were purchased for them by Epstein, during this first stint at the Star Club. However it is likely that that reverted back to their leather jackets for the rough and vocal German audience the band was always trying to please.

After their residency ended, the Beatles flew home on June 2, first to London, then to Manchester before being driven to Liverpool. It's undocumented but extremely likely that the airfare was paid by Epstein, who was investing a fair amount of money into his new prospects.

The band was scheduled to audition for EMI records on June 6, and after their failure with Decca they wanted to make sure they were as good as possible. They spent two days rehearsing at an empty Cavern Club in the late afternoon, from 3-6:30 p.m. on June 2, and for several hours beginning at 7 p.m. on June

who even at this extremely early era of recording had a clear idea of how a song should be presented.

Young adds very much to the song, including a fine piano solo which was complimented by Sheridan when he recorded the vocals the following month saying "this group is absolutely marvelous for the piano, don't ya think so?"

Sheridan would re-record the vocal track of the song in January 1964 adding "In Liverpool she even dared, to criticize the Beatles' hair, with their whole fan club standing there, ah, meet Sweet Georgia Brown" and some other more timely lyrics.

"Swanee River" was also recorded this day, although the Beatles recordings were never released, and no

3, a Monday which had no acts scheduled to perform.

The day before the EMI session the band traveled down from Liverpool to be certain that there would be no issues complicating their arrival. They stayed at the upscale Capitol Hotel in London the night before, heading to EMI studios for the very first time to arrive early for their 7 p.m. appointment which would prove to be monumental in the history of the band.

On this historic day, June 6, 1962, the four Beatles entered the studio. The first order of business was getting their amplifiers up to a professional grade.

Norman Smith was a sound engineer at EMI, hired in 1959 after his career as a jazz musician failed to progress. When the Beatles were first brought into the studio it was Smith who helped them get their best sound. He was also intrigued enough to alert George Martin, who was likely dealing with several bands at once. John Lennon quickly named Smith "Normal" which was a kind term of endearment for an engineer they quickly grew to trust, based on his experience with Martin.

Smith was the engineer for that day's session and recalls how battered their amplifiers were, particularly McCartney's. After fixing up Paul's amp, tying a string around Lennon's to prevent it from rattling, and sorting out whatever drum problems they had, the band was ready to begin.

Ron Richards was Martin's assistant producer during their recording years as well, working closely with the band throughout the decade, also discovering and producing the Hollies. He was the

initial producer for this session until Martin was summoned to the control room by Smith, impressed with Love Me Do, which was of course an original.

Tape operator

Stu de Staël

Chris Neal was sent to retrieve Martin, who was possibly overseeing a different artist test at the time. Throughout the day there were artist tests for Darien Angadi, Jill and the Boulevards, Elaine Truss, and the Long Riders. It was unlikely that Martin attended any of these recordings; there must have been a certain something special about the Beatles.

The Beatles were gaining confidence as songwriters, presenting three relatively new compositions, "Love Me Do," "Ask Me Why," and "P.S. I Love You," as well as the curiously selected "Besame Mucho," which was notably a bit of a novelty considering the band was trying to improve their image in the hopes to be taken a bit more seriously.

Session notes don't reveal the order of the recordings.

While standard practice for a test session such as this was to simply erase and reuse the tape, somehow miraculously "Besame Mucho" and "Love Me Do" survived.

Tape operator Ken Townsend was also present, and recalls how they weren't exactly amazed by the band,

The Beatles with Ron Richards

but it was apparent that there was an indescribable "something" about them, most certainly the same charisma that impressed Epstein.

There remain conflicting reports and speculations over whether the Beatles were already signed to a contract prior to this first meeting, or when it was decided that they would indeed get the coveted record deal prize, as it was most unusual to have a producer attend these sessions.

Townsend also recalls that in spite of the impression the band did make, it must not have been huge because the following week Norman Smith couldn't recall the name "Beatles" and had to ask while labeling a reel of tape.

The band actually took a couple of evenings off before returning to the Cavern on Saturday, June 9 for their "Welcome Home" show, which broke the attendance record by jamming around 900 fans into the underground venue.

On June 11 the band headed back to Manchester for their second appearance on "Here We Go," rehearsing in the early afternoon and taping in the evening. This recording was broadcast June 15 on the BBC "Light Programme," with the Beatles performing "Ask Me Why," "Besame Mucho," and

"A Picture of You."

"A Picture of You" was composed by John Beveridge and Peter Oakman and was a current hit for Joe Brown and his Bruvvers at the time of the band's recording, with Harrison taking lead vocals. This song would mark the first time that Harrison performed a lead vocal on a BBC performance.

"Besame Mucho" was performed as well, as was "Ask Me Why" which was the first Lennon/McCartney song to be performed and broadcast for the BBC. The band was slowly becoming more confident and comfortable performing their original material for "important" events.

They performed at the Tower Ballroom supporting headliner Bruce Channel, who was backed by the Barons, which featured Delbert McClinton on harmonica.

McClinton was born in Lubbock, Texas, which greatly impressed the Beatles due to the fact that is also the hometown of their hero Buddy Holly. After relocating to Ft. Worth, Texas as a child, McClinton grew to become an accomplished player who was a member of the Straightjackets, musicians who supplied background for blues artists Howlin' Wolf, Lightnin' Hopkins, Jimmy Reed, and Sonny Boy Williamson, who was also a highly regarded harmonica player.

McClinton was said to have given Lennon some pointers on playing harmonica during the time they spent together which Channel claims was where Lennon got the inspiration for "Love Me Do."

"Hey Baby" was a hit in 1962, released in December of the previous year by Chanell, with McClinton playing harmonica. His sound on the song has a similar tone and feel to that of "Love Me Do," which was recorded after the release of "Hey Baby'" but prior to the meeting between the harmonica players.

Lennon was probably a fan of the song and may have taken inspiration from it, however what is likely the case is that both McClinton and Lennon took inspiration from similar sounding harmonica performances, Lennon's most likely being Frank Ifield's version of "I Remember You," also released in '62.

The band played their final performance at the Casbah Coffee Club on June 24, which was closed after this night.

Sunday, July 1 was a great thrill for the band as they shared a bill at the Cavern Club with Gene Vincent, who headlined show. There is said to be a recording of the Beatles joining Vincent on stage, possibly the other way around, to perform "What'd I Say."

"What'd I Say" was a two-sided Ray Charles single from 1959 which fused blues and gospel, introducing a brand new style of soul music that would be important to the creation of rock and roll, as well as the Beatles.

While on the road for an exhausting tour, Charles requested that his background singers (the Cookies, also known as the Raelettes) and his band just "follow Ray" as he "fooled around" on some electric piano riffs. The band fell in and Ray spontaneously came up with simple "baby don't you treat me wrong" and other "hey and ho" call and response lyrics. That feature slowly and only slightly developed before it was recorded for Atlantic Records in February 1959 on a brand new 8-track recorder by engineer Tom Dowd, who considered it a quick and easy recording, with no overdubs.

Due to the extreme length of the song it was divided over two sides of a 45 to fit it all in, including the the strategic placement of a pause with Ray telling the band to "hold it" midway through the performance.

The Beatles joined Vincent was backed by Sound Incorporated for the occasion, which was the first Sunday that wasn't Jazz night at the Cavern. Times were clearly changing as rock and roll and the Mersey sound continued to pick up steam simultaneous with the Beatles' rise to fame.

The Beatles had met Vincent during 1961 and were very impressed with him, not just as a musician but as a stylish and professional performer who was also very charismatic. They certainly considered him another early role model to emulate, while still maintaining their own identity as a band.

As they had the previous year, the band performed aboard the MV Royal Iris, a Mersey River craft also known as the "fish and chip boat." These Riverboat Shuffle events were put on by Ray McFall who was the owner of the Cavern Club. In 1962 the Beatles performed on the MV Royal Iris July 6, August 10, and September 28.

Throughout July, with the band's fate at EMI still uncertain, they continued to play almost daily, most frequently at the Cavern Club during the lunchtime and evening shows.

On August 15 the band would perform at the Cavern and it would be the final performance for Pete Best.

After the show Best and the band discussed their usual arrangements for the following day. Generally Aspinall would pick up Best, and then round up the other band members. Best said to Lennon "I'll pick you up tomorrow?" and Lennon replied that they "had other plans" (for the following day).

Epstein also asked Best for him to come to his NEMS office that morning, nothing which seemed unusual to him.

After the EMI session Martin discussed with Epstein the fact that he wasn't especially impressed with the drummer. He felt that a rock band needed a stronger and more consistent "beat" behind them and informed him that they would be using a session drummer the next time the recorded.

On August 16 Best showed up as requested and was informed by Epstein that "The lads don't want you in the group anymore," explaining to him that

Clockwise from bottom: George Harrison sporting a black eye; the Beatles with Gene Vincent in Germany; Pete, George, Paul and John in their matching suits; Paul and John at the Cavern with unknown fans

thought their fame was about to fade away, and he didn't enjoy Lennon's sense of humor.

Epstein had also asked the opinion of Cavern Club DJ Bob Wooler, who was outraged about Best's dismissal. He reminded Epstein that not only was Best dependable and knew how to "fall in place," but was also popular among the fans, both the females who found him attractive and the males who enjoyed his "mean, moody, and magnificent" attitude.

After agonizing over the decision, Epstein, who was reluctant about changing the membership of the band just as their individual personalities were beginning to emerge, was finally told by the other members that they would like to change drummers.

There was a divide in the level of musicianship between the ever improving Harrison, Lennon, and McCartney and the floundering Best, who hadn't shown much sign of improvement in a while. McCartney was said to have been especially critical of Best, with rumors that he was envious of the attention the drummer was getting from the lady fans.

Contrary to that was Paul defending the drummer, saying that the producer was used to big band drummers who kept time very precisely, and that he didn't understand the sense of spirit and emotion that a Liverpool drummer would bring, unique and passionate, but not necessarily with the greatest sense of time.

McCartney's hindsight seems to be especially kind to Best.

With very few high quality recordings of Best's work, it is difficult to judge his playing. Aside from his talents as a musician, however, there was a certain closeness among the other three Beatles that wasn't shared with Best, not just their sense of humor, but also a kinship among them.

There was also a level of immaturity and lack of professionalism from the otherwise very conscientious band, having their manager do the "dirty work."

Best had become friends with Aspinall, who rented a room in the Best home and became romantically

Ringo was the new drummer.

Epstein asked a very upset Best to perform a couple more shows until Ringo was ready, which Best initially agreed to, later rethinking and changing his mind, never playing with the Beatles again. He was notably upset, feeling betrayed by the band as well as Ringo, whom he considered a friend.

Prior to this meeting Epstein had allegedly approached the Earl Preston and the TTs drummer' Ritchie Galvin about filling in or possibly joining the Beatles. Galvin declined, stating he thought it was the wrong choice to fire Best from the band, he linked with the drummer's mother Mona. Aspinall was furious about Best getting "sacked" and was going to quit his job with the Beatles organization, but was talked out of it by the bruised drummer.

During the next performance following the decision Aspinall asked Lennon about the situation. John reportedly replied "It's got nothing to do with you, you're only the driver."

Lennon was friendly with the generally quiet Best, however Harrison and McCartney were reportedly not especially close with him, rarely associating with him when they were off stage. While in Hamburg the three would frequently go off on their escapades leaving Best behind, excluding him from many of their inside jokes and adventures.

It was also reported that Epstein offered the drummer job to Johnny Hutchinson of the Big Three, but he refused, stating his loyalty to his friend Pete and saying he couldn't "do the dirty on him."

Starr played his last shows as a Hurricane while Hutchinson filled in with band on August 16-17 as the band played three shows in two days.

On Saturday, August 18, 1962 at Hulme Hall at Port Sunlight after a two hour rehearsal, the Beatles performed their first show with Ringo as their official permanent drummer.

This would be the final membership change for the band.

Ringo wasn't a stranger to the band, first meeting the Quarrymen on March 13, 1959 when he was a member of Al Caldwell's Texans, who would become Rory Storm and the Hurricanes. This was the opening night of the Morgue Skiffle Cellar in Liverpool.

The Hurricanes and the Beatles frequently shared space, including an extended residency at the Star Club where Ringo occasionally sat in with the band and became increasingly close with John, Paul, and George, enjoying a camaraderie among them.

The Beatles had reached a status as an excellent

band and were taken very seriously by mid '62, which of course was their wish. The Hurricanes had a bit less of a reputation, so Ringo would quickly blend in with the other Beatles, who all shared common goals and levels of talent.

Ringo's first official show as a Beatle was August 19 at the Cavern Club, and the band faced many angry fans who were upset over the firing of Best.

Bob McGrae, who was a DJ at the Cavern Club recalls there were girls crying on Mathew Street over the firing of Best, vowing to never enter the Cavern again. Ringo received a rude awakening with crowds hissing and booing, chanting "Pete Best forever, Ringo never" and "Ringo out, Pete in!"

The band played through the shouting, with George Harrison "mouthing off" to a fan who head-butted George, giving him a black eye.

On August 22, while wearing matching vests, the band was filmed for their first television appearance during their lunchtime appearance at the Cavern.

Manchester-based Granada Television kept hearing more

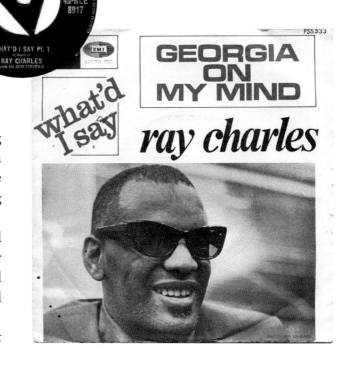

about these Beatles from Liverpool and set out to investigate this "mania." The Beatles performed while a crew filmed with an enthusiastic crowd on hand, including a few protesters. At the end of the audio a male voice can be heard shouting "we want Pete." The film quality was very poor, as was the audio which was recorded with one single microphone.

On August 23 John Lennon was married to Cynthia Powell, who was expecting a child fathered by Lennon. Epstein served as the best man, George and Paul were in attendance, as were Cynthia's half-brother and his wife.

Not in attendance was Ringo, who wasn't invited primarily due to the intended secrecy of the marriage, at least for the fans, and the newest band member wasn't completely proven to be trustworthy as of yet. Also absent was John's Aunt Mimi, who disapproved of the union.

Afterwards, courtesy of Epstein, the party celebrated with a dinner, and then prepared for their show at the Riverpark Ballroom in Chester.

It was very clear that Lennon was driven to succeed, and very little was important to him other than performing in a band. However very few acts or artists demonstrated the level of dedication as performing the night of his wedding.

This same compulsion to flourish contributed greatly to Lennon's success, but sadly this never-fading passion for the Beatles is also what ultimately led to the demise of his first marriage.

The band returned to EMI Studios in London on September 4, notably making their first recording to feature Ringo. September 4 was also the first day on the job for novice engineer Geoff Emerick, who was 15 years old when hired to assist Richard Langham. Emerick was immediately impressed with the band, and he worked alongside the Beatles very well, becoming extremely important to them as they learned together about the recording industry.

On this evening the band would record a song for what would become their debut single. In this era, before bands like the Beatles changed the way the recording industry worked, they would frequently get assigned the songs they were going to record.

Given the songwriting ability of Lennon/McCartney, as well as their ability to perform their own music, a little more consideration was given to them when selecting which song to record. Ultimately, however it was "How Do You Do It?" that was chosen for them.

Written by songwriter Mitch Murray in 1963, the song was originally offered to Adam Faith, who turned it down. Faith was a British teen idol that had great success in the U.K., with more than a dozen Top 20 hits between 1959 and 1964. His last hit was song called "A Message to Martha," a Burt Bacharach/Hal David composition which Faith recorded as "Kentucky Bluebird."

As the Beatles and other British Invasion groups began to dominate the charts, Faith had less and less success throughout the decade, sporadically releasing new music until his death in 2003.

The song was then offered to Brian Poole, of

the Tremoloes, who also rejected it, although the Tremeloes would have success in the '60s along with the Beatles and the current wave of young, pop music on the U.K. charts. The Tremeloes (occasionally Tremelo) continued to record throughout the '80s and were still an active touring band as of 2018.

Mitch Murray had great success throughout the '60s as well, writing successful hits for Freddie and the Dreamers including "I'm Telling You Now" and "You Were Made for Me" in 1963.

Along with Peter Callander, Murray had success writing for the Tremeloes with "Even the Bad Times are Good," from 1967 and "The Ballad of Bonnie and Clyde" for Georgie Fame in 1968.

After "How Do You Do It" was turned down by Faith as well as by Poole and the Tremeloes, it wound up on the desk of Ron Richards, who offered it to Martin to be the debut release for the Beatles.

On September 4 Beatles went to the EMI studios on Abbey Road to record their first single.

Presented to them sometime between June 1962 when they auditioned and the time of this first formal session, the band learned "How Do You Do It" from acetate, adding an intro, some vocal harmonies, and a guitar solo.

They expressed their dislike of the song and told Martin that they didn't think it fit the image they wished to present. However the band members knew their place, and although they objected they professionally agreed to record the song, quickly completing it in order to make more time to focus on their own "Love Me Do."

Murray apparently disliked the changes the band made, specifically the slight lyric changes and removal of the half-step modulation. It is not known if this is why the song was never officially released by the Beatles.

Ultimately "Love Me Do" and its B-side "P.S. I Love You" became the debut single. "How Do You Do It" was offered to fellow Liverpudlians Gerry and the Pacemakers, who had a hit with it in early

John and Cynthia Lennon

'63 when it was No. 1 until knocked out of the top spot by "From Me to You," the Beatles' third single.

Martin still considered releasing "How Do You Do It" for the second single, convinced of its potential, deciding to allow them to continue to release their own compositions, which was certainly proving to be successful.

While the song was certainly catchy and commercial, the band felt that releasing a blusier song that was an original gave them much more credibility than the fluffy and breezy "How Do You Do It?"

On September 5 a Granada Television sound tech captured a second performance, this time using three separate microphones, resulting in a better quality recording. Along with "Some Other Guy" the band reportedly performed "Kansas City/Hey Hey Hey Hey."

After being edited the film wasn't broadcast until November 1963 when Beatlemania was beginning to rapidly spread across the U.K.

"Some Other Guy" was written by Leiber and Stoller along with producer, performer, and songwriter Richie Barrett.

Barrett was born and raised in Philadelphia and was a vocalist for the Valentines in the mid '50s. The group released "Lily Maebelle" backed with "Falling for You" in 1955, "Why" backed with "The Woo Woo Train" on the flipside in 1956, and "Don't Say Goodnight" and "I Cried Oh, Oh" in 1957, all for the Rama label.

As a promoter and a talent scout Barrett discovered Frankie Lymon and the Teenagers, Little Anthony and the Imperials, as well as the Chantels. He also produced several song for the Chantels, including their 1958 single "Maybe" on which he plays the piano, bass, and drums.

Under the name Dickie Barrett he released a version of "Smoke Gets in Your Eyes" in 1958 and a cover of "Come Softly to Me" (as originally done by the Fleetwoods) with the Chantels singing

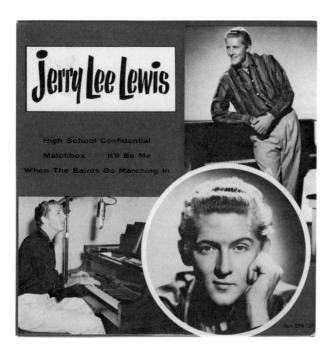

background in 1959.

On his version of "Some Other Guy," Barrett plays an electric piano, which was an uncommon instrument for 1962, and the solo is definitely inspired by Ray Charles.

Shortly after Barrett's release, the Big Three, also a Liverpool based band, covered "Some Other Guy" for their March 1963 debut release on the Decca label.

The Beatles, and very possibly the Hurricanes, quickly began doing the song as did many other English bands who were starting to attract attention during this period of music that was called the British Invasion.

The Beatles also played at the Cavern that evening, continuing to work as often as possible.

The band flew from Liverpool to London the morning of the session, and checked into the Chelsea Hotel, arriving at EMI shortly after noon. They rehearsed under the direction of Ron Richards, who had them run through six songs.

Although unconfirmed, it is likely that the songs they ran through were the newly introduced "How Do You Do It?" "Love Me Do," and the originals that they had and were considering recording "Ask Me Why," "Tip of My Tongue," "P.S. I Love You," and "Please Please Me."

A slower, bluesier version of "Please Please Me" was presented to Martin on this day as well. He immediately recognized its hit potential and suggested they "pep it up" and have a go at it the next time they recorded.

This rehearsal wasn't recorded and there is no EMI documentation. It is also possible that "Hello Little Girl," "One After 909," "Love of the Loved," or "Like Dreamers Do" were rehearsed or auditioned for Richards and possibly Martin as well.

It was "How Do You Do It?" that was forced upon them, and although they wanted to have an original as their first single, they also understood they didn't have the clout to make demands.

After recording the song a bit halfheartedly, the

band then got to work on "Love Me Do," which they were hoping would become the A-side. After finishing up the song, Martin promised that he would think very seriously about selecting it as the single, deciding that it was indeed the right choice although it needed a bit of reworking.

During the break Martin took the band, as well as Neil Aspinall, out for a spaghetti dinner, where Martin impressed them with his tales of recording with Peter Sellers and Spike Milligan.

The following Tuesday, September 11, the band traveled back to London once again to attempt to record their debut single. There is great speculation over why Andy White was booked as a session drummer for this session.

White was a Scottish drummer and session musician who, as well as performing with the Beatles, also appeared on tracks recorded by Herman's Hermits, Tom Jones, Bill Haley, and Chuck Berry. In 1952 White joined the Vic Lewis Orchestra and toured the U.S., becoming a well-liked and highly-skilled session player throughout the decade. During the 1960s he played on Bill Fury's debut album, as well as several tracks from Herman's Hermits, and on Lulu's version of "Shout!"

White was also part of Marlene Dietrich's backup band at the same time Burt Bacharach was the pianist, which led to White drumming on the *What's New Pussycat?* soundtrack LP in 1965, as well as Tom Jones' "It's Not Unusual," which featured session guitarist Jimmy Page.

White's first wife was Lyn Cornell, a member of the Carefrees, who would score a No. 39 hit with the novelty "We Love You Beatles," based on a chant sung in the 1960 musical *Bye Bye Birdie*.

White joined the BBC Scottish Radio Orchestra in Glasgow until it disbanded in 1983, when he then

Rock legend Chuck Berry

moved to the United States and settled in New Jersey.

In 2012 during the filming of "Not Fade Away," musical director Little Steven Van Zandt hired White as a consultant to teach the young actor/musicians how to perform as an early '60s band would for the period piece.

White passed away in November 2015.

Martin and Richards were concerned about the drumming for the Beatles and decided to hire a session player strictly for the studio. They didn't especially concern themselves over how they sounded live, but were acutely aware of what the recorded product sounded like. ◆

THE BRITISH INVASION

THE BRITISH INVASION WAS WHAT THE PRESS TITLED THE OVERPOWERING WAVE WHICH TOOK ROOT IN THE EARLY 60S AND SOON DOMINATED THE CHARTS IN THE UNITED STATES, PUSHING MANY ESTABLISHED ACTS TO THE LOWER PART OF THE TOP 50. SEVERAL OF THOSE DISPLACED ACTS INFLUENCED THE BEATLES, WHO WERE FORMING THEIR INDIVIDUAL SOUND.

These assorted British Invasion bands, literally hundreds in England, were recruited and recorded quickly, then released and exported, all experiencing various levels of success. Some enjoyed a run extending well through the decade and beyond, while others had success into the middle of the decade, only to be left behind by their limitations as the musical landscape changed rapidly.

The Kinks scored a Top 10 hit in August 1964 with "You Really Got Me," an early example of harder rock which would slowly evolve into heavy metal. Throughout the '60s and far beyond the band, led by brothers Ray and Dave Davies, would have wide success and great critical acclaim. Also in late '64 was "All Day and All of the Night" (note the use of "Day" and "Night" in the title, sounding similar to the title of the Beatles' first film) which followed the formula of their first successful hit with intense and powerful guitars.

As the Beatles progressed and developed as creators of music, the Kinks did as well, with the two bands mutually inspiring each other. Ray would also compose songs to give away throughout the decade, offering songs to Herman's Hermits ("Dandy") as well as "All Night Stand" for the Thoughts.

The Tornados were an English instrumental group who recorded and performed as Bill Fury's backing band, as well as on their own productions. "Telstar," titled for the satellite of the same name, was the band's first and biggest hit, becoming a No.1 in both the U.K. and the U.S. in 1962. That made the Tornados the first British act with a No. 1 on the American charts since World War II. Joe Meek, the song's composer and producer, oversaw a vocal version called "Magic Star" sung by Kenny Hollywood, also in '62. The B-side of "Telstar" was another Tornados original called "Jungle Fever."

In 1963 the Tornados would have a hit with "Globetrotter" b/w "Locomotion with Me" followed by "Robot" b/w "Life on Venus," "The Ice Cream Man" b/w "The Scales of Justice Theme" (from a series of theater-only featurettes), and "Dragonfly" b/w "Hymn for Teenagers." The following year the Tornados released "Joystick" b/w "Hot Pot," "Monte Carlo" b/w "Blue, Blue Beat," and "Exodus" b/w "Blackpool Rock," none of which would repeat the success of "Telstar."

Georgie Fame and the Blue Flames was a reputable jazz, blues, R&B, ska, and pop combo from the Invasion. Like the Tornados, Fame and the Blue Flames also served as a backing band for Fury, who is yet another example of a solo singer who had success in the first few years of the '60s, but became less marketable as the Invasion took over, led of course by the Beatles themselves.

In 1964 Georgie Fame and the Blue Flames released a trio of singles, "Do The Dog" b/w "Shop Around" in January, "Do-Re-Mi" b/w "Green Onions" in April, and "Yeh, Yeh" b/w "Preach and Teach," with "Yeh, Yeh" hitting No. 1 in the U.K. in December.

As was the case with many acts from the era, there would be numerous lineup changes, including drummer Mitch Mitchell briefly being a Blue Flame before joining the Jimi Hendrix Experience in late '66 when Fame disbanded the group.

The Zombies released "She's Not There" in July

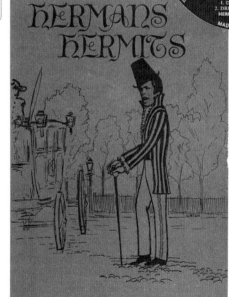

1964 as their debut single, loosely based on a John Lee Hooker composition called "No One Told Me" from 1962. Later in December 1964 they would release "Tell Her No," which was written by keyboardist and leader of the band Rod Argent (who would go on to form Argent after the Zombies' breakup in 1967). He did his best to copy a standard Beatle cut, using the word "no" 63 times in the song.

More common than the success of the Kinks or the Zombies would be the "one hit wonders" or bands with a handful of releases, each with sporadic or generally declining success.

Freddie and the Dreamers had a string of hits beginning in May 1963 with their arrangement of "If You Gotta Make a Fool of Somebody" followed by "I'm Tellin' You Now" in August and "You Were Made For Me" in November. The band would regularly release EPs and singles as the Invasion was ramping up, often borrowing from the Beatles catalog, as with their version of "Money (That's What I Want)" and their take on "Kansas City" and "Some Other Guy."

In 1964 the Dreamers had a run of singles for the Columbia label on both sides of the Atlantic with varying degrees of success, including "Over You," "You Were Made for Me," "I Love You Baby," "Just for You," and "I Understand (Just How You Feel)." The Dreamers (led by Freddie Garrity) would also cover the Coasters tune "I'm A Hog For You," drawing inspiration from the same sources the Beatles did when they performed songs as done by Buddy Holly ("It Doesn't Matter Anymore"), Eddie Cochran ("Cut Across Shorty"), and Chuck Berry ("Johnny B. Goode").

Throughout the decade the Dreamers would have success with their poppy brand of music. However as the Beatles evolved to develop and compose songs with more depth, the Dreamers were still doing "The Freddie" and covering material from others, including an all-Disney album in 1966.

The Honeycombs scored a No. 1 hit with their debut "Have I the Right" in June 1964, which was their greatest success. They sputtered and disbanded by early '66.

The Searchers were a Liverpool skiffle act who took their name from a 1956 John Wayne movie of the same name. "Sweets For My Sweet" (originally recorded by the Drifters in 1961) b/w "It's All Been a Dream" was their debut release in 1963, followed by "Sweet Nothings" (originally recorded by Brenda Lee in 1959) b/w "What'd I Say" (originally recorded by Ray Charles in 1959) and "Sugar and Spice" (originally done by Tony Hatch in 1963) b/w "Saints and Searchers," (a customized rendition of "When the Saints Go Marching In"), all in 1963.

During the height of the British Invasion, the Searchers continued to hit with "Needles and Pins" (written by Sonny Bono and Jack Nitzsche, originally recorded by Jackie DeShannon in 1963), "Don't Throw Your Love Away" (originally recorded by the Orlons in 1963), "Someday We're Gonna Love Again" (originally recorded by Barbara Lewis in early 1964), "When You Walk in the Room" (also originally recorded by

DeShannon in 1963), "Love Potion No. 9" (originally recorded by the Clovers in 1959) b/w "High Heel Sneakers" (originally recorded by Tommy Tucker in 1963) and "What Have They Done to the Rain" (an anti-nuclear protest song written and originally recorded by Malvina Reynolds in 1962). Reynolds would also pen "Little Boxes" and "Morningtown Ride," all from 1964.

The group's full-length debut LP *Meet the Searchers*, released in August 1963, included "Farmer John" (written by Don "Sugarcane" Harris and Dewey Terry, who released it as Don and Terry in 1959), "Stand By Me" (Ben E. King in 1961), "Da Doo Ron Ron" (the Crystals in 1963), "Where Have All the Flowers Gone?" (written by Pete Seeger in 1955 with additional verses added by Joe Hickerson in 1960), as well as "Money (That's What I Want)" and "Twist and Shout."

Sugar and Spice was the title of the Searchers' second U.K. LP in 1963, featuring "Listen to Me" (Buddy Holly from 1958) and "All My Sorrows" (written by Glenn Yarbrough in 1957), showing a folk side that was slightly unusual for a first wave British Invasion band. *It's The Searchers* and *Sounds Like The Searchers* would be rush-released in 1964, both comprised primarily of second-hand songs, generally American R&B and soul covers.

In '65 the musical landscape would drastically change, with bands trying to compose more original material, and using fewer pre-written and recorded songs.

The Searchers would continue to record and perform with frequent lineup changes and minimal success.

The Remo Four, also from Liverpool, formed in 1958 as the Remo Quartet, changing their name in 1959 as they performed vocal harmony songs as well as instrumentals.

The Shadows (formerly the Drifters, not to be confused with the American band with the same name) were Cliff Richard's backup group throughout the 60s and beyond, and also performed as an entity of their own.

The Merseybeats were another of the Liverpool or

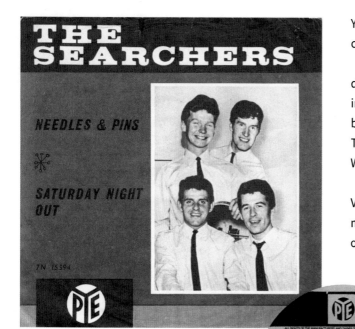

Merseyside "beat" groups which rose to brief, minimal acclaim as the Beatles climbed in fame. The Merseybeats performed alongside the Beatles at the Cavern Club, releasing "It's Love That Really Counts" b/w "The Fortune Teller" (the B-side written by Allen Toussaint under the pseudonym Naomi Neville and recorded by Benny Spellman in 1962) and "I Think of You" b/w "Mr. Moonlight" (also recorded prior to the Beatles version), both in 1963. The following year the Merseybeats would cover the Hal David and Burt Bacharach composition "Wishin' and Hopin'" which was hit for Dusty Springfield, backed with "Milkman."

After several more unsuccessful attempts they would disband, reforming simply as the Merseys in 1966.

The Big Three, formed in 1959 as Cass & the Casanovas in Liverpool, would be represented by Brian Epstein. In March 1963 they recorded "Some Other Guy," which would be a common song for several Merseyside bands to perform in their live acts. "By the Way" b/w "The Cavern Stomp" and "I'm With You" b/w "Peanut Butter" were both released in 1963, and "If You Ever Change Your Mind" b/w "You've Got to Keep Her Under

Your Hand" were released in 1964, none of which would chart. The group eventually disbanded in 1966.

Chad Stuart and Jeremy Clyde were an English vocal duo who hit with "Yesterday's Gone" b/w "Lemon Tree" in 1963, followed in 1964 by "Like I Love You Today" b/w "Early in the Morning," "A Summer Song" b/w "No Tears for Johnny," and "Willow Weep for Me" b/w "If She Were Mine."

The duo appeared on a 1965 episode of "The Dick Van Dyke Show" as the Redcoats (Fred and Ernie) that mirrored Beatlemania, and also were in an episode of "The Patty Duke Show" where they portrayed the fictitious Nigel & Patrick. The following year they played themselves on "Batman," as Catwoman (portrayed by Julie Newmar) attempted to steal their voices.

On their 1964 debut album *Yesterday's Gone*, Chad & Jeremy recorded "September in the Rain," possibly knowing that it was a song that the Beatles didn't write but would perform once and leave behind.

In 1965 the duo would cover "From a Window," recorded by Billy J. Kramer with the Dakotas the previous year. In 1966 they would have "Teenage Failure" b/w "Early Mornin' Rain" which was released to coincide with their *Distant Shores* album. That single release marked last time the band would chart.

Throughout the decade Chad & Jeremy continued to record and release singles and albums, staying with the times and developing (releasing two full-length psychedelic "concept albums"), although achieving only moderate results.

Peter and Gordon would have considerably more success with the help of the songs that were

written and given to them by Lennon and McCartney, which was a definite advantage. Similar bands would have success largely based on their association with the composition credit of Lennon/McCartney, including the Fourmost and Tommy Quickly.

Billy J. Kramer with the Dakotas would certainly benefit from their association with the Beatles, also achieving prominence on their own, as would Gerry and the Pacemakers. The Pacemakers would have a great deal of success, but always garnered a second-level band status, just "beneath" the Beatles. This designation came not from the Beatles themselves, but more from the press.

The leader of the Pacemakers was Gerry Marsden, forming the group with his brother Freddie Marsden, also the drummer. The band was formerly known as Gerry Marsden and the Mars Bars until the chocolate company threatened litigation. Gerry would eventually become the primary songwriter for the band, although they took a path similar to that of the Hollies and Beatles, beginning by covering songs that were primarily American rock and roll or country records. Like many British Invasion bands, they would not have the extended success. Just as the Beatles did, the Pacemakers revealed their broader view of music with covers such as "Maybelline" by Chuck Berry and "Jambalaya" by Hank Williams, as well as American theater standards such as "Summertime" from *Porgy and Bess* and "You'll Never Walk Alone" (also the title of the band's first LP), from *Carousel*.

The Pacemakers would also record "A Shot of Rhythm and Blues," "Where Have You Been All My Life," and "Slow Down" - all part

of the Beatles' repertoire - for their debut album, and likely "claimed" by many as their own as the Mersey Beat boom began to explode.

After Gerry and the Pacemakers' success with "How Do You Do It" in March 1963, they released two more records that would reach No. 1 with "I Like It" and "You'll Never Walk Alone."

In 1964 the Pacemakers would achieve further success with "I'm The One" in January, "Don't Let the Sun Catch You Crying" in April, "It's Gonna Be Alright in September, and "Ferry Cross the Mersey" in December, all written by Gerry Marsden and produced by George Martin. That combination would yield success, but not the same amount of recognition that the Beatles would achieve.

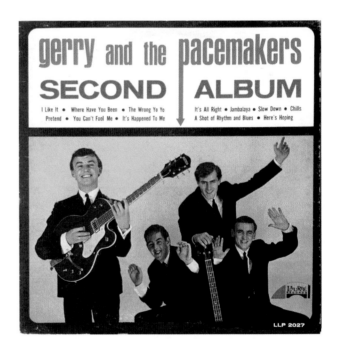

In early '65 the Pacemakers would release "I'll Be There," a version of a 1960 Bobby Darin song, but the band was never quite able to repeat their success of the prior two years. They disbanded in late '66.

A band that consciously tried to avoid being too much like the Beatles was Manfred Mann, a five-man band named after the keyboardist. They had released two

singles in 1963 ("Why Should We Not?" b/w "Brother Jack" and "Cock-a-Hoop" b/w "Now You're Needing Me") before striking with "Doo Wah Diddy," written by Jeff Barry and Ellie Greenwich, and originally done in 1963 by the Exciters, a vocal pop group with three females and one male. Manfred Mann's follow up, "Sha La La," was also a cover of a hit by a soul girl group, this time the Shirelles, whom the Beatles similarly had covered with "Baby It's You" and "Boys." While the band wrote a small percentage of their album output, they largely filled out their first record with covers (as the Beatles had done), primarily American blues and soul, again trying to avoid the appearance that they were "copying" the Beatles.

In 1965 Manfred Mann would score with a cover of a Bob Dylan composition titled "If You Gotta Go, Go Now." They repeated the recipe of covering a Dylan song with a "pop" feel with "Just Like a Woman" in 1966 (the same year as "Pretty Flamingo") and "The Mighty Quinn" in 1967, keeping a reputation as a viable rock act amidst the extremely competitive English music scene.

The Blue Jeans were a band that had similar start as the Beatles, beginning in 1957 as a jazz/skiffle act then becoming fans of rock and roll and adding a "Swinging" in front of their name. The Swinging Blue Jeans would strike in late '63 with their cover of "Hippy Hippy Shake," following with a cover of "Good Golly Miss Molly," first done by Little Richard, and "You're No Good," originally performed by Dee Dee Warwick and popularized by Betty Everett, both in 1963.

For their debut album in November 1964, *Blue Jeans a'Swinging*, they would cover a wide range of American soul and R&B music including Chuck Berry's "Around and Around," The Drifters' "Save the Last Dance for Me," Lloyd Price's "Lawdy Miss Clawdy," as well as "Tutti Frutti" and "Long Tall Sally" from Little Richard.

Both the Beatles and the Stones had released versions of songs on that appeared on *Blue Jeans a'Swingin'*. "It's All Over Now" was written by Bobby and Shirley Womack for the Valentinos in June 1964, with the Rolling Stones quickly recording their own version to score their first No. 1 in July.

The Swinging Blue Jeans could not sustain the success they had in '64, and they fell into the shadow of many of the more popular bands of the era, eventually retiring to the cabaret circuit in 1968 after several lineup changes.

The Escorts were a Liverpool-based band led by Terry Sylvester. They had a half dozen singles during their four years together, achieving minimal success. "Dizzie Miss Lizzy" was their debut release in April 1964, recorded a full year before the Beatles would also record and release the Larry Williams composition. The Escorts also covered the Drifters' "I Don't Wanna Go on with You," "Let It Be Me" as done by the Everly Brothers, and Smokey Robinson and the Miracle's "Head to Toe" before Sylvester left the band and went on replace Graham Nash in the Hollies.

The Hollies also originated as a skiffle act, this time a duo, formed by Allan Clarke and Graham Nash in 1962. They modeled their harmonies after the Everly Brothers, taking on the names Ricky and Dane Young, then joining forces with the Fourtones (not to be confused with the similarly names Fortunes) as well as members of the Deltas, and eventually morphed into the Hollies. Their name stemmed from their love for Buddy Holly (as was the case with most of the younger English bands from this era), as well as an affinity for Christmas, according to Nash.

The band's first two singles were covers of Coasters songs, "Ain't That Just Like Me," and "Searchin'," both from 1963. At the height of the "first wave" of the Invasion they would strike with "Just One Look," originally performed (and co-written) by Doris Troy in 1963, produced by Ron Richards who was Martin's direct assistant at Parlophone.

Stay with The Hollies was the band's debut LP, named from their cover of Maurice Williams and the Zodiacs' "Stay" and was mainly comprised of covers of American R&B records. The LP includes "I'm Talking 'bout You" and "Memphis," both Chuck Berry compositions, also songs that the Beatles performed but never recorded (possibly excluding themselves from doing songs that others would cover prior to them).

"Mr. Moonlight," however, would be recorded by the Beatles several months after the Hollies' version was released as the Beatles broke their self-imposed "rule" for the occasion.

Alongside several original compositions, the bulk of the album (released and repackaged in several forms with different titles) included the Hollies' takes on "Do You Love Me," by the Contours, "You Better Move On," an Arthur Alexander composition (which was also a hit for the Stones in January 1964), "Rockin' Robin," which was Bobby Day's one and only hit single, and "Lucille," which was considered by some a Little Richard song and by others an Everly Brothers song.

Conway Twitty's "It's Only Make Believe" was a country hit in America, a selection that displayed the Hollies' depth as performers beyond pop or simple

soul music.

The band's second full-length LP of 1964, *In The Hollies Style*, again produced by Ron Richards, would be made up of only a few covers and a large amount of originals written by Allan Clarke, Tony Hicks, and Graham Nash, and credited to L. Ransford. As the decade continued, this team would have great success as writers of original music, with Nash leaving in 1968 to form a singing trio with David Crosby and Stephen Stills.

The Animals were a Newcastle band led by Eric Burden. While they were gaining success and notoriety during the period when the Beatles were exploding, they were more inspired by American blues. They too were greatly moved by Dylan, covering his version of a traditional song "The House of the Rising Sun" from his eponymous 1962 debut LP *Bob Dylan*.

The Yardbirds were a band with loves similar to those of the Animals, both deeply influenced by American blues. They were among the first in what would be referred to as the English Blues Invasion or the second wave of British Invasion bands.

Formed in London in 1963, the Yardbirds would cross

paths with the Beatles as they were performing together, with George Harrison and Eric Clapton meeting and becoming close friends. Neither "I Wish You Would" b/w "A Certain Girl" or "Good Morning Little Schoolgirl" b/w "I Ain't Got You" in 1964 would chart, but they would earn the Yardbirds a reputation as the premier band in London threatening to knock the Beatles from their "biggest band" status. "For Your Love" was a Top 10 hit for the Yardbirds in early '65. It was a more pop-oriented song that wasn't "bluesy enough" for Clapton, who left the band as it wasn't headed in the direction that he wanted it to go.

The Dave Clark 5, originally the Dave Clark Quintet, was formed in 1957 by Clark, the band's drummer. After several unsuccessful releases they struck big with a cover of the Contours' 1962 hit "Do You Love Me?" followed by "Glad All Over" (written by Dave Clark and Mike Smith of the band, not to be confused with Carl Perkins' composition with the same title) both in 1963.

In 1964 The Dave Clark 5 would continue to have great success on both sides of the ocean with "Bits and Pieces," "Can't You See That She's Mine" and "Anyway You Want It." Their 1964 debut LP *A Session with The Dave Clark Five* featured a combination of originals and recordings by others ("Rumble" by Link Wray, "On Broadway" from the Drifters, and "Zip-a-Dee-Doo-Dah" from the 1946 live action and animated Disney film "Song of the South."

While the band remained one of the more successful acts of the Invasion, they would not adjust to the times of psychedelic rock, and by 1970 the DC5

would disband.

The Rockin' Berries were a Birmingham band who formed initially as the Berries, after their love for Chuck Berry (at one time boasting future Fleetwood Mac keyboardist Christine McVie, still Christine Perfect in 1963). They released "Wah Wah Woo" b/w "Rockin' Berries Stomp" and "Itty Bitty Pieces" b/w "The Twitch" in 1963, and "Didn't Mean to Hurt You" b/w "You'd Better Come Home" and "What in the World's Come Over You" b/w "You Don't Know What to Do" in 1964. "He's in Town" b/w "Flashback" was their biggest hit, reaching No. 3 in November 1964. The A-side was a Gerry Goffin/Carole King composition first recorded by the Tokens earlier in the year.

While the Rockin' Berries' vocal group quality seemed to prevent them from achieving wide success, the band still continued to perform well into the new millennium as a comedy and music review.

Adam Faith was an English pop singer who teamed up with the Roulettes in 1964 in hopes of competing with the Beat sound that was seemingly taking over. Faith was "assigned" to the Roulettes who together released "So Long Baby" b/w "The First Time" with declining results for each release.

The Roulettes released material of their own, the "Hully Gully Slip and Slide" b/w "La Bamba" and "Soon You'll Be Leaving Me" b/w "Tell Tale Heart" in 1963 for Parlophone, neither of which hit. In 1964 they had a minor hit with "Bad Time" b/w "You Can Go."

Herman's Hermits, a Manchester based band led by frontman Peter Noone, would debut in late 1964 with their cover of Earl Jean's (also with the Cookies) "I'm Into Something Good," written by Goffin and King. The song hit No. 1 in the U.K., again threatening to "take the Beatles out" as the top band. In subsequent years

(written by Chris Kenner and Allen Toussaint, originally recorded by Kenner in 1961) was the debut single for the Nashville Teens, originally formed as Surrey in 1962. As the decade wore on, the Nashville Teens would fail to have much further success.

Also part of the British Invasion in 1964 were the Mojos and the Bachelors.

It is interesting to note that English bands were trying to sound more American by using terminology from the States, while North American bands were trying to sound more British. This was the case with Chicago's Buckinghams and Paul Revere and the Raiders (formed in Iowa) wearing British costumes and taking advantage of the fact that Paul Revere was a band member as well as an American Revolution patriot and founding father.

As 1965 began, a substantial number of British Invasion acts would continue, including the Ivy League (not the be confused with the Iveys who formed in 1961 and later became Badfinger), the Hullaballoos, who covered Buddy Holly's "I'm Gonna Love You Too," and Sounds Incorporated, who did "In the Hall of the Mountain King," a modernized version of a Edvard Grieg classical composition.

the Hermits would have a string of successful singles on both sides of the Atlantic.

Lulu and the Luvvers would also hit with "Shout!" in 1964, followed by "I Can't Hear You No More," credited solely to Lulu, also written by Goffin and King. The tune was originally recorded as "I Can't Hear You" by Betty Everett, also in 1964. That would be followed by "Here Comes the Night" (also recorded by Them) and "I'll Come Running Over," both in 1964.

Also in 1964 the Moody Blues would strike a hit with their second release "Go Now" written by Jerry Leiber and Mike Stoller, first done by Bessie Banks in 1962.

This would launch a lengthy career for the band mostly associated with progressive rock as opposed to the British Invasion.

"Tobacco Road" b/w "I Like It Like That"

More releases: "The Game of Love" by Wayne Fontana and the Mindbenders, "Road Runner" (the Bo Diddley version) by the Pretty Things, and the Fortunes with "You've Got Your Troubles," also all in 1965. That same year the Mindbenders would hit again with "Groovy Kind of Love," first done by Diane and Annita earlier in '65.

Unit 4 + 2 would have "Concrete and Clay" in 1965, the Walker Brothers would have "Make it Easy on Yourself" while "Everyone's Gone to the Moon" was from Jonathan King. All were developing as artists and attempting to make a "new sound," only to be left behind by the Beatles, who were developing at a much faster pace.

Prior to the Beatles and their contemporaries taking over the U.K. charts, the American sound was the dominant force for English music. Many British releases were covers of songs originally recorded across the Atlantic.

With the presence of all this music from the "golden land" of the United States (the toppermost of the poppermost?), it's no wonder that the Beatles considered the place to shoot for to be America.

Examples of English bands recording influential American music in 1960 included Tommy Bruce and the Bruisers with "Ain't Misbehaving," Bert Weedon's cover of "Apache," and the John Barry Seven with "Walk Don't Run."

"Shakin' All Over" was done by Johnny Kidd and the Pirates, as the follow up to "Please Don't Touch" from '59. Both had an early "rock" sound with prominent lead guitars and big drums that would stand out above the rest for the young Beatles, as well as hundreds of other young English musicians.

The Pirates would also cover "You Got What it Takes," first done by Marv Johnson in 1959 and the aforementioned "A Shot of Rhythm and Blues" written by Terry Thompson, recorded by Arthur Alexander and

later performed by the Beatles themselves.

As the record companies had done in America, English acts would take American "race records" and re-record a sanitized version, as was done with Michael Cox and "Sweet Little 16" in 1961, the same year that Doug Sheldon quickly covered Kenny Dino's "Your Ma Said You Cried in Your Sleep Last Night."

In 1962 just as the Beatles were beginning to increase their popularity, the British musical landscape was similar to, but slightly behind, the American scene. Several English "family-friendly" white singers, both male and female, re-recorded American R&B in a much cleaner and passionless fashion.

Howie Casey and the Seniors re-did Little Richard's "True Fine Mama," first done in 1957 by Penniman as the B-side to "Ooh My Soul" and Carol Deene covered "Johnny Get Angry First" recorded by Joanie Sommers earlier in the year.

Jackie Lynton redid "All of Me," an American jazz standard first sung on the radio by Belle Baker and recorded by Ruth Etting, in 1931. Later Dean Shannon would redo the "Ubangi Stomp," a 1956 Warren Smith rockabilly song released on Sun Records.

Joe Brown and the Bruvvers would also have "A Picture of You," which was quickly picked up by the Beatles as part of their act.

As English children born during the war were coming of age, a very different style of music would quickly develop throughout the country, with London becoming the central location for music, art, and culture.

In the same fashion, America was ready for a new unifying type of nationwide pleasure and source of pride. The Beatles and their remarkable timing would be the proper component needed. ∎

CHAPTER II: PROFESSIONAL RECORDING ARTISTS

THE LARGE QUESTION THAT REMAINS IS: WAS THE EMI STAFF DISPLEASED WITH THE DRUMMING OF PETE BEST, WHO THEY WORKED WITH IN JUNE, OR WITH RINGO, WHOM THEY HAD JUST MET THE PREVIOUS WEEK?

ONE LIKELIHOOD IS THAT after seeing Best they knew they had to book a drummer and did it far in advance, not realizing there would be a membership change within the band, and since they had to pay White anyway they might as well use him.

The other possibility is that they weren't especially impressed with Ringo and booked White for the following week.

On September 11, 1962 a dejected Starr was demoted to shake maracas while John, Paul, George, and Andy recorded 10 takes of "P.S. I Love You" and Ringo shook the tambourine on 18 takes of "Love Me Do."

After briefly considering "P.S. I Love You" to be the A-side, the debut single was decided upon, and it was "Love Me Do," backed with "P.S. I Love You," both Lennon/McCartney originals. The band considered this to be a victory.

Ultimately the first pressing of the single, released on October 5, 1962, featured the version recorded September 4 with Ringo on the drums. Subsequent pressings featured the White version from the September 11 session.

Also on this day the band attempted to record a slightly reworked "Please Please Me" with White on drums (and Ringo observing from the control room), which sounded more like the version that would become the single. However, time ran out before the song was completed to everyone's satisfaction.

When the band would return to EMI in late November, it was Ringo who was back behind the drum kit, where he remained (with slight exceptions) for the remainder of the band's recording years.

On September 12, after their return home to Liverpool, the band performed at the Cavern, even acting as the backing band for 16-year-old Manchester singer Simone Jackson. Also on the bill that evening were Freddie and the Dreamers, also from Manchester, who were impressed by the Beatles after hearing them perform their rendition of James Ray's "If You Gotta Make a Fool of Somebody" which they quickly adopted as part of their own act, releasing it as their debut single later in the year.

The Beatles were a bit insulted and miffed at the Dreamers for "nicking" their arrangement of the song without giving them credit, but were quick to forgive them as the Dreamers appeared on their 1964 Christmas show.

On October 1, the band signed another contract with Epstein, negating the previous one which included Pete Best. The first contract from January 1962 was unsigned by Epstein, which would allow the band to "walk away" if he failed to deliver on his promise of securing a record contract.

At long last on October 5, the band's first official single was released. "Love Me Do" b/w "P.S. I Love You" peaked at No. 17, which is a very strong ranking for a debut release.

There are persistent rumors, quite likely true, that one of the main reasons the single charted so well, particularly in the Liverpool area, was that Epstein ordered an overabundance of the record (possibly more than 10,000 copies) for his NEMS record store. This of course would greatly inflate its ranking.

On October 6 the band held two separate autograph signings, the first at Dawson's Music Shop, the second at The Music Shop, both in Widnes. Later that evening they performed at Hulme Hall

Recorded by FREDDIE and THE DREAMERS on Tower Records

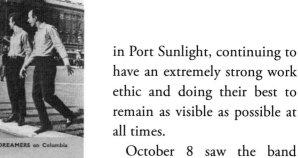

Recorded by FREDDIE and THE DREAMERS on Columbia

B. FELDMAN & Co. Ltd.   64 Dean Street, London, W.1

in Port Sunlight, continuing to have an extremely strong work ethic and doing their best to remain as visible as possible at all times.

October 8 saw the band recording their first interview for "The Friday Spectacular" which was recorded at EMI headquarters known simply as EMI House in London.

The band promoted their new single as they were interviewed in front of an audience of about 100 spectators. They didn't perform although invited to, instead choosing to play the studio versions of both sides of the 45.

Their first appearance on "The Friday Spectacular" was aired October 12 on Radio Luxemburg, later that same day the band had the opportunity to perform on the same bill as one of their biggest influences.

Little Richard and the Beatles crossed paths in Hamburg and would again on this night, which was a bill that also included Lee Curtis and the All-Stars, Pete Best's new band. Apparently there were some awkward moments between the All-Stars and the Beatles.

Shortly after that, on October 17 they made their television debut on Grenada TV, appearing on the local Manchester show "People and Places." They performed "Some Other Guy" and "Love Me Do."

On October 25 the Beatles were on "Teenager's Turn/Here We Go" for the third time, the first for Ringo Starr. This time they performed their new single, as well as "P.S. I Love You," "A Taste of Honey," which would be recorded for the debut album, and "Sheila" which was edited out of the broadcast and was also never recorded officially by the band.

As the band continued to garner more and more attention they recorded their first-ever radio interview on October 27. Monty Lister was presenter on Radio Clatterbridge, a community hospital radio station based in Wirral, a peninsula in northwest England.

Lister's interview with the band played on two shows, "Music With Monty" and "Sunday Spin." The four Beatles discussed their new drummer, their debut single, their debut television performance, a bit about their history, and their upcoming visit to Hamburg. All of the members of the band were remarkably calm as they politely answered the questions that were asked of them, presenting themselves as

Little Richard and the four Beatles

courteous and polite young men, who also had very sharp senses of humor.

After the interview they performed at Hulme Hall in Port Sunlight, their fourth appearance there in 1962, once again performing ahead of Little Richard.

They then appeared once again on Grenada TV's "People and Places," which was recorded on October 29 before their departure for Hamburg the following day, and later broadcast on November 2. For this appearance the Beatles performed "Love Me Do" and "A Taste of Honey."

The band flew to Hamburg ahead of their two week residency at the Star Club, their first German performances with Ringo as a Beatle. During these shows, which would last about three and half hours each night, the four Beatles got the opportunity to really relax and fine-tune their arrangements with their new drummer.

Starr was a better time keeper than his predecessor and considerably more imaginative, adding an extra element to the chemistry of the band and raising all of the players in the union, as opposed to holding them back.

With confidence and camaraderie, this is where the band really bonded and became close to Ringo, who had been a good friend but now was part of their

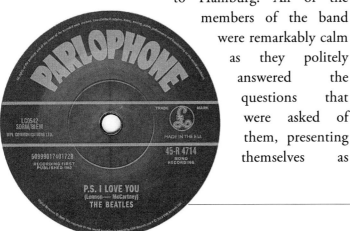

gang. He instantly proved that he could "keep up" with the other members, not just musically but with his wit, and they quickly included him as an equal.

During this second Star Club residency the Beatles also occasionally had the privilege to share a bill with Little Richard, whom they were also getting to know much better, learning a bit about both the music business and performance from a seasoned veteran.

Paul referred to this second visit as being uneventful, and mentioned that the band considered Hamburg, or at least the music scene there, "dead."

Upon their return to England the band again appeared on Radio Luxemburg's "Friday Spectacular," pushing their single and being interviewed at EMI house in Manchester.

On November 17 they played what Paul referred to as "the worst show ever" at the Matrix Hall in Coventry, where the Beatles headlined a show for about 80 people.

They also failed an audition for BBC television, although they would appear the following year.

In spite of these minor setbacks the band continued to play shows around England, and they looked forward to returning to the studio for their next recording session, hoping for more success than they had with their first release.

On November 26 the Beatles returned to EMI to record the follow-up single to "Love Me Do," with Ringo behind the drums yet again.

"Please Please Me" had been reworked to Martin's suggestions and it was taped in 18 takes, with John's harmonica being overdubbed after the initial recordings. After the song was just about finished Martin declared that they had just recorded their first No. 1, which of course was true depending upon which single chart was considered official.

In *Melody Maker*, *New Musical Express* and *Disc* the single reached No. 1 after being released in January of the following year. On the *Record Retailer* chart, which was the one used by *New Record Mirror*,

it only reached as high as No. 2.

After recording the A-side of the next single the band moved on to "Ask Me Why," which they performed for their first session in June as well, this would ultimately become the B-side. They completed the song in six takes then also attempted yet another original composition, Paul's "Tip of My Tongue," which would eventually be given to Tommy Quickly record, also the following year.

On December 2 the Beatles performed at the Embassy Cinema in Peterborough on a bill with Frank Ifield, who had a current hit with "I Remember You," which the band would perform in their own act later in the month.

Around this time they also began appearing on television and radio more frequently. In London they were on "The Talent Spot," which was broadcast on the BBC "Light Programme," "Discs a Gogo" on ITV television as well and "Tuesday Rendezvous" on the London ITV station Associated-Rediffusion. They also were also on "People and Places" for a third time in December, performing "Love Me Do" and "Twist and Shout."

Beatlemania was beginning to spread.

George Martin attended an appearance at the Cavern Club with his assistant and future wife Judy Lockhart-Smith on December 9. Martin had heard of the band's exciting live show and considered recording a performance at the Cavern, an idea that was scrapped as he feared for the safety of the EMI recording equipment in the hot, humid, and sweaty basement club.

On December 15 they played at the Majestic Ballroom in Birkenhead, after that they performed at *The Mersey Beat* poll awards show, where they won the popularity poll for the second consecutive year. The Beatles took the stage at about 4 a.m., following Lee Curtis and the All-Stars, which was Pete Best's new band.

Before the year was finished they would travel to Hamburg for one final residency at the Star Club. Between the December 18-31 the band would perform for 13 nights, taking a day off on Christmas.

They felt that they had surpassed the questionable German district in terms of notoriety, landing several television and radio appearances. They were reluctant to leave England to fulfill this previously agreed upon engagement, but knew that professionalism was important to success, and that news of a negative status could spread quickly.

While there they stayed at the Hotel Pacific, which was a well-known center for traveling bands. ◆

BEATLES' BIGGEST INFLUENCES

WHEN JOHN, PAUL, GEORGE, AND RINGO MET AND STARTED TALKING ABOUT WHAT MUSIC THEY LOVED AND WHAT MOVED AND AFFECTED THEM, THEY FOUND A FAIR AMOUNT OF SIMILARITIES AND COMMON INTERESTS.

As each individual Beatle began to discover their own love of music, they all had favorite bands, artists, and musicians who attracted their attention. An impressive list of these influences would play a special part in the overall sound of the Beatles as they developed as a band.

CHUCK BERRY

Innovative and iconic rock and roll guitarist Chuck Berry was born Charles Edward Anderson Berry on October 18, 1926 in St. Louis to a middle class and well-educated family. Berry's father was a deacon at a Baptist church where the young and clever "Chuck" sang in the choir, his mother was an educator who greatly encouraged his interest in music.

Berry gave his first public performance in 1941, when he played in a student music showcase. However, he turned to a life of crime soon afterward and spent three years in an intermediate reformatory where he formed a singing group with several of the other musically-inclined inmates.

Upon release on his 21st birthday, Berry spent a few years working at a his father's construction business, then as a janitor at a local auto plant and later as a part-time photographer.

In 1951 Berry joined a band with a former high school classmate, and Chuck quickly earned a reputation as an energetic and exciting showman.

After spending a year playing at local black nightclubs Berry met pianist Johnnie Johnson and joined his band, originally known as Sir John's Trio. He quickly took over as the front man. Not only did Berry perform jazz and contemporary standards with the band, he added a raw energy with his version of blues and country music. The new and seemingly unusual style of music attracted a wide following and appealed to both white and black audiences, which was uncommon for the 1950s.

In 1955 Berry would meet blues guitarist Muddy Waters who would refer him to Leonard and Phil Chess, founders of Chess records in Chicago. The Chess brothers would quickly help launch Berry's career with his first single "Maybelline," a unique combination of blues, R&B, folk, and country.

"Maybelline" (backed with "Wee Wee Hours") was the first in a series of hits for Berry which also included "Thirty Days," "No Money Down," "Roll Over Beethoven," "Brown Eyed Handsome Man," "Too Much Monkey Business," "You Can't Catch Me," "School Days," "Rock and Roll Music," "Sweet Little Sixteen," "Johnny B. Goode," "Beautiful Delilah," "Carol," "Almost Grown," "Little Queenie," "Back in the U.S.A," "Memphis, Tennessee," "Let it Rock," "Bye Bye Johnny," "I Got to Find My Baby," and "Jaguar and Thunderbird."

The Beatles especially enjoyed the consistently high quality of Berry's output, not just the A-sides but also the flip-sides and other tracks from full-length albums as well.

After a string of successes coupled with television and movie appearances, Berry was arrested in December 1959 for violating the Mann Act by transporting an underage girl across state lines. After a lengthy trial and an appeal Berry served a year and a half in prison, spending his time learning more about the financial side of the music business.

After his 1963 release from prison Berry continued to write, perform, and record, scoring lesser hits with "Nadine," "No Particular Place to Go," "You Never Can Tell," and "Promised Land."

While continuing to tour and record, Berry had very little chart success and became one of the earliest "oldies acts" (along with Carl Perkins). On this "oldies" circuit Berry earned a reputation as a difficult performer, insisting on a non-negotiable contract, showing up consistently at the exact moment of show time, demanding to be paid in cash in advance, and expecting a backing band that "knew what they were doing" (as to insinuate that if you don't know how to play Chuck Berry music, you do not know what you are doing).

After switching record labels Berry returned to Chess in 1970, scoring his first and only No. 1 hit with "My Ding-a-Ling," a novelty cover of a tune written and recorded by Dave Bartholomew in 1952.

Throughout the decade Berry continued to tour, playing erratically and out of tune on many occasions. A couple of the "pick up" bands he performed with included the Steve Miller Band and Bruce Springsteen. In June 1979 Berry was invited by President Jimmy Carter to perform at the White House, also that year he released his last album of all new material on the album *Rock-It*.

Likely due to the fact that he was frequently paid in cash, the IRS audited Berry and discovered he had evaded paying taxes. He pled guilty, serving four months in jail and performing benefit shows as community service.

In the 1980s Berry purchased a restaurant in Missouri. The investment ultimately cost him more than $1 million in legal fees and fines after a camera was discovered in a ladies restroom where he had set it up to

"catch a thief."

After touring the world in 2008, Berry continued to play sporadically around the country and monthly at Blueberry Hill, a restaurant near St. Louis, until 2014. He died March 18, 2017 at his Wentzville, Missouri home.

Although Berry's mainstream fame had diminished, his impact was shown almost immediately with virtually hundreds of bands around the world citing him as a great influence and a favorite. He is widely considered to be among the first rock and roll acts in the world, and a pioneer.

Berry's colorful guitar playing combined with his articulate lyrics all about girls, cars, and the American lifestyle both inspired the Beatles and propelled them to write and perform originals of their own. The band performed 11 of his compositions early in their career, and four more during the *Let It Be* sessions.

They recorded only two Berry originals for official release. "Thirty Days, Vacation Time," "Almost Grown," and "Maybelline" were recorded during the *Let It Be* and *Get Back* sessions of January '69, although the performances were sloppy and uninspired.

It's interesting to note that even late in the stages of the Beatles as being a fully-working band, when they wanted to "get back" to basics, Chuck Berry was one of the ways they went.

In 1969 John would use the phrase "Here come old flat top" for "Come Together" and would be sued by Berry. Lennon would also record several of Berry's songs for his *Rock and Roll* album, released in 1975.

Berry's rock and roll poetry encouraged the band to write and perform their own stuff and many elements of his music can be heard in much of the bands work both with the Beatles, as well as solo artists. His contribution to the Beatles, as well as music in general, is insurmountable. Many artists are lauded as the creators of rock and roll, and although few can reasonably accept such accolades, Berry and his body of work is high upon the list.

CHUCK BERRY SONG BY SONG
"ROCK AND ROLL MUSIC"

All four Beatles were enamored with Berry, but Lennon was the most vocal about it, even from the very early days. In later years Berry and Lennon would meet both on stage and in court.

Berry wrote "Rock and Roll Music" in April 1957, just as the term "rock and roll" was beginning to be shunned by the older generation. His message of "it's gotta be rock and roll music" appealed greatly to the young Quarrymen, who began performing it in September 1959. The lyrics mention the song "All Shook Up," and the young Beatles found it to especially clever to mention one song within another.

The Beatles continued to perform the song frequently throughout their touring days with John singing lead. It was performed for the BBC only once in December 1964 on "Saturday Club," shortly after its release on the *Beatles for Sale* album.

Starting in June of 1966 it became their live show opener, remaining in that position until the end of their touring days, including their final show at San Francisco's Candlestick Park in 1966.

"SWEET LITTLE 16"

"Sweet Little 16" was never officially recorded by the Beatles, but it was part of their live act for quite a while. Berry recorded the song in late December 1957, releasing it the following month again on the Chess label.

As soon as the band heard the song they learned it and it became a sporadic part of their act. They performed it infrequently during the days of the Quarrymen, and of course the Beatles. As with most of the Berry songs the band performed, John took lead.

Similar to many of Berry's other songs, the band enjoyed the fact that "Sweet Little 16" includes specific places in the United States. This again is a songwriting tool that they would use in the future.

The song was performed and recorded by the Beatles on New Year's Eve 1962 in Germany, as well as for "Pop Go the Beatles" in June 1963 for the BBC.

"JOHNNY B. GOODE"

Berry wrote the song in 1955 although it wasn't recorded until January 1958, then released the following March. The song is semi-autobiographical; however the name Johnny comes from piano player and member of Berry's band Johnnie Johnson who is not the actual pianist on the Berry version.

John and Paul were massively impressed by the Berry records that they got from the States. Paul recalls listening to them in John's bedroom at aunt Mimi's house. George enjoyed Berry's music as well, but was more focused on his guitar technique. They noted the consistent use of proper nouns as well as the story progression (from poor country boy to star) and of course John enjoyed the "Johnny" aspect of the song.

Berry would ultimately write about 30 songs about Johnny including "Bye Bye Johnny," "Go Go Go," "Johnny B. Blues," and "Concerto in B. Goode."

"MEMPHIS, TENNESSEE"

Released in June 1959, "Memphis, Tennessee" was Berry's B-side to "Back in the U.S.A.," again on the Chess label. It is a song about a man on the phone with an operator trying to track down Marie, who has been trying to get in touch with him but couldn't leave a number.

The operator is not of much help and the singer tells her about the fun that Marie had before her mother pulled them apart. In the final verse it is revealed that Marie is only 6 years old, so is therefore presumably his daughter, or at least the daughter of a love interest, a very unique narrative, complete with a reveal in the final verse of the song.

The Beatles certainly took notice of these traits in the song (a pay off or punchline) and were very aware of the story telling and uniqueness of a song about a man's child.

It's very likely that the first version of the song they heard was by Dave Berry and the Cruisers, which was also released in June 1959. The Beatles quickly sought out and found the original, adding it to their repertoire shortly after.

In 1962 on New Year's Day (with Pete Best on drums) they attempted it for the ill-fated Decca Records audition. Decca, interestingly enough, was the label that released the Dave Berry (no relation) version.

The band also performed it for the BBC in March 1962 (still with Best on drums) and four other occasions with Ringo. In October 1963 for "Saturday Club" they performed the song for the last time, moving on to focus on more of their original compositions.

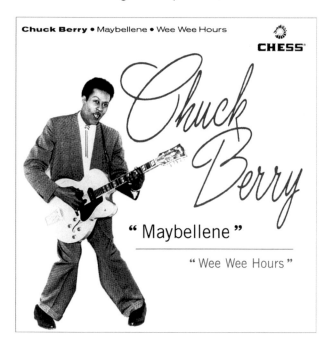

"TOO MUCH MONKEY BUSINESS"

In September 1956 Berry composed and recorded "Too Much Monkey Business," with "Brown-eyed Handsome Man" as its B-side. Following his formula Berry delivers clever lines about being young and working hard and dealing with salesmen and women and fighting in the war of Yokahama and going to school and working at the

gas station with all its many ungrateful tasks, all of which is what he calls monkey business. He even uses the word "botheration." All of this, along with his rapid delivery appealed greatly to the Beatles.

While singing the song he is also sort of speaking the verses, this also helped influence Bob Dylan to write his "Subterranean Homesick Blues."

Starting in about 1960 the Beatle played it frequently, keeping it around for several BBC performances, four in all throughout 1963.

"I GOT TO FIND MY BABY"

When the Beatles were looking for songs to cover they would search endlessly for hidden treasures. Berry's 1960 release "I Got to Find my Baby" couldn't be a more perfect fit for the eager young band. In August 1960 the single came out in the U.S., but not in the U.K. A copy of the record made its way to the hands of the Beatles, they learned the song and likely included it in their live act between 1960-63. It's also likely the song was played infrequently in '62 if at all, only being revived for the BBC in '63.

The song was originally composed by blues man Peter Clayton in 1941 on Bluebird Records, and re-recorded for the Chess label in May 1954 by Little Walter.

Berry reworked it a bit and did his own version, which was the one that the young Beatles would learn. They performed it for the BBC on two occasions, both in June 1963.

"ROLL OVER BEETHOVEN"

Originally recorded by Berry in 1956, the song was eventually performed live, recorded, and officially released by the Beatles. As with most of their Berry covers, John handled lead vocals until 1961 when George took over that role. George is the vocalist on the version included on their second U.K. release *With The Beatles* in November 1963 (released in the U.S. on Capitol as *The Beatles' Second Album* in April 1964).

On July 30, 1963 during the quick and efficient session for the album, the band was ready to commit the song to tape. They did "Roll Over Beethoven" in five takes with a slight edit at the end, and then quickly moved on. They had performed the song so many times in the years leading to this recording that the session was nearly seamless. In August they edited in the final guitar chord.

The Beatles continued to perform the song, including multiple times for the BBC, until late 1964 when it was replaced by "Everybody's Trying to Be My Baby" as the George song in the live act.

While the song kicks off side two of the U.K. release, in America the Capitol Records version of the album had it as the first track on side one.

"I'M TALKING ABOUT YOU"

Phrases like "walking down an uptown street" (using both directions in close proximity) and internal rhyming like "mine" and "fine" were highly inspirational to Bob Dylan, the Beatles, and virtually every band to discover Chuck Berry and rock and roll.

Berry released the song in February 1961 with "Little Star" as its B-side, and once again, the young Beatles quickly learned the song and began performing it.

It was recorded at the New Year's Eve '62 show in Germany, and they performed in for the BBC on March 16, 1963. As was the case with many covers, this one fell off their set list for more original songs and other covers, but the Berry influence on the Beatles is shown throughout every phase of their career.

EDDIE COCHRAN

Born in 1938, Eddie Cochran was a native of Minnesota, although he would frequently boast of southern roots since his parents were from Oklahoma. As a youth Cochran learned to play piano and drums as well as guitar, his primary instrument.

The Beatles were very impressed with the American rockabilly musician, who possessed a country sound that also had the energy of early rock and roll.

Cochran relocated to California with his family in 1952. He dropped out of high school during his first year to work as a professional musician, becoming a session guitarist and performing in a duo with country singer Hank Cochran. Eddie and Hank called themselves the Cochran Brothers; although they shared a bill and last name they were not related.

Eddie released a string of hits beginning in 1955, most were original compositions including "Twenty Flight Rock." It was co-credited to Ned Fairchild, pen name of Nelda Fairchild, who came up with the initial form of the song.

"Twenty Flight Rock" has a narrative about the singer not being able to make it all the way up 20 flights of stairs to be able to "rock" with his girl, a unique type of song, one that intrigued the young Beatles.

Cochran created a rebellious pre-punk anti-establishment teenage image, as would be reflected in "C'mon Everybody," about having a party when the parents are away, "My Way," which was about telling the parents who the boss is, and "Summertime Blues" about the struggle with trying to enjoy the summertime while oppressive adults try to ruin the fun.

In 1959 Cochran's contemporaries Buddy Holly, Ritchie Valens, and J.P. Richardson (professionally known as the Big Bopper) died in a plane crash. This led to Eddie attempting to get away from touring to focus on his work in the studio as a session player, performer/composer, and as a producer for other artists.

Several days after the plane crash Eddie would record a song called "Three Stars" about his fallen friends, which eerily would remain unreleased until after his own death.

Sadly Cochran would suffer a similar fate in 1960 as he himself was killed at a young age in an automobile accident. As Cochran was an extremely creative and prolific songwriter, several of his songs were left behind to be released after his death.

The early Beatles were greatly influenced by Cochran, however they never recorded any of his material. One song was captured on tape in 1960, and it is likely that they performed several of his songs throughout their formative years.

LITTLE RICHARD

Another important influence on the band, particularly McCartney, was Little Richard.

On the first day that John and Paul met, Paul "auditioned" by performing an Eddie Cochran song ("Twenty Flight Rock"), a Gene Vincent song ("Be Bop a Lula"), and few songs of Little Richard's which immediately impressed the skeptical young John Lennon.

Born in Macon, Georgia in 1932, Richard Wayne Penniman was an innovator of modern rock and roll, gaining notoriety with his flamboyant and exciting delivery in the mid-1950s.

He grew up heavily involved with his church, singing and learning to play piano in the presence of his grandfather and two of his uncles who were preachers. He was called "Lil Richard" by many due to his small frame and delicate features.

His father was very stern and was especially harsh on young Richard when he began to show signs of homosexuality in his pre-teens. One of 12 children, Penniman was kicked out of his home at the age of 13,

moving into the home of a white couple who owned a club in Macon.

This is where he would develop his talents and become "Little Richard," the self-proclaimed creator, innovator, emancipator, and creator of rock and roll.

By 1955 he had hooked up with Specialty Records based in Los Angeles and had a string of hits including "Tutti Frutti," "Slippin' and Slidin'," "Rip it Up," "Ready Teddy," "The Girl Can't Help It," "Keep a Knockin'," "Good Golly Miss Molly," "Kansas City," and "Hey Hey Hey Hey."

In mid-1957 when Paul joined the Quarrymen, they immediately started performing Little Richard songs in their act. Paul has said that in the very early days of the Beatles they considered themselves to be Buddy Holly and Little Richard, with John emulating the glasses-wearing Buddy and while Paul was screaming like Richard.

By the end of the '50s Little Richard's success started to diminish and he quit the rock and roll business to form his own church. After performing strictly gospel for a while he returned to the music business in 1962 and had a large amount of success touring in Europe, where his records were still selling very well.

In '62 the Beatles and one of their greatest heroes crossed paths as they opened several shows for Little Richard, who at the time boasted Billy Preston as part of his background band. While together in Germany, Paul was able to learn at the foot of the master and received some advice on perfecting his patented scream.

Little Richard was very impressed by the young, soulful Beatles, saying "If I hadn't seen them with my own eyes I'd have thought they were a colored group from back home."

As the band began to write and record strictly original material, they would frequently write songs that they were trying to attempt to emulate. A prime example of song like this is "I'm Down," recorded in June 1965, which accurately and warmly conveys the excitement of a Little Richard record.

The time that the band shared with little Richard was life changing for them, specifically Paul, who referred to him an idol. The Beatles never did outgrow Little Richard's influence. Instead, they took some elements of his style and made them their own by adding their own unique touch.

Throughout the 60's Little Richard focused primarily on his live shows as opposed to further recordings. In 1969 he performed to wide critical acclaim at the Atlantic City Pop Festival, where he outshined performers like the Byrds, Canned Heat, Joe Cocker, Creedence Clearwater Revival, and Janis Joplin.

Also in '69 at the Toronto Rock and Roll Revival Little Richard along with some of his fellow rock and roll pioneers Chuck Berry, Bo Diddley, Gene Vincent, and Jerry Lee Lewis were perhaps even better received than Lennon as well as the Doors and Alice Cooper, who received positive reviews themselves.

Throughout the '70s Little Richard continued to tour worldwide, and developed a drug and alcohol habit (famously saying "they should have called me Little Cocaine"). He eventually gave up drugs and alcohol in 1977.

After suffering some health issues, Little Richard occasionally performs, although rarely. He still frequently boasts loudly of being the originator, emancipator, creator, and architect of rock and roll, and there are few who ever disagree with him.

LITTLE RICHARD SONG BY SONG

Songs originally done by Little Richard were a frequent staple during the band's live performance days. Many of these performances were widely reported yet loosely documented, and very few are actually recorded or available. The list of Little Richard songs which the Beatles performed, recorded, and/or simply enjoyed includes both rock and roll mainstays and lesser-known tunes.

"LUCILLE"

"Lucille" was performed for the BBC in 1963 and was also part of the band's set list as early as 1957. Not only were they familiar with "Lucille" as a Little Richard 45, but they also knew it as an Everly Brothers song from their 1960 album A Date with the Everly Brothers, which was a strong selling point for the band. Written by Little Richard, along with Albert Collins (not the blues guitarist of the same name) in 1956, the song was released on the

Specialty label in February 1957.

There is some confusion about who wrote the bulk of the song, as the initial pressing did not bear Penniman's name. However while Collins was in prison Little Richard purchased half the songs rights, even though he claims to have written the lyrics by simply singing about a common name.

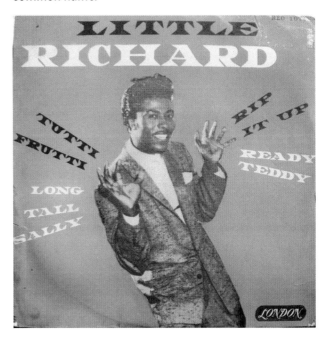

"Lucille" is loosely based on another Little Richard song (recorded with Johnny Otis' band) called "Directly From My Heart to You," which was recorded as a ballad in 1956 as the B-side to "Little Richard's Boogie," released on the Peacock label.

The song was given a new set of lyrics and the tempo was drastically sped up, imitating the rhythm of the trains that would pass by Richard's home as a young child.

"Lucille" reached No. 1 on the Billboard R&B charts, and its electrifying delivery became a rock and roll standard almost immediately.

The song was said to be part of the Beatles' act from late 1957 until 1962, with a revival September 1963 when they performed it twice for the BBC on "Pop Go the Beatles" and "Saturday Club."

As is the case on many of the Little Richard songs the Beatles performed, Paul sang lead on this driving rocker that the band enjoyed so much. McCartney would record his own solo version of the song in 1988 released on the *Choba B CCCP* album, which was a selection of Paul's rock and roll favorites from the '50s.

"SEND ME SOME LOVIN'"

"Send Me Some Lovin'" was written in '50s by John Marascalco and recorded in February 1957 by Little Richard. It was performed as early as 1959 by the Quarrymen although there are no known recordings.

While the band knew of the Little Richard version of the song, and very likely they knew it was also a Buddy Holly number released in November 1957.

In 1975 Lennon would release *Rock and Roll*, an album comprised of covers of his favorite rock and roll standards from the '50s. It included several covers of Little Richard songs, one of which was "Send Me Some Lovin'."

Without the benefit of a recording, it's difficult to know for sure which Beatle sang lead on the song when it was performed. Lennon may have just recalled doing the song during the 1974 recordings and took lead since it was his song now, or it may have always been his and is a rare Lennon vocal on a Beatles' cover of a Little Richard tune.

"RIP IT UP"

"Rip it Up" was performed as early as 1959 and very likely sung by Paul, again there is no evidence of who sang lead at this point. The song quickly fell off the setlist (1961) but the band briefly revived it in January 1969 during the *Get Back/Let it Be* sessions.

During this recording which was ultimately unreleased, the four Beatles along with Billy Preston clumsily move through a medley of rock hits (a concept that would be utilized by all four Beatles as solo acts) including "Rip it Up" with John and Paul rather inharmoniously sharing lead vocal duties.

The song was also revisited for Lennon's 1975 *Rock and Roll* album.

Originally the song was written by frequent co-collaborators John Marascalco and producer Robert "Bumps" Blackwell and recorded by Little Richard in

June 1956. Later in the year Bill Haley and the Comets recorded a version as well, the Beatles likely knew of both versions when they were learning it.

"READY TEDDY"

"Ready Teddy" was also part of the band's act between 1959 and 1961, and also written by Marascalco and Blackwell, originally released on the Specialty label in 1956. There was also a popular version of the song by Elvis Presley in '56, as well as Buddy Holly in '58.

The song was briefly performed during the January 1969 recording sessions which ultimately yielded the *Let It Be* album, again with John and Paul sharing a lyric to minimal success. It's uncertain who they were trying to be when they performed the song, which fell off of their set list rather early.

"MISS ANN"

Also a part of their set list for 1960 and 1961 was "Miss Ann." Like several of the other songs that the Beatles covered by Little Richard, were revived during the *Get Back/Let It Be* sessions when the band was trying to revisit their roots in an attempt to harmonize the group. Originally the song was released in 1957 as the B-side to "Jenny Jenny."

This is an excellent example of the Beatles selecting songs which they enjoyed but weren't necessarily certain the audience would recognize. The band let the crowd presume it was one of their own.

From the time John started a band until the time the Beatles stopped touring there were always Little Richard songs around. "Tutti Frutti" was written by Penniman along with Dorothy LaBostrie, who claims to have written it completely by herself, although it was credited to both of them.

The song was Little Richard's breakthrough hit in 1955 and is considered by many to be one of the first rock and roll songs to be created. It was almost immediately covered by white American singer Pat Boone, who brought attention to Little Richard even though his version surpassed the original in chart success.

"LONG TALL SALLY"

The first song Paul ever performed in public was "Long Tall Sally." Officially recorded by the band in 1964, it was the song that the band performed the longest, playing it during their final concert in August 1966.

"TUTTI FRUTTI"

An iconic song identified with Little Richard, "Tutti Frutti" was played by the Quarrymen between 1960-62 until it fell out of the band's set list.

"KANSAS CITY/HEY HEY HEY HEY"

Little Richard combined two of his songs into a medley, "Kansas City/Hey Hey Hey Hey," which the band performed live in 1960 and '61, and then revived for the *Beatles For Sale* album in 1964.

"GOOD GOLLY MISS MOLLY"

"Good Golly Miss Molly" was written for Little Richard by Marascalco and Blackwell in 1956 and released in early '58. It was also recorded by a group named the Valiants, who released the song before Richard, but recorded it after. The young Beatles quickly learned the song which was a known crowd pleaser, and it is likely Paul again

was the lead singer. This song, too, was retired quickly, likely by 1962.

"CAN'T BELIEVE YOU WANNA LEAVE"

Another example of a rare and relatively unknown song by Little Richard that the Beatles performed in their act is "Can't Believe You Wanna Leave." The song appeared on the full-length Here's Little Richard album from 1957 which the band may have heard because they lived in a port town which frequently brought them access to American albums. They performed "Can't Believe You Wanna Leave" between '60 and '62, again the singer is unknown.

"OOH! MY SOUL"

"Ooh! My Soul" was released in May 1958 to minimal success but once again the band quickly learned it for the act reportedly as soon as 1960 with Paul singing lead. A version of the song was performed for the BBC on August 1, 1963 with McCartney recording one of his finest vocal scream deliveries.

GENE VINCENT

Another early inspiration for the young Beatles was Gene Vincent, particularly during the period when they were first getting to know one another and finding their common musical loves, attempting several of his songs in the very early days of the band.

Born Vincent Eugene Craddock in 1935, the Norfolk, Virginia native received his first guitar when he was 12 and developed an interest in country, gospel, as well as classical music at an early age.

After changing his name to Gene Vincent, he formed a band called the Blue Caps, named after a term used to describe sailors in the Navy, where he had served after enlisting at age 17. Although he never saw combat, while in the Navy he shattered his leg in a motorcycle accident, an injury which left him with a limp and in pain for the

rest of his life.

Vincent had a string of singles throughout the '50s including "Race with the Devil," "Blue Jean Bop," "Crazy Legs," "Rocky Road Blues," "Git It," "Say Mama," "Over the Rainbow" and "Summertime." His biggest hit was "Be-Bop-a-Lula," actually the B-side of his first single, "Woman Love."

He also released several full-length albums which displayed depth and diversity, with old standards as well as American country tracks being done in a more updated "rock" fashion while still retaining their original charm. This list includes "Ain't She Sweet," "Up a Lazy River," "Wedding Bells are Breaking Up This Old Gang of Mine," "Unchained Melody," "By the Light of the Silvery Moon," "In My Dreams," "You Belong to Me," "Your Cheatin' Heart," "The Wayward Wind," "I Can't Help It (If I'm Still in Love With You)," "Greenback Dollar," "Accentuate the Positive," and "Blue Eyes Crying in the Rain."

As young musicians the Beatles were impressed with Vincent's ability to cover wide range of music, playing "old music" while still retaining his coolness. He also was very influential on the band wearing the leather suits, prior to that it was "nothing but blue jeans."

In 1960 while on tour in the U.K., Vincent was involved in the accident that killed Eddie Cochran. Vincent reinjured his previously broken leg and breaking several bones, never fully recovering.

He returned to England the following year where he was greatly received, permanently moving there in '63. Throughout the decade Vincent enjoyed stretches of moderate success, but his health deteriorated rapidly due to an alcohol addiction. He died in 1971 at age 36.

The Beatles never officially recorded any of Vincent's material, but did perform "Wildcat" when Paul borrowed a reel-to-reel tape recorder early in their career and "Be-bop-a-Lula" was recorded in Hamburg in 1962.

They were said to have performed about a dozen of his songs during their early live shows, including many songs Vincent covered, although the naive young singers only knew those as Vincent songs.

It's uncertain who sang lead for the band when they would perform "Be-Bop-a-Lula," but it was likely John. The only known recording of it from the Beatles features guest vocalist Fred Fascher, brother to Horst, who co-ran the Star Club. It is evident that the band knew the material very well, particularly Harrison who shines with a very skilled guitar solo.

FATS DOMINO

Antoine Dominique "Fats" Domino was born in Louisiana in 1928, and like several of the Beatles' rock heroes he grew up in modest circumstances and learned to play music at a young age.

Domino was the son of a well-known violinist and his brother-in-law was a jazz guitarist, who taught the young Louisiana French Creole-speaking Antoine to play piano.

In 1947 Domino joined the Solid Senders. Bandleader Billy Diamond nicknamed his new pianist "Fats" after Fats Waller, a very animated performer in his own right, as well as Fats Pichon, another popular piano player in the 1920s.

Domino's first single for the Imperial Records was

Detroit City Blues backed with "(They Call Me) the Fat Man" in 1949 which immediately gained attention for the charming, soothing, and pleasant sounding singer.

He had a string of hits on the R&B charts from 1950-55 including "Boogie-Woogie Baby," "Every Night About This Time" "Rockin' Chair," "Goin' Home," "Poor Poor Me," "How Long," "Going to the River" b/w "Mardi Gras in New Orleans," "Please Don't Leave Me," "Rose Mary," "Something's Wrong," "You Done Me Wrong," "Where Did You Stay," and "Don't You Know."

"Ain't That a Shame" was a crossover hit in 1955 for Domino, which refers to a song from the "black charts" which becomes a hit on the Hot 100 or pop charts, frequently referred to as the "white charts."

The Domino version only reached No. 10 while a milder version by Pat Boone went to No. 1 shortly after, achieving greater airplay in an era of massive racial segregation.

Dave Bartholomew was a musician, bandleader, producer, and an A&R man for Imperial Records who co-wrote "Shame" with Domino. Bartholomew produced it in an attempt to make the singer sound "more white" as the partnership did with "I'm in Love Again," "Blue Monday," "I'm Walkin'," "I'm Gonna Be a Wheel Someday," and "Let the Four Winds Blow."

Bartholomew also wrote "I Hear You Knocking" in 1955, which Domino would do in 1961 and "One Night" in 1956, which would be recorded by Elvis Presley in 1959. Both songs were originally done by Smiley Lewis.

Continuing with a string a releases, Domino achieved consistent success on both the white and black charts with hits that included "Blueberry Hill," "Walking to New Orleans," "When My Dreamboat Comes Home," "Honey Chile," "What's the Reason I'm Not Pleasing You," "I'm in the Mood for Love," "The Big Beat," "Whole Lotta Loving," "When the Saints Go Marching In," "Margie, I Want to Walk You Home," "Ain't That Just Like a Woman," and "Let

the Four Winds Blow," his last visit to the U.S. Top 20, many of which were produced by Bartholomew.

"Valley of Tears" was a March 1957 release by Domino, co-written by producer-arranger Bartholomew and re-recorded by Buddy Holly the following year.

Having a song of a slow and sensitive nature recorded by two of their heroes further endorsed the band's belief that thoughtful and less rock-style songs were acceptable to perform. "Red Sails in the Sunset" was a song that the Beatles would perform in late 1962, and that Domino himself would record the following year.

While the band always avidly championed Domino and his style, they never recorded any of his songs during any of their documented sessions. Any songs they may have performed or attempted by him are pure speculation, although solo Beatles would record his material many years later,.

Lennon claims that "Ain't That a Shame" was the first song he learned how to play on guitar and he and Paul both have said if it wasn't for Fats Domino there would be no Beatles. This is possibly a slight over-exaggeration on their part, but the accolades were sincere for a musician the Beatles all individually enjoyed for his sheer pleasantness. Domino himself said his goal was to make happy songs that people could remember and sing along.

As the '60s wore on Domino's chart success dwindled. He continued to record and tour, changing labels on several occasions. In 1980 he decided he would never again leave New Orleans, as he disliked touring and was never able to get the food that he loved anywhere else.

Domino declined invitations to perform at his Rock and Roll Hall of Fame induction in 1986, as well as the White House in 1998. He would remain in his home until 1985 when he would briefly tour Europe, returning to his Lower Ninth Ward mansion that was sadly destroyed in the heavy flood left behind from Hurricane Katrina in 2005.

In 2006 President George W. Bush, knowing Domino's policy on traveling, personally visited him to replace his National Medal of Arts, which was awarded to him by President Bill Clinton in 1998 and washed away in the natural disaster that claimed many of Domino's possessions and personal memorabilia.

In his last decade, Domino rarely performed in public, saying he'd rather spend his time in his Louisiana hammock. He died at home of natural causes on October 24, 2017 at age 89.

ELVIS PRESLEY

Despite the fact that they never officially recorded his songs, Elvis Presley was not only a strong early influence for the Beatles, he is possibly the most important one of all.

Born to meager conditions in Tupelo, Mississippi, Elvis was the surviving brother as his identical twin Jesse was stillborn. Elvis was very close with his parents growing up, and they raised him to always be graceful and polite, encouraging his interest and natural ability to perform.

When Èlvis was 13 the family relocated to Memphis, where the young musician got off to a rough start. An eighth grade music teacher tried to tell him he had zero aptitude for singing. Elvis attempted to convince them otherwise by bringing in his guitar and performing again, telling the teacher "you just don't appreciate my kind of singing." The teacher agreed. The sensitive and fragile Presley was picked on by some of his older classmates for his appearance which included sideburns and an oiled hairstyle.

In his teens Elvis performed in a band with Dorsey and Johnny Burnette and was heavily exposed to the blues music of the Memphis area. This experience, combined with Elvis's gospel upbringing, greatly influenced his sound, in much the same way Elvis' music helped mold the sound of the Beatles.

In August 1953 Elvis booked time at Sun Records to make a record for his private use, possibly as a gift and likely in the hopes of being discovered. His hopes came to fruition as Elvis was signed to the label. While at Sun he recorded some of the most influential music in the history of rock and roll through 1954, when his contract was sold to RCA records.

During this period Elvis recorded some of the songs that became the Beatles' favorites, including "That's When Your Heartaches Begin," "That's Alright," a "revved up" version of "Blue Moon Over Kentucky," "Just Because," "Good Rockin' Tonight," "Baby Let's Play House," "I Got a Woman," "I'm Left, You're Right, She's Gone," "Mystery Train," and "I Forgot to Remember to Forget."

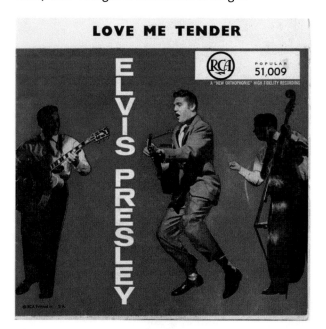

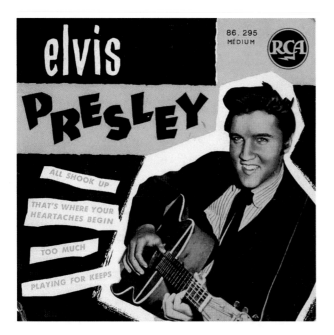

These monumental recordings were all produced by Sun's owner Sam Phillips featuring Elvis, guitarist Scotty Moore, and upright bass player Bill Black, and were the songs the Beatles drew from in their early performing days. Presley's early music, including the songwriters behind those songs, left an indelible mark on the musical tastes of the individual Beatles in their youth, thus played an essential role in the formation of the Beatles.

It is notable that during this era consumers of imported music had to wait quite a while after the release date to acquire a record. Generally the only way to receive imports was via trans-Atlantic ships, which would bring records from the States to port towns such as Liverpool.

In 1955 Elvis released his first single on the RCA label, which had a much greater distribution system and it became one of the most influential records of all time.

"Heartbreak Hotel" was written by Tommy Durden and Mae Boren Axton, and was inspired by an article about a man who committed suicide by jumping out the window of his hotel. As soon as the young Beatles heard the song they were all individually moved by it, as were literally millions of other kids around the world.

"Hotel" was followed with a string of hits including "Blue Suede Shoes," "I Want You, I Need You, I Love You," "Hound Dog," "Don't Be Cruel, "Love Me Tender, "All Shook Up," "(Let Me Be Your) Teddy Bear," "Jailhouse Rock," and "(You're So Square) Baby I Don't Care."

In 1956 Elvis began his acting career, appearing in four films before being drafted into military service, serving in the U.S. Army between and 1958-60. He gracefully served and wished to be treated "just like a regular guy," which his fellow soldiers greatly agree was how it was in reality.

While in the service Elvis would become interested in karate, which he would continue to study seriously after his tour of duty was complete. Sadly, he would also be introduced to amphetamines which would be a part of his world for the rest of his days.

Prior to Elvis' departure for the Army and during a two-week leave, many songs were recorded so that there would be an ample supply of new stuff to be released in his absence. This quickly-produced period of songs that were hastily arranged and impacted the quality of the music that was being released. Sales remained far above average, however, and were responsible for a large percentage of the label's total sales.

After his honorable discharge from the Army on March 23, 1964, Elvis continued to record while filming a series of low-budget musical films. While the Beatles remained fans of several of his films, they felt that some of the spark had left the building. The band would get to meet the king the following year, leaving them a bit disillusioned about their hero.

Elvis' comeback special and a return to the road spurred a resurgence of interest in 1968. He performed live frequently (although never playing outside of North America) until his death in on August 16, 1977. An autopsy showed 14 different drugs in Elvis' system.

Elvis had a great influence on all four individual Beatles, who were impressed with his charisma and persona, as well as his success. Not only did emulating Elvis seem like a good way to "get chicks," the Beatles were also big fans of his music. They performed several of Presley's songs throughout their career, although none for their official recordings.

Up to 30 different Presley songs were said to be played by the Beatles/Quarrymen throughout their performing years. They focused almost primarily on material from the "pre-army Elvis" period, clearly their favorite era of his music. They grew out of Presley as his music became very manufactured and his films became his priority. While the band seemingly lost interest in Elvis as they progressed as songwriters, his inspiration was unsurpassed, both musically and in what they considered "cool."

ELVIS PRESLEY SONG BY SONG
"I FORGOT TO REMEMBER TO FORGET"

"I Forgot to Remember to Forget" is one of many Sun Records-era recordings from Elvis that the Beatles enjoyed, studied, and learned. They performed it in 1964 for an episode of "From Us to You."

The song was written by Stan Kesler and Charlie Feathers, or at least that's where the credit is pointed. Kesler was a producer/guitarist/ songwriter who began writing songs for his band, the Snearly Ranch Boys, to perform. After several of his songs were recorded by Sun Records artists, he was hired by Sun owner and producer Sam Phillips as a session man.

Kesler co-wrote "Forgot" and "I'm Left, You're Right, She's Gone" as well as both sides of the "Signifying Monkey" b/w "Listen to Me Baby" from Smokey Joe, all released on Sun Records in 1955. "I'd Rather Be Safe Than Sorry," recorded by Warren Smith, and both sides of the "I Need A Man" b/w "No Matter Who's to Blame," a Barbara Pitman single from 1956, were also written by Kesler, all on the Sun label.

Kesler also played in the house band at Sun Records, performing for sessions with Carl Perkins, Roy Orbison,

and Jerry Lee Lewis, playing bass on "Great Balls of Fire." In the late '50s and early '60s Kesler continued as a recording engineer at Sun, and started several of his own labels. He found success with his XL label, where he produced "Wooly Bully" as well as other singles and album tracks for Sam the Sham and the Pharaohs.

Feathers was also a session musician at Sun Records who got credit on "Forgot" after Kesler asked him to help record a demo. As a singer and theatrical performer, Feathers recorded "I've Been Deceived" and "Peepin' Eyes" for the Flip label, also owned by Phillips, as well as "Defrost Your Heart" and "Wedding Gown of White" for Sun in 1956.

In 1964 the Beatles recorded "Forgot" at the BBC Paris Studio in London with George on lead vocal. Each Beatle had their own casual specialty when it came to covering music by others, but it appears they all took turns singing Elvis tunes.

The band enjoyed several qualities about the song: Elvis' youthful and soulful voice, the sparse but intense rhythm section, the use of two different forms of the word "forget," as well as the antonym in the title, a unique writing tool.

"I'M GONNA SIT RIGHT DOWN AND CRY (OVER YOU)"

"I'm Gonna Sit Right Down and Cry (Over You)" was a song that the Beatles performed frequently, and several recordings exist. Roy Hamilton recorded the original version, which was released in 1954 as a soulful swing tune featuring a horn solo along with Hamilton's classically trained operatic voice. Presley did it shortly after that, releasing it on his 1956 self-titled debut LP on the RCA label. His rendition had a more up-tempo, country rockabilly style.

When the Beatles adopted "I'm Gonna Sit Right Down and Cry (Over You)" as part of their act as early as 1960, they did it as a hectic rocker, much in the same style as many of their originals from that time. The song must have been performed on multiple occasions, and certainly was played more consistently and more enthusiastically once Starr joined the group, as tapes reveal.

From the December 1962 Hamburg performance we hear the band confidentially and energetically playing the song live for an excited German crowd. They performed it again on July 13, 1963, during one of the band's lengthy sessions for the radio show "Pop Go the Beatles." It is unknown if the song was ever considered for an official recording.

"THAT'S ALL RIGHT (MAMA)"

The band performed "That's All Right (Mama)" for "Pop Go the Beatles," this time their rendition of the song was more similar to the Elvis version.

Arthur "Big Boy" Crudup first wrote and recorded the song in 1946 as "That's All Right." It was then re-recorded in Chicago for RCA/Victor, becoming the first single released as a 45 rpm on the label. The composer's rendition of the song was much slower than the one the

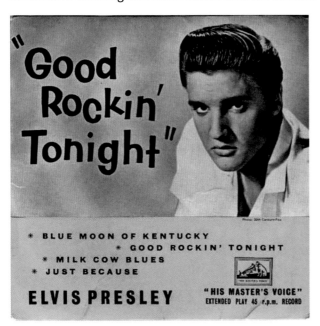

* BLUE MOON OF KENTUCKY
  * GOOD ROCKIN' TONIGHT
* MILK COW BLUES
* JUST BECAUSE

ELVIS PRESLEY   "HIS MASTER'S VOICE"
EXTENDED PLAY 45 r.p.m. RECORD

Beatles would perform, which was largely based on the Presley record.

In 1954 Presley, along with guitarist Scotty Moore and upright bassist Bill Black, starting performing an impromptu and up-tempo version of the Crudup song. Sun owner/producer Phillips immediately became intrigued and asked the trio to start over so he could get it on tape. The single was released in July 1954 as Elvis' first for Sun.

When the young Beatles heard this song, as well as dozens of others, they immediately became fans and followers. From the formation of the Quarrymen through mid-1963 the Beatles performed dozens of Elvis songs, and although they never officially recorded one for EMI, during their BBC sessions they took the opportunity to perform several.

McCartney took the lead on "That's All Right (Mama)," although it's likely that John, George and he would all take turns singing lead on Elvis songs, not "claiming" him as territory as they did with other acts they covered. Harrison shines brightly on the BBC recording of "That's All Right (Mama)" from 1963, suggesting that they had performed this song frequently over the past five years or so.

"THAT'S WHEN YOUR HEARTACHES BEGIN"

Presley first performed and recorded "That's When Your Heartaches Begin" in 1953 when he paid about $4 for enough studio time at Sun to record a two-sided acetate record (very similar, yet a bit more sophisticated than the Percy Phillips record from 1958) that had "My Happiness" on one side and "Heartaches" on the other. It was written by Fred Fisher, William Raskin, and Billy Hill and was first recorded by the Shep Fields Rippling Rhythm Band in 1939, then by the Ink Spots in 1941.

In January 1957 Elvis would more formally record "That's When Your Heartaches Begin" with the Jordanaires. It was released as the B-side to "All Shook Up."

Fisher, a songwriter born in Germany in the late 1800s, wrote "Come Josephine in My Flying Machine" in 1910, "Who Paid the Rent for Mrs. Rip Van Winkle?" in 1914, "They Go Wild, Simply Wild, Over Me" in 1917, and "I'd

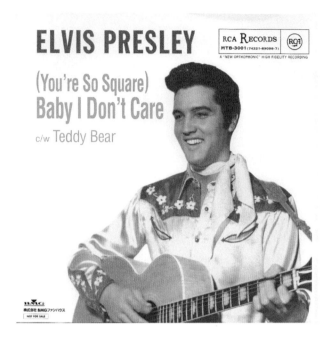

ELVIS PRESLEY

RCA RECORDS
MTB-3001 (74321-89098-7)
A "NEW ORTHOPHONIC" HIGH FIDELITY RECORDING

(You're So Square)
Baby I Don't Care
c/w Teddy Bear

"Sleepy Head" for Sam Lanin and His Orchestra in 1929, "Home on the Range," "Only a Bum," and "The Last Round Up" for Bing Crosby, "There's a Wild Rose that Grows on the Side of the Hill" for Herb Cook and His Three Little Words, all in 1933, "Wagon Wheels" for Sam Robbins and His Hotel McAlpin Orchestra in 1934, and "'Til the Clock Strikes Three" for Larry Kent and His Orchestra in 1937, all of which were recorded dozens of times by dozens of artists.

When the Beatles recorded "That's When Your Heartaches Begin," it was likely as a trio. John would take lead, doing what he might refer to as his "Elvis voice" on the sad tale of a man being despondent over losing his love to his best friend, a theme that Lennon himself would revisit several times as a songwriter.

John and Paul appeared to be focusing on slower songs to record while they had their hands on the controls, likely trying to help bass playing Stu improve as a musician. Another slower paced, more traditional song they rehearsed during this era was a standard by Liverpool crooner Michael Holliday. "I'll Always Be in Love with You" was sung by John when they performed it on this occasion, displaying his sense of showmanship, as well as a love for music from his youth, much of which was introduced to him by his mother. The song itself was written by Sam Stept, Bud Green, and Herman Ruby, first published in 1929 and recorded by band leader Morton Downey (father of disc jockey and "trash tv" pioneer Morton Downey Jr.), Jack Pleis, and a band called the Ravens.

Rather Be Blue" in 1928. He also composed "Your Feet's Too Big" in 1936, which would be recorded by the Ink Spots as well as Fats Waller, and performed by the Beatles as well.

In 1949 a greatly exaggerated biographical film called "Oh, You Beautiful Doll" (oddly not a Fisher composition) was made based on the life and music of Fisher, and featured his songs "Peg o' My Heart" from 1913, "Dardanella" from 1919, and "Chicago (That Toddlin' Town)" written in 1922.

One co-writer of "That's When Your Heartaches Begin" was Raskin, who also penned "Fifty Million French Can't Be Wrong" for Jack Kaufman in 1927, "Wedding Bells (Are Breaking Up That Old Gang of Mine)" for Gene Austin in 1929, and "They Cut Down the Old Pine Tree" for Gene Autry in 1930.

The other co-writer was Hill, a classically-trained violinist born in Boston in 1899. He headed west to work as a jazz musician and cowboy before returning to the music business in the late 1920s. Hill became a successful songwriter in Tin Pan Alley, the area of New York dominated by songwriters and music publishers for the first half of the 1900s.

Some of Hill's more successful compositions include

Russian-born Stept emigrated to America at age 3, growing up to write over 500 songs for stage and film. His most famous work is "Don't Sit Under the Apple Tree" (With Anyone Else but Me)," made popular by the Glenn Miller Orchestra and the Andrew Sisters in America during World War II. His other notable compositions include "I Beg Your Pardon, Mademoiselle" in 1932, "Breakin' in a Pair of Shoes" in 1936, "This is Worth Fighting For" and "I Came Here to Talk" in 1942, and "Blame it on Paree" for the Nelson

Riddle Orchestra in 1957.

A very small sampling of Stept's work also includes "We Must Have a Song to Remember" for the Peerless Quartet and "And That Ain't All" for Billy Murray in 1919, "That's My Weakness Now" for Ukulele Ike in 1928, "Please Don't Talk About Me When I'm Gone" in 1930, and "By a Lazy Country Lane" in 1931, all collaborations with Green.

Green was an Austrian native who came to New York as an infant, first writing songs for Vaudeville before becoming a staff writer for music publishers who wrote songs for Broadway musicals. Green's catalog includes "Lo-Nah" from 1926 (with Stept), "Moonlight Lane" in 1928, and "Under the Sweetheart Tree" for Jack Payne and his B.B.C. Dance Orchestra in 1930, also with Stept. The latter is unrelated to "Don't Sit Under the Apple Tree," although both songs use a similar theme.

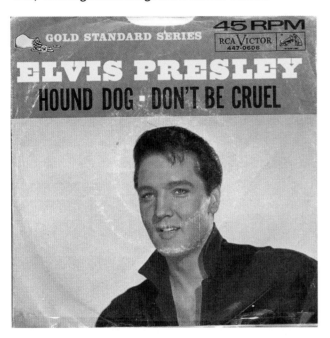

Green was also a writer on "A Sentimental Journey," first published in 1944, as well as "Alabamy Bound" which was made famous by Al Jolson in 1939.

Ruby was an American songwriter who composed songs in the 1910s and 1920s for Broadway plays, moving to Hollywood to write songs and screenplays in the 1930s. His first recorded composition is "My Sunny Tennessee" which was released as a 78 rpm in 1921

on the Little Wonder record label. The performers are unknown, listed only as a tenor duet.

He also penned "Feelin' Kind O' Blue" for the International Novelty Quartet in 1925, "Since I Found You" for Frank Keyes and His Orchestra in 1929, and "My Honey's Lovin' Arms" for Wingie Manone and His Orchestra in 1943.

It is possible that band members were familiar with several of the recorded versions by Kay Starr, Ella Fitzgerald, Benny Goodman, Lawrence Welk, Joe Williams, Sonny King, the Jonah Jones Quartet, or the Savage Beat of Augie Colón.

Born in Lancashire, England (before it became Liverpool) in 1924, Holliday had recently recorded the song "I'll Always Be in Love with You" in 1958. He gained sizable local attention, likely heard by the individual Beatles as well as their parents, who were all musically aware.

Holliday's version is a bit brighter with a more optimistic tone than some of the other more overly emotional performances with which the band members were more familiar. The lyrics find the singer crooning of being forever in love with a woman, or more specifically a gender neutral sweetheart, who may stray a million miles away, and finding bliss in someone else's kiss.

Once again a theme of undying love would be prevalent for the Beatles even at this formative stage for the songwriters/performers.

Lennon's performance is intense and sincere, with a slow and somber tempo, displaying a familiarity with the material, both musically and lyrically. There is a guitar solo which may possibly be played by George, or perhaps Paul, who also may sing the bridge of the song. With similar accents and a poor quality recording, the young Liverpudlian singers sound very similar to one another.

It has been stated that the song was a part of the band's live repertoire in 1960-61, although documentation is extremely spotty and inconsistent. A song of this class would certainly be one they wouldn't avoid performing live, as show tunes and "old standards" were always part of the fabric of the Beatles and their open mindedness to many types and styles of music.

"BABY LET'S PLAY HOUSE"

Recorded by Elvis for Sun Records in 1955, "Baby Let's Play House" was a song that Lennon performed on the first day he met Paul. The song likely stayed around as part of the Beatles' set until late 1962, and in late 1965 Lennon would liberally borrow a lyric of "Baby Let's Play House" for an original composition.

Prior to that, it was Elvis who heard the version by Arthur Gunter, the man who wrote the song and recorded it the previous year. Gunter's version uses a different verse/chorus pattern, and there is a slight variation in the lyric as Elvis changed "you might get religion" to "you may have a pink Cadillac." Elvis also added the "baby baby baby" part at the beginning. It is extremely unlikely that the Beatles would have had access to the original version during this era, so they knew it strictly as an Elvis song.

Guitarist Jimmy Page calls the Elvis version of "Baby Let's Play House" the record that made him want to play guitar, and he was especially impressed with Scotty Moore's work on it.

In addition to the list above, "I Got a Woman" was covered by the Beatles twice for the BBC, and is an original Ray Charles composition; however the Beatles likely thought of it as an Elvis song.

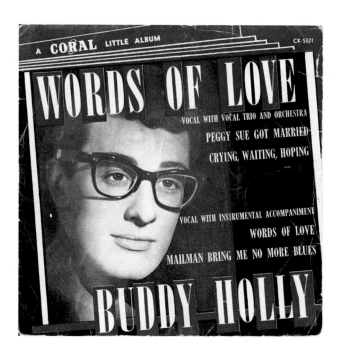

BUDDY HOLLY

Buddy Holly was another very important early influence for the band, and like Elvis he impacted them stylistically as well as musically.

Born Charles Hardin Holley in Lubbock, Texas, Holly (as he would professionally become when his name was misspelled on a contract) was raised listening to country acts like Hank Williams, Bob Wills, Hank Snow, and the Carter Family. "Buddy" was the nickname of the youngest of four children in his very musical family, and he was also exposed to gospel music in his family's Baptist church.

Holly's band name, the Crickets, was also a great inspiration for the Beatles' name. They enjoyed the fact that a cricket was an insect as well as a game, although unbeknownst to them the Texas musician had no knowledge of the British game.

Buddy performed while still in high school, and after graduation he decided to become a professional musician with full support from his family. He was greatly inspired after seeing a young performer named Elvis Presley, whom Holly would go on to open for on several occasions in 1955.

Holly was signed and then soon released from a contract with Decca Records in February 1956 (when Holley became Holly). The band was named Buddy and the Two Tones or, as they were later called, the Three Tones before becoming the Crickets.

The Crickets were comprised of Niki Sullivan on vocals and guitar, Jerry Allison on drums, and Joe Mauldin on bass. They were one of the bands that made the Beatles take notice as they wondered where that sound came from, they also set the lineup for the Beatles with two guitars, bass and drums.

While recording with Norman Petty, Buddy had considerably more control over the recordings, and achieved the sounds he was hearing.

Beginning with the release of "That'll Be the Day" in 1957, Holly along with his new band the Crickets had a string of international tours, television appearances and albums. Releases included "Words of Love," "Peggy Sue," "Every Day," "Oh! Boy!" "Not Fade Away," "Maybe Baby," "Rave On," "Think it Over," "Early in the Morning," "It's So Easy," "Real Wild Child," and "Heartbeat," which was the last song of his released during his lifetime.

With each new single Holly was trying to move ahead and make progress with his music, a pattern similar to the one the Beatles would follow in their recording career.

As the sessions shortly prior to his death reveal, Holly was intrigued by adding uncommon musical instruments into a rock and roll sound such as violins, cellos, and other more traditionally classical or "pop" instruments, as well as unique rhythms and use of percussion.

He had done this in the earlier part of his very brief career with the celesta solo on "Everyday" (played by Norman Petty's wife Vi). He continued to use odd forms of percussion (knee slapping and cardboard boxes), organ, other keyboards, and technological innovations throughout his recordings, including multi-tracking on his version of "Words of Love" as a primary example.

Holly was also exploring different styles, including big band and soul music, also collaborating with musicians who weren't similar to him. He did a 1958 session with an 18-piece orchestra yielding four rather non-rock and roll sounding pop songs, "It Doesn't Matter Anymore," "True Love Ways," "Raining in My Heart," and "Moondreams."

Holly would relocate to New York with his wife to be closer to the music and publishing scene, and he brought a home reel-to-reel recording unit with him.

He also had sights on producing for other musicians, overseeing a session for disc jockey and songwriter Waylon Jennings in late '58. Jennings would join Holly's touring band when the original members of the Crickets along with producer/manager Petty split with Holly amidst financial and legal disputes.

In February 1959 Holly was part of the Winter Dance Party tour. After a performance in Clear Lake, Iowa he chartered a plane for himself and his band, who at the time consisted of Tommy Allsup, Carl Bunch, and Jennings. Allsup lost his seat in a coin toss with Valens, and Jennings gave up his seat in sympathy to the Big Bopper. Tragically, the plane crashed shortly after takeoff into snowy conditions, killing all four on board.

Holly's newlywed widow, Maria Elena Holly, was pregnant at the time of her husband's death and lost the baby afterward due to psychological trauma.

The ever-ambitious and prolific creator had several unfinished or abandoned songs that were completed and concluded after his death, these records include "It Doesn't Matter Anymore," "Raining in My Heart," "Peggy Sue Got Married," "Crying, Waiting, Hoping," and "True Love Ways," as well as "Reminiscing," which was a partnership with King Curtis.

LONNIE DONEGAN

Frequently called the King of Skiffle, Lonnie Donegan was one of the most popular artists in post-war England with his American country-fueled act. He scored hits with covers of Lead Belly and Woody Guthrie songs.

Born Anthony James Donegan in Scotland, he relocated to England during the second World War. His father was a professional violinist who performed with the Scottish National Orchestra. He grew up listening to traditional jazz and took up guitar, also developing a keen interest in country and western, folk, and blues. Donegan was a very "open-eared" musician, similar to the Beatles themselves.

While studying music he heard on the radio, Donegan would learn whatever standards he could, and started to perform professionally while still in his teens. He joined Ken Coyler's Jazzmen who would eventually become the Chris Barber Jazz Band. Donegan would sing and play banjo during the Dixieland set, also known as the skiffle break, with the name inspired by Dan Burley & His Skiffle Boys.

He subsequently formed the Anthony (later Tony) Donegan Jazz Band, eventually changing his name to Lonnie in honor of bluesman Lonnie Johnson, who the band opened for in 1952.

Donegan's debut recording was in 1955 on the Decca label, "Rock Island Line" backed with "John Henry," both of which he learned from Lead Belly records.

Donegan was quickly snapped up by the Columbia Graphophone Company (not to be confused with Columbia Records) and he briefly recorded at EMI studios

In July 1957 Donegan had a hit with a double A-side, consisting of "Gamblin' Man," a Woody Guthrie song Donegan reworked, and "Puttin' on the Style," which was a cover of a song from Vernon Dalhart, an influential country artist from the 1920s.

With continuing success in England as well in the United States, Donegan became a model of how to succeed for the young Beatles. Once again they were thinking of the U.S. as a holy land beyond their wildest fantasies.

The Lonnie Donegan Showcase, his 1956 debut LP, was made up of songs written/passed on by Lead Belly, as well as American blues pianist Leroy Carr and other traditional folk and country songs with slightly updated and personalized lyrics.

This debut release was an astonishing success, selling hundreds of thousands of copies in the U.K. In the United States his music was not as well received, his biggest hit being "Does Your Chewing Gum Lose its Flavor on the Bedpost Overnight?" a cover of "Does the Spearmint Lose its Flavor on the Bedpost Overnight?" first released in 1924 by the Happiness Boys. Donegan changed the title in 1959 because Spearmint is a registered trademark and would not be played by the BBC.

Donegan's success, as well as the skiffle craze, would diminish greatly as the "beat groups" rose in notoriety.

He recorded only sporadically throughout the '60s and most of the '70s.

In 1978 Donegan recorded an "all-star" album called *Putting on the Style* with Ringo, Rory Gallagher, Elton John, and Brian May which led to a bit of a comeback, or at least more exposure for the aging artist.

Until his death in 2002, Donegan would sporadically appear with artists who were influenced by him over the years. He left behind a generation of young English kids whom he influenced greatly, with an impact that was at the time far beyond that of the Beatles.

ARTHUR ALEXANDER

While the Beatles were greatly influenced by artists such as Elvis, Chuck Berry, Little Richard, Buddy Holly, and Gene Vincent, who all had a fair deal of success, the band was certainly not beyond searching deep to find other inspiration. A wonderful example of this is Arthur Alexander.

Widely considered a country soul artist, Alexander was born in Sheffield, Alabama in 1940. He was billed as June Alexander (short for Junior) on his first single "Sally Sue Brown," released on Judd records, which was owned by Sun Records owner Sam Phillips.

The following year he recorded "You Better Move On" in Muscle Shoals, Alabama and released it on the Dot label based out of Gallatin, Tennessee. This, along with its B-side "A Shot of Rhythm and Blues" yielded attention in the R&B as well as the country world.

Released on the London label in the U.K., the Beatles, among others, quickly picked up on the originality of the soulful record which still had a country western feel about it. This very American sound was indicative of what the Beatles loved and they were striving to write songs of the same caliber.

While the Rolling Stones would ultimately cover the A-side of the record (1964) the Beatles snapped up the

B-side as their own.

"A Shot of Rhythm and Blues" was written by Nashville-based songwriter Terry Thompson and it had all the elements that the Beatles, especially John, would look for in a song, specifically the fact that it is about loving music.

In the song the singer tells the "symptoms" that you may have, as if it was an illness, but the chorus reveals it's not something to be avoided, but more importantly it will bring a lot of joy and pleasure.

These were elements that the band loved, and took note of the fact that the song was not about love, although finding a dancing partner, a major component of "I Saw Her Standing There," was a prevalent theme. The band would enjoy similar elements of "Rock and Roll Music," written by Chuck Berry and recorded for the *Beatles For Sale* release in 1964.

The band performed "A Shot of Rhythm and Blues" on three occasions for the BBC in summer 1963. John proudly sang the lead vocal with George and Paul supplying some wonderful harmonies. Ringo was quickly gaining confidence and provides especially excitable "Beatle-esque" drumming. George also adds a nice bit of lead guitar work, not over playing, but adding just the right touch.

"A Shot of Rhythm and Blues" never became an official release for the Beatles, but would have fit very nicely alongside the originals on any of the first four albums.

"Solider of Love (Lay Down Your Arms)" was co-written in 1962 by Nashville-based singer songwriter and session man James "Buzz" Cason and Tony Moon, who went on to become a successful publisher.

As soon as the Beatles heard the song they added it as part of their act, imitating the piano on guitar and adding harmony background vocals, courtesy of Paul and George. John again passionately interprets the song and delivers an impressive vocal on the performance available from the BBC, recorded June 18, 1963 for "Pop Go the Beatles."

"Anna (Go to Him)" was recorded for the Beatles' debut album, and there are also recordings of the band performing the song live for the BBC. However there was nothing from Alexander on the list for the Decca auditions.

"Where Have You Been All My Life" was the B-side to "Solider of Love" and immediately part of the act as well.

A recording was made of the Beatles performing "Where Have You Been All My Life" on New Year's Eve, 1962, shortly before they stopped performing it in their act with Lennon once again taking lead vocal in a passionate performance.

It was co-written by husband and wife songwriting team Barry Mann and Cynthia Weil (yet another female who contributed to the Beatles' formation) who also penned songs for the Righteous Brothers, the Ronettes, Mama Cass Elliot, and the Monkees (among others).

During the January 1969 sessions the band briefly performed the song in an unsuccessful attempt to get back to their roots. They also stumbled through "A Shot of Rhythm and Blues" and "Soldier of Love."

Some influences were more prevalent during different stages of the band's growth as songwriters and performers.

Lennon, with enthusiastic support and reinforcement from the other Beatles, again learned a considerable amount about projecting emotions into a performance to reflect the lyrics. An energetic and enthusiastic delivery is needed when singing about the love of music, but a sadder and more somber tone is needed when singing about letting your love go to another man.

The Rolling Stones, the Beatles, and Bob Dylan have all recorded covers of songs written or performed by Alexander, as have the Hollies, George Jones, Humble Pie, Joe Tex, Dusty Springfield, Ike and Tina Turner, Jerry Lee Lewis, and Elvis Presley.

After limited success in the mid-'60s and a brief comeback in 1972, Alexander left the business, becoming a bus driver for a center for disadvantaged kids in Cleveland.

In 1993 Alexander began performing again and he released the *Lonely Just Like Me* album. Sadly he suffered a heart attack and passed away on June 9, 1993, only three days after his final performance.

McCartney says that in the early days they wanted to sound like Arthur Alexander, again revealing very specifically where their earliest inspirations came from.

In many of the early Lennon/McCartney (or McCartney/

Lennon) compositions they were trying hard to emulate such soul artists as Arthur Alexander, Wilson Pickett, or Smokey Robinson and other Motown artists.

SMOKEY ROBINSON

Smokey Robinson was born in Detroit in 1940 to a lower-income family. His mother passed away when he was an infant, and he was raised by his eldest sister and extended family.

William was nicknamed "Smokey Joe" as a child by his uncle and quickly adopted the name. As he grew up he was a gifted athlete who did very well in school, but mainly his interests were in music. Smokey started his own vocal/doo-wop band called the Five Chimes, later to be the Matadors, eventually called the Miracles.

Diana Ross, later of the Supremes, was a neighbor of Robinson as a child, and the two worked together during the mutual heights of both their careers.

In 1957 after Robinson failed an audition with Brunswick Records he met songwriter and entrepreneur Berry Gordy, who was impressed with the young and ambitious songwriter's already large collection of material. With Gordy's help the Miracles released "Got a Job" in late 1958 (the answer to the Silhouettes' "Get a Job" from 1957).

Robinson dropped out of college to focus on becoming a professional musician, and was one of the earliest acts to sign on the Berry Gordy's Tamla/Motown label.

In late 1960 "Shop Around" was released and became Motown's first million seller, kicking off a string of hits for the Miracles which would include "You've Really Got a Hold on Me," "Mickey's Monkey," "Ooh Baby Baby," "Tracks of My Tears," "Going to a Go-Go, "I Second That Emotion," and "The Tears of a Clown."

More impactful for the Beatles was the large list of songs that Robinson had written for others, composing "Who's Loving You" for the Supremes in 1961 as well

as "Your Heart Belongs to Me" in late 1958, followed by dozens of others for Motown acts throughout the decade. These included the Temptations ("I'll Be in Trouble," "I Want a Love I Can See," "My Girl," "Get Ready," "Don't Look Back," "Since I Lost My Baby," "The Way You Do the Things You Do," "You've Got to Earn It"), Mary Wells ("Two Wrongs Don't Make a Right," "My Guy," "Operator," "The One Who Really Loves You," "What's Easy for Two is Hard for One," "When I'm Gone," "You Beat Me to the Punch"), Marvin Gaye ("Lucky, Lucky Me," "Ain't That Peculiar," "I'll Be Doggone," "One More Heartache"), the Marvelettes ("My Baby Must Be a Magician," "Don't Mess with Bill"), the Four Tops ("Still Water (Love)"), the Contours ("Whole Lotta' Woman," "First I Look at the Purse," "That Day When She Needed Me"), and dozens of others.

While the Beatles were very aware of Robinson, they likely only understood his influence on the Motown slightly, not realizing just how influenced they were by his writing, direction and production.

In the early 1970s Smokey would leave the Miracles, briefly retiring from recording to focus on his higher level position as vice president of Motown Records. Robinson returned as a solo artist in 1974.

Robinson has continued to sporadically record and consistently tour for the last several decades, releasing several albums of new material. In 2014 *Smokey and Friends* was released, which featured duets with Elton John, James Taylor, and Linda Ronstadt, among others.

CARL PERKINS

Carl Perkins was an American rockabilly singer/songwriter who immensely influenced the sound of the Beatles. McCartney stated "if there were no Carl Perkins, there would be no Beatles," a statement he and John also made about Fats Domino. While McCartney's accolades may be slightly overstated, Perkins' catalog of music undoubtedly brought great inspiration to the band.

Perkins was born into a family of sharecroppers in Tennessee, where he was raised being exposed to white southern gospel music as well as African American work chants which he would pick up from the field workers he labored alongside as a child.

The Grand Ole Opry was a weekly routine for Carl, as well as his brother Jay and their parents, who while financially deprived always encouraged their children's interest in music. After building a crude instrument from a cigar box and a broom, Carl acquired a poorly cared for Gene Autry model guitar from a neighbor, teaching himself some rudimentary skills.

John Westbrook was an African American field worker who played jazz and blues guitar and became friends with the young and enthusiastic youngster, who affectionately called him Uncle John. Westbrook encouraged Perkins to play from his soul, and "feel the sounds vibrate through the strangs."

When Perkins was a teenager, his family moved closer to Memphis enabling him to listen to a wider range of music in their house with electricity. At age 14 Carl and his guitar-playing brother Jay began performing strictly for tips in some occasionally rough bars in the area, eventually persuading their brother Clayton to join them on the upright bass.

When Carl's job at a local bakery was reduced to part-time, Perkins' wife Valda Crider encouraged him to try to make performing music his entire career.

The Perkins Brothers, along with drummer W. S. Holland continued to play consistently. They eventually relocated to Memphis after hearing Elvis Presley and learning about Sun Records and Phillips.

Success led to Perkins performing on bills with labelmates Elvis and Johnny Cash.

"Blue Suede Shoes" was written by Perkins in late 1955 and was released on Sun where it earned gold record status and created interest in the country-leaning early rocker.

In March 1956 on their way to a national appearance on "The Perry Como Show," which would mean broad public exposure, the Perkins brothers were involved in an automobile accident. While Carl was recuperating from his injuries, including a broken collarbone and three fractured vertebrae, Elvis released his recording of "Blue Suede Shoes." Presley's version wasn't as successful as the Perkins' version in terms of sales, but it became extremely well-known due to Elvis' frequent national television appearances, most notably on "The Milton Berle Show."

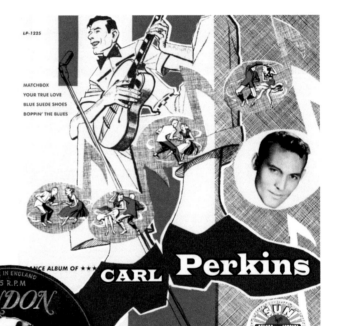

Jay Perkins suffered internal injuries as well as a fractured neck. Tragically, he never fully recovered and he passed away in 1958.

After Carl was fully healed he continued to record for Phillips and Sun Records, including "Boppin' the Blues," "Everybody's Trying to Be My Baby," "Dixie Fried," and "Matchbox," which featured pianist and labelmate Jerry Lee Lewis.

After "Matchbox" was completed, Lewis along with Perkins, Cash, and a visiting Elvis Presley recorded a spontaneous and unrehearsed performance which came to be known as "The Million Dollar Quartet."

Perkins would have moderate success after leaving

Sun, finding a long-term position as an opener for Cash as well as a player in his touring band.

In the mid-'60s when Perkins was touring England with Chuck Berry, they were thrilled with new interest in their older music due to the success of many of the British Invasion bands. Also while in England in 1964, Perkins was introduced to the Beatles, and the musicians informally performed or "jammed" together.

After leaving Cash's revue, Perkins started a new band with his sons Carl Stanley on guitar and Gregory Jay on bass. Also in the '70s while on the "country circuit" Perkins cut off the tip of his left pinky after getting it caught in the blades of a fan, and later the same year he was shot in the ankle in a hunting accident.

In later years Perkins would continue to perform as an "oldies" act and would frequently work with some of the musicians he inspired, most notably McCartney, Harrison, Eric Clapton, Dave Edmunds, "Slim Jim" Phantom and Lee Rocker of the Stray Cats, John Fogerty, Tom Petty and the Heartbreakers, Duane Eddy, Paul Simon, Chet Atkins, Joan Jett, the Jordanaires, Paul Shaffer, D.J. Fontana, Willie Nelson, and Bono.

After battling throat cancer for several years, Perkins suffered several strokes and died in January 1998.

PERKINS SONG BY SONG

Perkins' early inspirations of gospel, country, blues, and folk merged together to create a very distinctive sound, which of course greatly appealed to the Beatles. Over the course of the band's career they performed a minimum of 11 Perkins songs, likely more.

"TENNESSEE"

"Tennessee" was a Perkins release from his 1957 LP *The Dance Album of Carl Perkins*. The song brags about the virtues of the southern state, which boasts of giving the world music, Eddy Arnold, and the atomic bomb, while lightly criticizing Kentucky for Red Foley and Texas for Ernest Tubbs.

The Beatles were said to have sung the song frequently

in their formative days, when America seemed like a perfect, unattainable world, greatly romanticized by the band. They dropped the song from their lineup in '61.

During their January 1969 *Let It Be* sessions, the Beatles performed "Tennessee" once more. It turned out to be one of the more "complete" takes from the sessions, with all three singing Beatles sharing the lead, George remembering the words best.

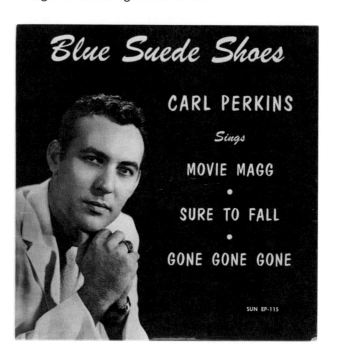

"BLUE SUEDE SHOES"

While the Beatles may have known it as an Elvis song, "Blue Suede Shoes" shared a similar path for the band. They performed it during the first shows they played as a band until sometime in 1962, reviving it for the 1969 sessions.

According to the loosely documented tale, which has frequent slight variations, Cash suggested in 1955 that Perkins write about the latest fad the kids were wearing - blue suede covered shoes. A short time later while playing a dance, Perkins overhead an argument from a dancing couple, the boy snapping at the girl saying "don't step on my suedes" (the details, such as what the color the shoes actually are greatly disputed).

It is said that using this inspiration Perkins immediately

began writing down lyrics on a brown paper bag, listing the things that are "allowed" (physical abuse, slander, theft, arson, and drinking the singer's booze) as long as nobody steps on the shoes.

The Beatles enjoyed the humor of the song (putting fashion ahead of all else) as well as the prominent guitar solos. Perkins plays the solo on his version while Moore plays two solos on the Presley version, released on the RCA label after Phillips sold Presley's contract in order to afford a wider stable of talent.

"Blue Suede Shoes" was also a rather complete and well-performed recording from the Beatles' 1969 sessions.

"SURE TO FALL (IN LOVE WITH YOU)" AND "LEND ME YOUR COMB"

"Sure to Fall (In Love with You)" and "Lend Me Your Comb" were both songs that the band was introduced to by Perkins and performed in their live shows. Both tunes remained part of their act beyond the early performances well into the recording era.

One quality that consistently impressed the Beatles was the ability of an artist to write, sing, and perform their own music. As they began writing songs of their own, these were the types of songs they were trying to create.

"Sure to Fall" uses the phrase "hold me tight" which was not exclusive to Perkins, however it was certainly part of the Beatles' terminology as they searched for ways to create songs of their own.

Similarly on "Lend Me Your Comb," they would also search for ways to be subtle as well as humorous. The song was released shortly after the Everly Brothers struck with "Wake Up Little Susie," and both songs have a similar innocent quality.

"BOPPIN' THE BLUES"

Although no records exist, "Boppin' the Blues" is a Perkins song that the band reportedly did very early in their performing days. However, a close look at the song clearly reveals why they might be attracted to it. A 1956 Sun label single for Perkins, "Boppin'" sings of the blues as the cure for a sickness, placing music on an even greater pedestal. It is a song about dancing which was certain to get the people moving, a frequent request from club owners.

SONGS FROM THE *LET IT BE* AND *BEATLES FOR SALE* SESSIONS

"Your True Love," and "Gone, Gone, Gone" were also Perkins songs performed early on and briefly revived during the *Let It Be* sessions.

From 1957 "Your True Love" was the B-side to "Matchbox," which the Beatles performed on multiple occasions and in many different situations. Both sides of the single were recorded on the same day the Million Dollar Quartet recordings took place.

Not to be confused with the Everly Brothers song of the same name from 1964, "Gone, Gone, Gone" was a Perkins single from 1955, which had a country as well as R&B quality to it. Again, it was exactly the type of song the Beatles were trying to create on their own.

"Honey Don't" and the aforementioned "Everybody's Trying to Be My Baby" would both be recorded for the Beatles' fourth LP *Beatles For Sale*, released in late '64. At that time "Everybody's Trying to Be My Baby" replaced "Roll Over Beethoven" as the George song in the live act.

EVERLY BROTHERS

Don Everly was born in Kentucky and his younger brother Phil was born in Chicago to a family that frequently relocated, including stays in Iowa, Kentucky, and Tennessee. Little Donnie and Baby Boy Phil were child entertainers and part of "The Everly Family" radio show featuring their parents.

In 1953 the family moved to Knoxville, Tenn., and two years later the brothers moved to Nashville to pursue their own career.

Family friend Chet Atkins, who was a guitarist and the manager at RCA's Nashville Studios arranged for the singing brothers to audition for competing record label Columbia who dropped the duo after their first single failed to chart. Atkins then introduced the Everlys to Wesley Rose of Acuff-Rose Music publishing company, who in turn helped get them signed to Cadence Records.

The duo recorded "Bye Bye Love," written by husband and wife songwriting team Felice and Boudleaux Bryant after dozens of other artists turned it down. It became their first million seller, hitting on the country, pop, as well as the R&B charts.

After three years of success with Cadence the band moved to Warner Brothers Records for a 10-year contract reported at $1 million, an astronomical sum in 1959. The Everlys' pay day was in reality less than this over-exaggerated account, but was still a substantial amount for a

musical act of the era.

In 1960 the band struck big with an original composition called "Cathy's Clown," which was the first in a string of early '60s hits including "So Sad (To Watch Good Love Go Bad)," "Walk Right Back," "Crying in the Rain," "That's Old Fashioned," "Lucille," "Ebony Eyes," and "Temptation."

The Everly Brothers were one of the Beatles' greatest influences, and the band no doubt recognized the Bryant/ Bryant credit on "Problems," "Poor Jenny," "Radio and TV," "Take a Message to Mary," "Bird Dog," "Devoted to You," "Nashville Blues," "Love Hurts," "Always it's You," "Donna, Donna", "A Change of Heart," and "So How Come No One (Loves Me)" on which John and George shared vocals when it was recorded for the BBC in 1963.

It's very likely that the band did the song, along with other Everly Brothers' tracks in their act from the time they first started performing together.

Vocal duties typically would have been shared by John and Paul, who were the two leaders of the group even in the very early days before Harrison joined, but it is George along with John who harmonize on "So How Come No One (Loves Me)," which was the only Everly Brothers song to be recorded by the Beatles, although not for an official album.

"When Will I Be Loved" and "Like Strangers" were leftovers that Cadence Records, who still retained the rights, released after the duo left their label.

A falling out with the publishers prevented them from recording any Acuff-Rose songs, which included many of their own compositions and the two dozen song written for them by the Bryants, the Everlys' success began to taper off.

In October 1961 they registered to serve in the Marines to avoid being drafted and to take advantage of the shorter stints served by enlistees. They appeared on "The Ed Sullivan Show" in mid-February 1962 while in their uniforms.

After their return to civilian life, the band continued to tour and record with very little success. They mended their argument with their publishers in 1964, releasing albums and singles with consistently low results.

Drug addiction and disappointment plagued the brothers' relationship, with the two departing after Phil smashed a guitar on stage and walked off during a 1973 performance.

Their individual solo careers were less successful than they were as a duo, and eventually the two would briefly reunite in 1984. They recorded the album *EB 84* with Dave Edmunds producing. The main single off the record was "On the Wings of a Nightingale" written by McCartney specifically for the reunited duo, which was the band's final charting song.

Over the next two decades the Brothers would work together sporadically, touring with Simon and Garfunkel who were also reunited in 2003. Sadly the Everly Brothers would again be estranged until the time of Phil's death in 2014, Don stating that while the brothers spoke to one another instinctively while singing as if they were "reading one another's minds" they had very serious conflicting political interpretations, as well as differences on "life."

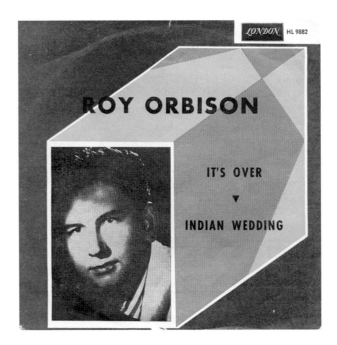

ROY ORBISON

Roy Orbison was an American singer/songwriter who was not only a major influence for the Beatles, but was close friend of the band as well.

During a period of American music that lacked a certain passion or energy, Orbison stood out above his contemporaries with his operatic and passionate performances.

Orbison was born and raised in Texas and learned to play guitar and sing after getting a guitar at age six. After that, Orbison said he was "finished for anything else" and music became his life. While attending Wink (Texas) High School, Orbison and some friends formed the Wink Westerners, later to be named the Teen Kings.

Johnny Cash performed in Odessa, Texas in 1955 and met Orbison, recommending him to contact Sam Phillips at Sun Records in Memphis. Orbison called Phillips who rudely informed him that "Johnny Cash doesn't run my label" and hung up.

Shortly after the Teen Kings recorded "Ooby Dooby" on the Je-Wel label, Phillips was impressed enough to offer them a contract with his Sun Records.

For several years Orbison would record with Sun, having minimal success with a rerecording of "Ooby Dooby" as well as "Go Go Go" and "Devil Doll," both B-sides.

Orbison wrote "Claudette" for his newlywed bride, and the Everly Brothers would record it as the B-side to their 1958 hit "All I Have to Do is Dream."

The Teen Kings disbanded after a dispute over songwriting credits. Orbison continued to live in Memphis, writing songs for Acuff-Rose Publishing, working with guitarist and producer Chet Atkins. Along with his "A-team" of musicians and the Jordanaires singing background, Atkins helped develop the Nashville sound, a well-produced and theatrical style of country music.

Orbison's wife Claudette and infant son Wesley lived in a small one-bedroom apartment and frequently Orbison would sit in his car to write songs in peace and quiet. One day Joe Melson noticed Orbison, approached him, and the two would immediately begin a songwriting partnership.

This brand of music helped Orbison survive the rock and roll crash of the late '50s, an era of rock and roll dominated by teen idols who performed very formulaic renditions of current hits. The "crash era" took the lives of Eddie Cochran and Buddy Holly, drafted Elvis Presley, put Chuck Berry in jail and gave religion to Little Richard.

After a bit of fine tuning, the songwriting duo of Orbison and Melson would have a monumental hit with "Only the Lonely (Know the Way I Feel)" recording it only after the Everly Brothers and Elvis Presley rejected it when offered.

Monument Records founder Fred Foster produced "Lonely" for Orbison. The hit would be followed up with "Blue Angel" and "I'm Hurting," all in 1960.

In 1961 the combination worked again with "Running Scared" backed with "Love Hurts," a cover of the 1960 Everly Brothers hit composed by the husband-wife team of Boudleaux and Bryant. Also in 1961 was "Crying" b/w "Candy Man," both sides again written, performed, and produced by the same "crew" of record makers, which were instinctively the type of records that attracted the Beatles.

In early 1962 Orbison would have "Dream Baby (How Long Must I Dream Alone)" that the Beatles would quickly learn and perform as part of their live shows.

Orbison had "In Dreams" (which uses the phrase "like dreamers do") and "Blue Bayou"/"Mean Woman Blues" in 1963. That year he also had an international tour that put him in close proximity with the Beatles, who were impressed with the power of his voice and the magnitude of his minimal stage performance.

Billy Dees and Orbison would co-write "It's Over" together, as well as "Oh Pretty Woman" which was taken from the phrase "a pretty woman doesn't need money" that Dees said after Claudette Orbison said she was "gonna head to Nashville for a bit." The song also employs a bit of what Orbison described as "Spanish bullfighter music."

As with many of the artists who inspired the Beatles, as their success became more dominating, Orbison's career would suffer.

Orbison endured several tragedies, including losing Claudette in a motorcycle wreck in 1966 and his two older sons in a 1968 house fire. He continued to record and perform over the next two decades with limited success, while remaining highly regarded by fans as well as his peers through his late 1980s comeback and collaboration as part of the Traveling Wilburys, until his death in 1988 at age 52.

The Shirelles

GIRL GROUPS

While many of the influences that young Beatles gravitated toward were masculine rock and roll types, the influence of girl groups was also vital to them.

During their recording years the band did five cover versions of songs originally done by girl groups, and many others in their live act or for the BBC.

For the first album Ringo sang lead on "Boys" and John does on "Baby It's You." Both songs originally done by the Shirelles.

Formed in 1957 in Passaic New Jersey, Shirley Owens, Doris Coley, Addie "Micki" Harris, and Beverly Lee were initially called the Poquellos, or Pequellos, likely named after the piquillo, a hot pepper.

After writing "I Met Him on a Sunday" for the Passaic

High School talent show, the group changed their name combining the "Shir" of Shirley Owens and the "elle" of the Chantels, a similar girl group from the Bronx. They were also briefly the Honeytunes.

The girls were managed by Florence Greenburg, who was the mother of a fellow student and owner of Tiara Records, which was ultimately sold to Decca Records, along with the Shirelles' contract. Greenberg approached Luther Dixon, who had worked with Nat King Cole, Perry Como, and Pat Boone to write and produce for the band.

Beginning in 1960 they had a string of Top 10 hits: "Will You Love Me Tomorrow?" (written by Goffin and King) reached No. 1 in 1961, its B-side was "Boys." Also in 1961 their cover of the 5 Royales' "Dedicated to the One I Love" reached No. 3, "Mama Said" hit No. 4, "Baby It's You" went to No. 8 and "Soldier Boy" became their first and only No. 1 on the Billboard charts in the States.

In 1962 they visited the Top Ten for the last time with "Foolish Little Girl."

A surplus of girl groups along with the pending British Invasion kept the group from garnering too much success after this. They continued to release music with numerous member changes including soul singer Dionne Warwick beginning in 1963.

Due to contract disputes the Shirelles sued the record company (Scepter) and were countersued. Ultimately they reached a mutual out-of-court agreement.

Their influence on not only the Beatles but on other female artists as well is extremely important. The Shirelles paved the way for women performers, specifically female African American artists, to be treated as true talents and to be taken seriously. It's unlikely that the band ever performed any other songs by the group beyond "Boys" and "Baby It's You," but they always considered the Shirelles to be among their favorites.

The Shirelles were inducted into the Rock and Roll Hall of Fame in 1996, and a stage musical called *Baby It's You* was performed in 2011, which also led to lawsuits from the Shirelles.

The Cookies, formed in 1954 in Brooklyn, New York, were the original artists of "The Devil in Her Heart," a track that Harrison sang lead on for the *With The Beatles* album in 1963. In 1956 "In Paradise" was a hit for them on the Atlantic label and through that they were introduced to Ray Charles, and they gradually became the Raelettes.

In 1961 they reformed with original member Dorothy Jones at the helm, which yielded them a small amount of success in 1963 with "Don't Say Nothin' Bad About My Baby" cracking the Top 10.

After "Chains," a Goffin/King composition which became a Top 20 hit in 1963, the band had few achievements. In 1967, after several lineup changes, they released their final record.

Another all-girl lineup that influenced the Beatles were the Marvelettes, formed in 1960 from glee club members at Inkster High School, in a suburb of Detroit. At one point the group was called the Casinyets, as in "can't sing yet." The following year after renaming themselves the Marvels, the group entered a talent contest and even though they only placed fourth, they still had the opportunity to audition for the newly-formed Motown records.

They were asked to find an original song to record, so when they returned to Inkster the band's senior member Georgia Dobbins contacted local songwriter William Garrett. He offered her an unfinished song called "Please Mr. Postman," which would be recorded by the Beatles in 1963.

Dobbins "unofficially" finished the song, but due to family obligations, as well her father's advice, she left the field of show business shortly before the band returned to Motown, where they were signed to the Tamla label and their name was officially changed to the Marvelettes.

After "Please Mr. Postman" was officially finished by Brian Holland, Robert Bateman, and Freddie Gorman, the Marvelettes recorded it in August 1961 with the rotating staff of Motown studio musicians named the Funk Brothers, who at the time included Marvin Gaye on the drums.

It was released in September and quickly became the label's first No. 1 hit.

The Marvelettes continued to release music on the Tamla/Motown label for the remainder of the decade with minimal success. They only hit the Top Ten on two other occasions with "Playboy" in 1962 (No. 7) and "Don't Mess with Bill," also No. 7 in 1966.

As labelmates like the Supremes and Martha and the Vandellas garnered more attention, the Marvelettes' output suffered in quality. Eventually the British invasion as well as a plethora of other girl groups pushed them out of the limelight that they achieved.

By the end of the decade after many personnel changes and legal disputes, the Marvelettes disbanded with occasional attempts at a comeback from various members of the band, each with their own claim to the name. In 2015 they were inducted into the Rock and Roll Hall of Fame.

Once again the Beatles were fans of this girl group, although they only included one of the Marvelette's songs as part of their set list. They performed "Please Mr. Postman" live frequently beginning in early '62, when the song was practically unknown in England. It was recorded by the Beatles in July 1963 for the *With The Beatles* album, released in November of the same year in the U.K.

They continued to perform the song live including several BBC performances until early '64 when they officially retired it from their repertoire.

The Beatles also garnered inspiration from other girl groups who were under the umbrella of the Motown sound, which had a huge impact on the band.

THE MOTOWN INFLUENCE

During their recording career the Beatles covered several songs that were initially on the Motown or Tamla record label, based out of Detroit. Founded in January 1959, Motown is a combination of the words "motor" and "town," named after the large population of vehicle factories in the area.

Initially it was named Tamla Records and Gordy housed all of its departments under one roof, including the administrative offices, sales, the recording studios, artists and repertoire, vocal coaches, and choreographers, all working together in a fashion that was similar to that of the assembly lines that produces the vehicles at the nearby auto plants.

Gordy applied the assembly line mentality to the production of his records, with each participant specializing in one fashion or another.

The soulful sound became synonymous with popular American soul music and the young Beatles quickly added songs from the label into their act.

During their early shows the band would perform "Money (That's What I Want)," "Please Mr. Postman," and "You Really Got a Hold on Me," all of which were recorded for their second album, *With The Beatles*. Much of their original material between 1962 and 1964 was inspired by the sounds that came from Detroit.

From the first album the song "There's a Place" came with Motown in mind, at least according to John; Paul claims it came from "West Side Story."

During the second half of '64 the band was especially in a Motown mood, covering the three songs for their *With The Beatles* album and writing others that were

The Four Tops

directly inspired by the Detroit label.

"All I've Gotta Do" and "Not a Second Time" were examples of the band, according to Lennon, "trying to be like Smokey," of course referring to Smokey Robinson and the Miracles.

Throughout the recording years the Beatles would use Motown influences on their originals, but they also used the label as a model for what not to do.

Paul said that they didn't wanna fall into the "trap" of having all of their songs sound too similar, stating that many of the Supremes songs sounded like the other Supremes songs, and many of the Four Tops songs sounded like other Four Tops songs.

With several Motown songs covered by the Beatles and other originals taking direct inspiration from the Detroit label (as well as covers of other soul or girl group music), the second album would crystallize the Beatles' credibility as a legitimate soul or R&B act.

Over the years several Motown artists who were admired by the Beatles would also cover songs of theirs, most notably Stevie Wonder, Supremes, Marvin Gaye, and the Four Tops.

Always looking for rare and unusual songs to perform, the Beatles certainly stumbled across a treasure when they discovered a record by the Donays on the Oriole label in Brian Epstein's NEMS store.

Very little is known about the girl group from Hamtramck, Michigan who had a very minor hit with "Devil in His Heart" in 1961 on the Correc-tone label. It was re-released on the Brent label in August 1962 as "(There's a) Devil in his Heart" as the B-side to a song called "Bad Boy," which was also released in England on the Oriole label, which is likely how the Beatles discovered it. They quickly made it part of their act with George taking the lead vocal duties, and changing the "his" to "her," eventually recording it for the *With The Beatles* album in July 1963.

The Donays only released these two songs and then faded into obscurity; however they have an interesting place in history thanks to the one and only Beatles.

By late '63 the Beatles had matured in their own writing styles and didn't record any further songs that were once done by girl groups. The girl group influence on the band remained extremely important however, especially in the harmonies the three singing Beatles would try to emulate.

Other minor influences that the band heard in their formative years include Bill Haley and the Comets and Duane Eddy, as well as numerous one hit wonders.

BILL HALEY

Bill Haley and the Comets weren't necessarily a band that the Beatles idolized or strived to be like, yet they still learned several songs by Haley as they scanned the charts record racks.

First as the Saddlemen, the country, swing, R&B act had several singles beginning with "Juke Box Cannon Ball" b/w "Sundown Boogie," "Dance with a Dolly (With a Hole in Her Stockin')" b/w "Rocking Chair on the Moon," "Icy Heart" b/w "Rock the Joint," and "Stop Beatin' 'Round the Mulberry Bush" b/w "Real Rock Drive" in 1952.

The following year he had "Crazy Man, Crazy" b/w "Whatcha Gonna Do," "Pat-A-Cake" b/w "Fractured," "Live It Up!" b/w "Farewell, So Long, Goodbye," and "I'll Be True" b/w "Ten Little Indians."

In 1954 Haley would have the "Chattanooga Choo-Choo" b/w "Straight Jacket" and "Green Tree Boogie" b/w "Rocket '88'," as well as his four-song *Shake, Rattle and Roll* EP which had the title track, the "A.B.C. Boogie," "Thirteen Women," and a song that would usher in a new era of rock and roll.

"(We're Gonna) Rock Around the Clock" was originally recorded by Sonny Dae and His Knights earlier in the year (loosely based on "The Syncopated Clock" written by Leroy Anderson) and Haley quickly re-recorded it. The song was selected for the 1955 film "Blackboard Jungle" which each of the Beatles enjoyed viewing, as they experienced the excitement generated by the song. On July 9, 1955 the song reached No. 1, becoming the first "rock and roll" record to reach No. 1 in the States. ∎

CHAPTER 12:
THE STAR CLUB RECORDINGS

DURING THIS FINAL GERMAN RESIDENCY A RECORDING WAS MADE OF A BEATLES PERFORMANCE BY STAR CLUB MANAGER ADRIAN BARBER. WIDELY BELIEVED TO BE FROM THE NEW YEAR'S EVE PERFORMANCE, IT IS LIKELY THAT THE RECORDING IS ACTUALLY COMPILED FROM SEVERAL DATES FROM THE SECOND HALF OF DECEMBER 1962.

KINGSIZE TAYLOR HAD REQUESTED that some of his performances be taped and Barber recorded him, as well as the Beatles on a Grundig reel-to-reel recorder with a single microphone. The recorder was likely one similar to the model that Paul borrowed from his neighbor in 1959.

There is much debate and speculation over the specifics of when the recordings were made, sources varying greatly. What is quite evident from the poor quality tape is an ambitious and talented band that was very professional and very "tight," as Harrison said of the Hamburg era.

Released in several forms (which included years of litigation) the exact order of the performance is unknown, however it is very likely that this is an excellent document of what a "typical" Beatles set may have been in the last month of this exciting year for the band.

"I'm Gonna Sit Right Down and Cry Over You" was written by Joe Thomas and Howard Biggs in 1953, originally recorded by Roy Hamilton in 1954, and also appeared on Elvis' first full-length album in 1956.

Biggs, born in Seattle in 1916, was a songwriter, pianist, and arranger for doo-wop, jazz and R&B records, becoming an important part in the dawn of rock and roll.

His first songwriting credit was for the Ravens' "Be on Your Merry Way" which was the B-side to "It's Too Soon to Know" in 1948. The Ravens also had "Send For Me If You Need Me" which was the B-side to their second single, "Until the Real Thing Comes Along," also in 1948.

Other important credits include "Got You on My Mind," by Buddy Morrow and His Orchestra in 1952, "Beginning to Miss You" from John Greer and His Rhythm Rockers in 1953 and "Your Mouth's Got a Hole in It" as recorded by Piano Red in 1953.

Joe Thomas was an American bassist who frequently co-wrote with Biggs, sharing credit with him on "Got You on My Mind" and "Ooo Wee" originally recorded by Louis Jordan and His Tympany Five in 1953, covered shortly after by Kitty, Daisy & Lewis.

It's unlikely that in this raw and naive stage the Beatles thought anybody other than Elvis wrote the song, not understanding how the songwriting field worked. They would drastically change the way things were done within a few short years.

Hamilton's version is slower than the Beatles would ultimately perform it, and it has a country as well as rhythm and blues quality about it, including horns. When Elvis recorded it shortly after Hamilton, his arrangement provided a rockabilly take on the song, sounding very country.

The Beatles likely performed "I'm Gonna Sit Right Down and Cry Over You" for quite some time before the December 1962 recording, as all four members deliver their precise contribution very skillfully, displaying yet again their solidarity as a band.

It is undocumented if the band did this song with Best on drums, prior to Ringo joining the band. Starr shines brightly on the performance with an extremely frantic, yet defined drum intro, clearly knowing where to "fill" the sound and when to quickly blend into the background.

"I'm Gonna Sit Right Down and Cry Over You" was the style of song that many of the area bands typically included in their set. Keeping in mind that being an Elvis fan was practically unanimous among the age group that would be the Beatles' peers, it's not outside the realm of possibility that the Hurricanes also had this as part of their act.

The Beatles play with a very straightforward delivery by John and Paul, similar to the arrangement on "Some Other Guy," sharing a lead vocal.

George shines on guitar as well, supporting all throughout the song and taking advantage of his windows as well.

McCartney's bass skills had progressed rapidly as well, as he was able to depend on the drummer more than he had with Best.

Paul and Ringo seemed to have fallen into place very quickly, with a certain chemistry between the two musicians that would be vital to the overall Beatle sound. This would be copied and emulated by countless musicians, literally around the world.

On July 16, 1963 the band would perform it during

their "Pop Go the Beatles Day" when they quickly and casually committed 18 songs to tape for future airings of their very own BBC program. This was possibly the last performance of the song, which never seemed to be considered as an official EMI recording.

"I Saw Her Standing There" was a relatively new song in late 1962, with the band very confidentially delivering a very well-rehearsed performance, which is clear even through the quality of the recording is poor.

There were also slight changes between the versions of the song recorded during the Cavern rehearsal just a few months earlier. By the time the band would record "I Saw Her Standing There" the following year it was a well-rehearsed number and reasonably quick to record.

"Roll Over Beethoven," originally done by Chuck Berry for the Chess label in 1956, had been part of the Beatles' repertoire as early an 1957. John initially took the lead vocals, eventually handing off those duties to George, who sings lead on the Hamburg recordings, the official *With The Beatles* album version, and seven separate BBC performances in less than a year.

"Hippy Hippy Shake" was written and recorded by Chan Romero for the Delphi label in 1959 and a was a popular number among Merseyside bands. It was performed five times for the BBC by the Beatles, but like several songs from the Hamburg recording, it was never officially considered for recording.

"Sweet Little Sixteen" was an early favorite of Lennon's, and one of many Berry compositions that the band would perform throughout their career. The Beatles would only perform the song once for the BBC but the December recording once again displays a confident singer who is reinterpreting a favorite artist respectfully, while also adding his own style.

When selecting songs to either perform live or record for BBC broadcasts, the band would frequently draw from Berry's catalogue.

"Little Queenie" was another Berry song that was a part of the band's set in late '62. There is no other evidence of the song being performed, although it is highly likely that it was a part of their act for several years

at least. What is unusual about the band performing this particular number is that Paul is taking lead on a Berry song, a territory generally reserved for John.

"I'm Talking About You," another Berry song with John singing lead, would again be performed during the Hamburg recording, as well as for the BBC in March the following year.

Berry's songs struck all of the band members in a profound way, so when they were looking for material to perform that would be enjoyable for not only the band but for the crowd or radio listening audience, they would frequently select from this category.

"Lend Me Your Comb" was a song by Kay Twomey, Fred Wise, and Ben Weisman, released on the Sun label in 1957 by Carl "The Rockin' Guitar Man" Perkins.

Twomey was an American songwriter who successfully wrote "Johnny Doughboy Found a Rose in Ireland" for Kenny Baker and "Better Not Roll Those Blue, Blue Eyes" for Shep Fields and His New Music. She also penned "Serenade of the Bells" for Jo Stafford in 1947, "There's a Music Box in the Moon" for the Three Suns in 1948, and "Gentle Johnny" for Doris Day in 1952.

Wise was frequent collaborator with Twomey, teaming up with her on "The Whistling Cowboy" for Horace Heidt and His Musical Knights in 1942. Wise also was partially responsible for "Sing Song Serenade" for Guy Lombardo, "The Bells of San Raquel" for Tony Pastor and His Orchestra, "Misirlou" for Woody Herman and His Orchestra, "Nice Dreamin' Baby" for Freddy Martin and His Orchestra and "You'll Never Know" for Bea Wain and Her Orchestra, all in 1941.

The following year he would bring "When Johnny Comes Marching Home" to the Andrews Sisters with Vic Schoen and His Orchestra, and "Nightingale" for Xavier Cugat and His Waldorf-Astoria Orchestra, also penning "A Flea and a Fly in a Flue" for Louis Prima and "Roses in the Rain" for Paul Weston and His Orchestra with Matt Dennis in 1946, "Life Lost its Color (When I Lost My Love)" for Hawkshaw Hawkins in 1949.

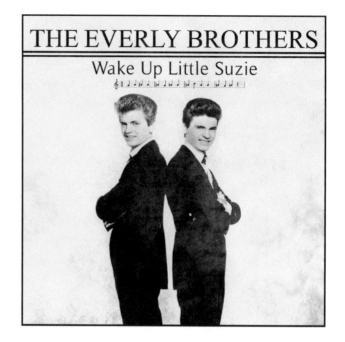

Weisman was an American songwriter who penned more songs recorded by Elvis Presley than any other composer. Weisman also wrote "The Wallflower Waltz" for Rosalie Allen and "Have A Little Sympathy" for Charles La Vere in 1949.

"Satisfaction Guaranteed" and "Who'll Buy My Heartaches" were both sides of a single written by Twomey-Wise-Weisman for Carl Smith. This trio also composed "Pretty Little Black-Eyed Susie" for Guy Mitchell in 1952, "Oo! What You Do to Me" for Patti Page, "Honey in the Horn" for the Commanders, "We're A-Growin' Up" for Tennessee Ernie and Molly Bee (Ernest Jennings Ford and Molly Beachboard) all in 1953, and "Beware" for Roy Hamilton in 1955.

The very prolific Weisman also co-penned "First in Line" for Elvis and "Red Light, Green Light" for Mitchell Torok in 1956, "Don't Leave Me Now" for Elvis and "Tiger Lily" for the Five Keys in 1957.

With that level of songwriting history it's no wonder why the young impressionable Beatles would be attracted to such a simple but effective, innocent sounding song.

"Wake up Little Suzie" was released by the Everly Brothers in September 1957, just two months prior to "Lend Me Your Comb" coming out. While they both share similar themes of fearing trouble from their parents upon their return home, it's unlikely that one inspired the other as curfews were very prevalent in this era, particularly among Americans.

On Perkins' version Carl sings lead along with his brother Jay, then Carl sings the solo bridges himself. The Beatles' version shared a similar arrangement with John and Paul harmonizing, then with Paul singing the solo Perkins lines.

Frequently the band would have their "turf" although they each appreciated the same things and at this creative point in their career there were few egos and they were always willing to share.

The A-side of the Perkins version of "Comb" was "Glad All Over" which was also a song that the Beatles would perform for several recordings throughout the formative years of the band. The Perkins version of the song is not to be confused with "Kookie, Kookie Lend Me Your Comb," from Connie Stevens and Edd Byrnes, which was released in 1959.

In July 1963 the Beatles would perform "Lend Me Your Comb" for the BBC. It was likely that the songs selected to be performed for radio broadcast were those already ruled out for the album, so the BBC recordings would be the final performance of these songs.

"Your Feet's Too Big" was another novelty song that the band would perform in their attempt to please as much of the crowd as possible, continuously trying to be more than just a rock band. Written by Fred Fisher along with Ada Benson, it was originally recorded by the Ink Spots in May 1936. It was later popularized by Fats Waller who had his own version from 1939.

The tune revolves around the singer complaining about the size of a girl's feet, which get compared to baby elephant feet. While at dinner the singer notes four attendees at the table including the singer, the girl, and her big feet. He goes on to discuss the fact that he enjoys everything else about the girl, from the ankles up.

Waller added his own contributions to the song, including the line "Your pedal extremities are colossal, to me you look just like a fossil" and his catchphrase "One never knows, do one?"

Fisher was a German immigrant who came to America in the early 1900s. He wrote the songs "When I Get You Alone To-Night" for Billy Murray in 1912 and "There's a Little Bit of Bad in Every Good Little Girl" for Jaudas' Society Orchestra in 1917, both released on a phonograph cylinder. He also wrote "Night Time in Little Italy" for Howard Koop and Lorraine for Henry Burr in 1917, "Chicago (That Toddling Town)" for the Georgians in 1922, and "Some Other Bird Whistled a Tune" for Jack Smith in 1926.

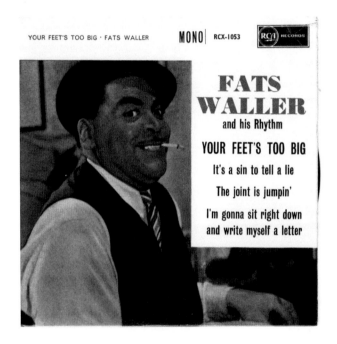

Curiously he would also compose "Red Sails in the Sunset" for the Casani Club Orchestra in 1935 and "That's When Your Heartaches Begin" for Shep Fields and His Rippling Rhythm Orchestra in 1937, later recorded by the Ink Spots as well as Elvis Presley. Both were songs that the Beatles would at one point include as part of their act.

Very little is known about Ada Benson, the co-writer of 'Feet," which is her only songwriting credit.

McCartney takes lead on the theatrical performance of "Your Feet's Too Big," which displays his natural ability for showmanship at a young age. His abilities would only improve as he and the band's confidence would increase.

"'Til There Was You" and "A Taste of Honey" were both songs that were part of the band's act for quite some time. Both songs provided chances for McCartney to show off his love for show tunes, and they were great crowd pleasers, giving spectators a chance to dance if that is what they were hoping to do. Both songs would be officially recorded for EMI.

"Twist and Shout" was also a crowd pleaser that the band would perform on many occasions, both before and after their fame spread throughout the world, and also eventually recorded for official release.

John took ownership of this song with each Beatle enthusiastically performing their own contribution.

The late 1962 version of "Twist and Shout" had a different arrangement, which didn't include the verses, just the crescendo near the end of the song, and the guitar intro. This slightly abbreviated version seems to be what the band would play when they opened a show, or a set with it.

The band performed the song on December 4, 1962 for the BBC in London on "The Talent Spot" radio show, however the recording no longer exists, making it impossible to know which arrangement was played on this occasion.

After the Beatles' success began to rapidly increase, which version of "Twist and Shout" they played seem to depend on its placement in a setlist. They would play the abbreviated version of the song when they would perform it first during their live shows, but if it came later in the set, they would play an arrangement similar to the official recording. Using this familiar song

as a bit of an intro, or theme song, displays the band's early abilities to present their music well, with strong songs beginning and ending each set performed.

"Mr. Moonlight" would be recorded in late 1964 for the *With The Beatles* album. This late 1962 performance displays the band having fun with a song they clearly knew well. By the time the band was ready to record the song they had performed it onstage on many occasions and were quick to perfect it in the studio.

Again, the band was trying to select unusual material to cover, occasionally so unknown the audience just might think it was one of theirs. While it's unlikely that the band ever took specific credit for a song that wasn't theirs, if nobody asked, they wouldn't volunteer the information.

On this live version all three singing Beatles share the bulk of the song, with John taking a rather commanding lead.

The primary difference between the arrangement of the December 1962 version and the official EMI recording is of course the guitar solo on the live recording, presumably George, in place of the organ solo on the 1964 version.

When selecting songs for the *Beatles For Sale* LP they picked "Mr. Moonlight" even though it had been dropped from their set list for most of the past two years. While promoting the album they performed many of the songs, both covers and originals, for several BBC performances, but "Moonlight" was not among them.

"Besame Mucho" was a consistent part of the band's repertoire throughout the year as they performed it on several key occasions, although they never released it until years after they stopped making albums. Humorous and just a bit silly, the song would certainly have its place in their Germany sets, but never quite made the cut for an official release. The arrangement they used throughout the year was reasonably consistent, with some extra added harmony from John on the Star Club version.

Ringo's drumming, as compared to the performance from Best on the January 1 recording is considerably

more energetic and exciting, certainly a more forceful contribution to the song.

Each of the young Beatles had their own love for Buddy Holly and would snap up any songs they could find with his name on the label. When they heard "Reminiscing" when it was released the previous September, it's very likely they immediately added it the act, having yet another "new" song from their guitar-playing hero.

The version of "Reminiscing" recorded from the Star Club spotlights George, taking lead vocal as well as playing the solo on the song, transferring the saxophone to the guitar seamlessly.

After the band's final German residency was finished, they no longer needed as many songs in their repertoire and this was among the many that were left behind.

"Kansas City/Hey Hey Hey Hey" was one of the songs that remained in the Beatles live act the longest, being performed during more than 100 performances between 1961 and late 1964. It was performed frequently in front of audiences as well as for the BBC, which they first did in August 1963, and it was ultimately recorded for the *Beatles For Sale* album.

Paul's love for raw rock and roll, specifically Little Richard, is what propelled his exciting rock and roll side, which he enjoyed showing off to the rough German audiences, who were always impressed with his ability to be sweet and kind, as well as rough and rowdy.

The arrangement on every recording of the Little Richard medley remained the same with hardly any variation at all, and exhibited an incredible amount of energy, which was well captured in the studio as well.

"Long Tall Sally" was another cover of a Little Richard song that remained part of the Beatles' live repertoire for a very long time. It was part of their live show throughout Beatlemania.

An extremely confident and enthusiastic McCartney was captured on tape in December 1962, backed by a band who is rivaling Paul's excitement. Throughout the poor-quality recording the Beatles and their fans display a genuine excitement, depicting a band that was on the brink of a major change.

"Where Have You Been All My Life" was the B-side of the Arthur Alexander single "Soldier of Love (Lay Down Your Arms)" which was also a song from the band's repertoire.

Barry Mann and Cynthia Weil were the husband and wife team responsible for this otherwise obscure track. They were also the co-writers on "Bless You" for Tony Orlando in 1961, and "A Girl Has to Know" for the G-Clefs, "If a Woman Answers (Hang Up the Phone)" for Leroy Van Dyke, "Uptown" for the Crystals, and "Conscience" for James Darren, all in 1962.

Like many songs from this era of the band, the Beatles never recorded it in any official capacity. In fact it's likely that the last time they played it for German audiences in late '62 was the final time they would ever perform it at all. Similar to other songs the Beatles left behind during this era, as songs fell off the Beatles live act other bands would pick them up and include them in their own acts.

It is also possible that several bands were also performing "Where Have You Been All My Life" at the time and the Beatles dropped the it consciously, not wanting to "share" with others. Gerry and the Pacemakers would record it in 1963 and the Searchers would do it the following year.

In the Beatles' minds they didn't need too many of one type of song, and "Where Have You Been" was a slower soul cover with John singing a passionate lead, much like the Beatles version of "Baby It's You," which would have won out for a space in the shows.

While several of these songs were forgotten by the band, the tunes certainly played their role in the formation of the Beatles as they learned how to interpret others' compositions in order to improve as performers of their own music.

"Hully Gully" is included on several versions of the Hamburg release, which is actually a performance by Cliff Bennett and the Rebel Rousers, possibly with guest appearances from any of the Beatles. As is the case with much music from this era, very few documentation exists other than memories.

The song itself was originally recorded by the Olympics in 1959 as "(Baby) Hully Gully," written by Fred "Sledge" Smith and Cliff Goldsmith.

"Road Runner" was briefly performed during this December 1962 Hamburg stint, seemingly as a sound check or test, possibly to a near empty house.

Bo Diddley released "Road Runner," complete with the "beep beeps," as to imitate the sadistic animated Road Runner who mentally tortured Wile E. Coyote in the Warner Bros. cartoons. The band was said to have included this as part of their act, at least for a short period of time.

"Crackin' Up," released in July 1959, was also reported yet sadly never confirmed to be performed by the Beatles during this time. Along with many other songs rumored but never confirmed, they may have been only occasionally attempted by the band.

Another stray recording from the Hamburg era is of "Money," which has an unknown singer. It is possible that the vocalist was Sheridan jumping on stage to join the band.

"Nothin Shakin' (But the Leaves on the Trees)" was an obscure single that the band found, possibly in Epstein's NEMS record store.

It was originally recorded and released by Eddie Fontaine, who was an American singer the Beatles were familiar with from his appearance in the 1956 musical "The Girl Can't Help It," starring platinum blonde bombshell Jayne Mansfield. The film featured highly influential performances from Little Richard, Gene Vincent, Eddie Cochran, Fats Domino, and the Platters as well as Fontaine.

Fontaine's influence on the band was minor, however the genre of rockabilly or as the Beatles occasionally called it "American hillbilly" was rather substantial. This style particularly impacted a young Harrison, who was especially attracted to it.

Once again, the band members each had their own area of expertise or turf, which wasn't strictly policed, but generally assigned to one of the singing Beatles.

In the 1956 musical, Fontaine performed the song "Cool it Baby" which was released as a single that same year, with the B-side "Into Each Life Some Rain Must Fall." Also in 1956 he released "Stand on That Rock" and "Here 'Tis." In 1957 Fontaine had "Honkey Tonk Man" and "Homesick Blues" before releasing his own composition.

Fontaine recorded "Nothing Shakin'" intending it to be a demo, however it was released as a single on the Argo label without Fontaine's knowledge. He also re-recorded it for the Sunbeam label in 1958. Fontaine was the solitary songwriter on it, although it is mysteriously credited to Fontaine/Colacrai/Lampert and Gluck.

Thematically "Nothing Shakin'" fits in with the songs the Beatles were enjoying from other artists, and trying to write on their own. The singer is simply discovering that his father indeed was correct when he told them that women would be trouble, and there would be "times like these." After spending money on the girl the singer gets no reward and is left frustrated, a rather innocent song.

It is interesting to note that the song includes the phrase "please please please." Also notable is that even though the girl offers no reason, the singer remains optimistic, a trait McCartney would draw from, although it was Harrison who takes charge of the song when they performed it.

The Hamburg recording features a slightly different arrangement of the song, similar to that of their slightly reworked "Twist and Shout." Both are listed as set openers, with the first verse omitted and the guitar solo as the intro.

When the band would record the song again in July 1963 for "Pop Go the Beatles" with George taking lead, they performed a rendition much more similar, almost identical, to the Fontaine recording, complete with a rather impressive and proficient solo from Harrison.

"To Know Her is to Love Her" was one of several girl group originals the Beatles would cover, and they also performed the song for the Decca auditions, although never for official release.

The performances from January 1, 1962, the Star Club Recordings from December of the same year, and the recording for "Pop Go the Beatles" in August of the following year were all very similar, displaying that the band clearly knew the song and were able to perform it well, even after what was likely an eight-month rest.

"To Know Her is to Love Her" is yet another song that was part of the Beatles' act and loved by many area bands as well. Other acts may have claimed it as their own after the Beatles stopped playing (in this case Peter and Gordon picked up the song), as the Beatles likely left it behind in favor of more compelling original songs.

"Ask Me Why" was an early original by the band, recorded on a few occasions in 1962, including during the December residency in Hamburg.

The late '62 performance once again displays the

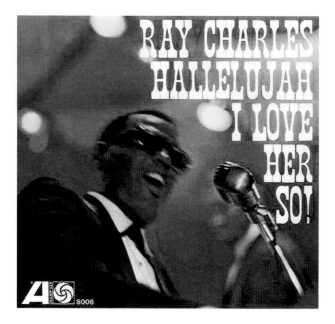

band's consistency, holding the tempo and the pace of the song while continuing to possess the same energy and passion throughout each performance.

"Falling in Love Again" was part of their act and is another show style song that Paul enjoyed performing, always determined to be more than just a rock and roll band.

Marlene Dietrich performed the song in the 1930 film also titled "Falling in Love Again," and as with many others from this era each of the four Beatles enjoyed the song and were familiar with it even before meeting their bandmates.

Many of the live songs of this era suffered the same fate, being left behind as the band continuing to progress rapidly as songwriters, got more famous, and needed to fill less time during an engagement. At this point it would only be about two years before performing other people's music would be a rarity.

"Be-Bop-A-Lula" was performed frequently by the Beatles who were substantial fans of Gene Vincent and his Blue Caps who originally recorded the song in May 1956. It also was included in the film the "The Girl Can't Help It."

Sources differ on who actually wrote the song and who gets the proper credit. The words were said to have been written by Vincent along with Donald Graves, while the two were in a naval hospital in Norfolk, Virginia at the same time. Vincent, who was recuperating from a motorcycle accident, wrote the tune while Graves was said to have written the words.

There is a song from 1945 called "Be-Baba-Leba" which was recorded by Helen Humes and was re-recorded as "Hey! Ba-Ba-Re-Bop" by Lionel Hampton later the same year.

While the phrase stems from the style of jazz music known as "be-bop" (exemplified by high tempo and complex compositions which featured many key changes, greatly challenging the musicians with improvisation) the song is a rather straightforward mid-'50s song with an early rock and roll sound.

Vincent's manager Bill "Sheriff Tex" Davis purchased the song lyrics from Graves for what is widely said to be "fifty bucks," although the exact amount is a source of debate.

It's not for certain where Graves specifically got the idea for the phrase, however Davis always (untruthfully) claimed he wrote it along with Vincent after hearing the Andrew Sisters 1958 song "Don't Bring Lulu."

Vincent would also occasionally tell the tall tale of how the song was inspired by the comic strip "Little Lulu," which may be somewhat true, but once again it's unable to be proven or disproven.

In 1956 the band members heard the song around the same time they saw it featured in the "Girl Can't Help It" film and they were all greatly attracted to it, quickly making it part of the Quarrymen's show.

Starr also "locked in" with the other members of the band quickly playing very well with them, and may have performed the song prior to joining the Beatles.

Many of the songs performed during this final residency in Germany were left off the band's set lists shortly after the calendar changed to 1963.

"Hallelujah I Love Her So" also features a singer that wasn't a Beatle, this time Horst Fascher, brother to Fred, who was a waiter at the Star Club. Originally a Ray Charles song from 1956, it was another tune the band knew from their very early days. The Beatles, and likely guest vocalist Fascher, were more familiar with the song as an Eddie Cochran number. It stands to reason that Beatles were very familiar with "Hallelujah I Love Her So" by the end of 1962, more than two years after their recording of the song from Paul's Liverpool home in 1960.

Fascher was a former boxer turned security guard/bouncer who became friends with the Beatles when they traveled to Germany, working with them first at the Indra Club, later the Kaiserkeller, and ultimately the Star Club, which Fascher ran along with Manfred Weissleder. As a towering and intimidating figure Fascher would help protect the band, both as they were playing as well as when they were off the stage. In exchange for his services in keeping them out of trouble with the locals, Fascher would occasionally sing with the band.

What is rather surprising on the recording is how well Fascher performs with the band, knowing when to sing, when to let the players play, and when to come back, displaying the fact that he must have joined them relatively frequently.

After the final Star Club residency, possibly even before, the song was no longer performed by the band. They may have just performed it one final time as a token of their esteem to their unofficial bodyguard.

"Sheila" was a song the band did throughout the year, also performing in for a BBC broadcast in October although it was edited out.

American pop artist Tommy Roe wrote the song in 1960, first recording it with his background band the Satins for Judd Records based out of Tennessee and run by the brother of Sam Phillips, who ran Sun Records based in Memphis. The original version didn't have the prominent drums that the re-recorded version had, and it featured a brief guitar solo, which was replaced in the 1962 version by an extended drum section.

In 1962 Roe re-recorded the song for the ABC-

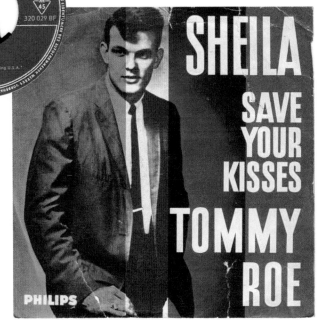

Paramount label, which was the version that the Beatles were familiar with and quickly copied.

Once again George takes the lead on the song that was originally by a "heart throb," Each singing Beatle had their own "turf" and George's seemed to be the young and good looking pop star that attracted the women. Harrison takes ownership of the song very well as he continued to grow in confidence as his playing and stage presence increased.

Starr yet again performs fantastically, consistent with his new band, quickly earning his role as a timekeeper. In just a few short months the Beatles would play on a bill that was headlined by Roe, along with Chris Montez. After the crowd's reaction to the Beatles they became the headliners as Montez and Roe were replaced.

"Sheila," as with many of the songs done by solo pop singers from this era, was dropped as they focused on cover versions of songs that they felt had a more substantial quality to them, primarily soul and rockabilly songs.

"Everybody's Trying to Be My Baby" was a Carl Perkins song that was a consistent favorite of the band and possibly one of the very first songs that Harrison ever learned.

While many of the songs from this recording were soon forgotten, the Perkins' numbers stayed around for a bit longer, a passion that the individual Beatles would never outgrow.

"Matchbox" was another a song that had a similar history for the band. It was introduced to them Carl Perkins, performed at an early stage with the band, and continued to be a part of their act through the era when they still recorded other music.

The December 1962 recording features Lennon singing lead, and the rest of the band falling into place spectacularly with another guitar solo from George that continued to help his confidence grow.

Ringo would take over vocals sometime after the final Star Club residency, singing lead when they performed it in July 1963 for BBC's "Pop Go the Beatles." Starr would also sing lead on the EMI version, recorded in June 1964 for consideration for inclusion on the *A Hard Day's Night* soundtrack LP.

"Red Sails in the Sunset" dates back to 1935 and very likely a song that McCartney's father introduced to him as a child. The music was written Austrian composer Hugh Williams, the stage name of Wilhelm Grosz, who fled from Vienna as World War II was unfolding.

Lyricist Jimmy Kennedy, inspired by a yacht named "Kitty of Coleraine" which had red sails and would navigate off the coast of Ireland.

"Red Sails" was recorded by Ray Noble and his Orchestra, Guy Lombardo, Bing Crosby, Jack Jackson, Leslie "Hutch" Hutchinson, Mantovani, Vera Lynn, Henry "Red" Allen, and Anona Winn, all in 1935. Nat King Cole had a very popular version of the song in 1957, and this is another version the band most likely heard.

A youthful McCartney may have been familiar with any of these versions, however it is most likely that the version the band was especially grabbed by was from Dinah Washington, whose '62 hit possibly "reminded" Paul about the song. The Washington version was considerably slower than the Beatles' take

Much of this is purely speculative, but what is known is the surviving audio reveals McCartney at a very exciting point in the development of his stage show, displaying a commanding presence as he delivers a rather "un-rock and roll" song in a very rock and roll way. The Beatles took ownership of it while simultaneously playing it as Buddy Holly might have.

Many of the standards that the band would include as part of their act ("'Til There Was You," "September in the Rain," "Falling in Love Again" would remain slower ballad-type songs, as opposed to doing them in a rock style (such as their take on "Ain't She Sweet"). This was the case with "Red Sails," which was likely only a brief part of the band's act.

The lyrics of the song are literally directed at the sails of the boat, asking them to take care of his, or her "baby," depending upon which gender is singing. Paul enthusiastically takes lead on the song with the other Beatles chiming in on occasion.

"I Wish I Could Shimmy Like My Sister Kate" also known as "Sister Shake," "Sister Kate" "Shimmy like Kate," or "Shimmy Shimmy" (or "Shitty Shitty" as a brave McCartney introduced the song) was a song that the Beatles learned after hearing the Olympics version from 1960.

The song itself dates back to the early 1900s and is said to have been a rather lewd tale of a murdered Madam of a brothel named Kate Townsend.

Either Anna Jones along with Fats Waller or Louis Armstrong were the alleged original performers, however it's Clarence Williams and Armand Piron who are credited on the sheet music as the publishers. What is most likely is that the song was passed on verbally over several years and became noticed when Williams and/or Piron heard the song performed live.

Although there were jazz and blues roots to the "I Wish I Could Shimmy Like My Sister Kate," it quickly became a favorite for the country and western crowd as well.

The song was recorded by the Cotton Pickers and the California Ramblers in 1922, Muggsy Spanier and his Ragtime Band in 1939, Wingy Manone's Dixieland Band in 1945, Bunk Johnson and His New Orleans Band in 1946, Bob Wills and His Texas Playboys in 1947, Claude Luter Et Ses Lorientai and Rushton's California Ramblers in 1948, Sidney Bechet's Blue Note Jazz Men in 1950, Turk Murphy and His Jazz Band in 1954, Ottilie Patterson and the Chris Barber Jazz Band in 1955 (which may have been a version that Paul or any of the other Beatles may have heard), Humphrey Lyttelton and His Band as well as the Dutch Swing College Band from the Netherlands in 1955, Brother Matthew with Eddie Condon's Jazz Band in 1956 and Wilbur De Paris and His New New Orleans Jazz Band in 1957, the Blue Rivers Jazz Band in 1958, and Shel Silverstein and the Red Onions also performed the song for the album *Hairy Jazz* in 1959.

After the Olympics recorded it in 1960 with the title "Shimmy Like Kate" and had a minor hit with this rather soulful doo-wop version of the song, the Beatles likely took notice. It is difficult to know if the song was a regular part of their act or just a song

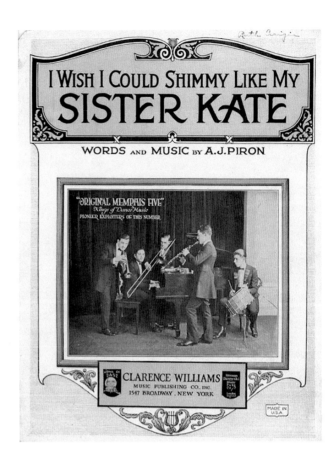

they would perform on occasion or perhaps just by request (or by demand as the tough German crowds may have considered it).

The lyrics are sung from the perspective of Kate's sibling, who wishes to dance, or shimmy, like Kate. While simple on the surface there is a bit of a sexual undertone involving the specifics of what exactly "shimmying" is. This is something that would definitely capture the attention of the young Beatles who grew up in a port town and were fans of the double entendre.

John takes the lead vocals with some help from Paul, while George shines brightly with a pair of guitar solos. Ringo and Paul can also be heard through the frustratingly poor-quality tape, playing along nicely as they continued to get more and more comfortable as a rhythm section.

The song certainly had promise and served the purpose of getting crowds to dance when the band performed at clubs, however it never seemed to be a steady part of their act, or considered for official recording sessions.

With "Shimmy like Sister Kate" we aren't specifically sure if the band was familiar with any other versions of the song, many of which were rather country and western.

"I Remember You" was an American country song done in a yodeling style by Frank Ifield in early '62. The Beatles seemed to cover it almost immediately, but then eliminated it from their rotation.

Victor Schertzinger wrote the music while the lyrics were penned by Johnny Mercer in 1941, first heard in the 1942 American film "The Fleet's In." Sung here by Dorothy Lamour along with the Jimmy Dorsey Orchestra, it was done with a relatively slow and somber tone. It's unknown if the Beatles were familiar with this version of the song, or if they even saw the Johnny Mercer-directed film. Mercer co-wrote all the songs from the film (including "Tangerine") along with Schertzinger who composed music for over a hundred movies between 1916-42. "The Fleet's In" was Schertzinger's last movie, released after his October 1941 death.

After the film and the release of the Jimmy Dorsey single with the vocal by Bob Eberly, "I Remember You" was quickly re-recorded by Freddy Martin and His Orchestra, with both those releases coming in 1942. The song was also done by Joan Edwards in 1944, as well as Jo Stafford, the Pied Pipers, and Paul Weston's Orchestra, also in '44.

Bing Crosby and the Charioteers along with John Scott Trotter and His Orchestra recorded the song as part of a medley of music from the film along with "Tangerine" and "Arthur Murray Taught Me Dancing" in 1947.

"I Remember You" was recorded by a remarkably long list of artists: the Lennie Niehaus Quintet and the Jackie Gleason Orchestra each recorded the song in 1954, the Four Freshman as well as Charlie Parker did it in 1955, Paul Smith, Ted Heath, Sonny

Rollins, the Bobby Jaspar Quintet, Arty Shaw and His Orchestra, and Doris Day all recorded it in 1956, and Italian nightclub vocalist Nicola Arigliano recorded it in 1958. Also in 1958-59 were Paul Weston, Dinah Washington, June Christy, and Julius La Rosa. 1960-61 heard versions of the song by André Previn, the Modest Jazz Trio, Peggy Lee, the Doug Watkins Quintet, and James Clay.

The Ifield version was recorded in 1962 and became a huge hit for the singer. It was unusual but not unheard of for an English singer to have a big hit with a country standard.

With "I Remember You" striking gold on the radio, the Beatles learned the song, this time with Paul singing lead and John performing the harmonica. The song was also said to be an inspiration for the band's debut single, which features a similar-sounding harmonica.

The band had been introduced to American country, primarily through English artists doing cover versions of songs from the good old romantic United States. Hank Williams was an artist who was introduced to the band in a similar fashion. Ifield had a minor hit with a cover of Williams' "Lovesick Blues" as the follow up to "I Remember You," which utilized a very Hank Williams-like yodel.

On December 2, 1962 at the Embassy Cinema in Peterborough, the Beatles were on a bill with Ifield, as well as Susan Cope, Tommy Wallis and Beryl, the Lana Sisters, and the Ted Taylor Four. Peterborough was located a bit further south than the Beatles were generally used to playing and they didn't go over especially well, having greater success in the northern part of the country.

These songs with a deep pedigree and a history always seemed to pique the interest of the Beatles, even if they came to them in unusual ways, and were only performed on rare occasion. Each of these songs contributed some sort of inspiration for the band, even as just a chance to try something "new" as a rehearsal for future performances they hoped were ahead, which of course they were.

After these historic tapes were made by Star Club's stage manager Adrian Barber he gave them to Ted "Kingsize" Taylor who attempted to sell them to Epstein after the Beatles' commercial breakthrough. Epstein considered the offer a waste of his time, counter-offering a small sum which Taylor turned down.

Paul Murphy, the head of Buk Records, finally purchased the tapes from Taylor and invested a large amount of money to clean up the recordings, eliminating hisses and clicks and making the product slightly more commercially viable.

After some legal battles and several releases with various track lineups, the songs are ultimately an enjoyable, albeit exasperating set to listen to due to the poor quality. They wonderfully serve their purpose as a historic look into a very important time for a band on the brink of world stardom.

Alan Williams reported that he had more than three hours of recorded material from this final trip to Hamburg, however much of this may have been Kingsize Taylor, or simply the time the band spent on stage doing nothing other than tuning or drinking or figuring out what to play next.

"Red Hot" was a 1955 yellow Sun record from Nashville written and originally recorded by Billy "The Kid" Emerson, who also wrote and recorded "When it Rains it Really Pours," also recorded by Elvis on the Sun label in 1957.

Billy Lee Riley & the Little Green Men also recorded "Red Hot," which consisted of the singer declaring his

girl is not just "hot" but "red hot" (which would be an especially attractive woman) and the background singers answered back that she ain't "dooley squat."

During the December '62 Hamburg recording, a brief version of the Beatles doing the song was taped, lasting about a minute, including an unknown organist which is possibly Roy Young. The tape is of such poor quality that it is actually uncertain if it is John or George singing lead.

As 1962 began the Beatles were optimistic about a chance to try out for a "big deal" record label. Ultimately that early opportunity would turn out to be a dead end, but the ever-persistent band kept doing what they did best, which was to play as often as they could believing they would become better and better the more they performed, with the hopes of eventually landing a recording contract.

As the year unfolded they secured a deal with London-based EMI, achieving success and excited to record more in the following year.

After completing their German obligations, the four Beatles spent their first day of 1963 traveling home from Hamburg. This time the band was flying, slowly becoming a bigger act with more "prestige" and no longer had to travel by train out of necessity.

Much of this success was thanks to the personal investment of their manager Epstein, who made a series of very good choices on behalf of the band, not only involving their fate as professional recording artists but with their image as well. ◆

BEFORE
THEY WERE
THE BEATLES

John Lennon (1940-1980) was born on October 9, 1940 in Liverpool during World War II to Julia Smith and merchant seaman Alfred Lennon, who was not present at the time of John's birth.

Julia and her husband would have a contentious relationship, and at the age of five Lennon was forced by Alfred to choose between his mother and father. John chose his father until his mother began to walk away and he began crying and quickly followed her. It would be 20 years before Alfred Lennon would see his son again.

As a child John was raised by his Aunt Mimi and Uncle George, who had no children of their own and did their best to nurture the clearly creative and intelligent, yet reckless and impulsive young Lennon.

The Smiths would encourage John to read and "keep his mind sharp" by drawing and exploring his love of cinema, although after age 14 when he got his first guitar he would quickly have little interest in anything else.

Lennon was accepted into Liverpool College of Art, however he was an uncommitted student and was eventually expelled, which he considered a gift so he could spend more time with his music.

At age 15 Lennon formed his first skiffle band. Tragically the following year John's mother was killed, which would become a source of bonding among Lennon and his friend and future partner Paul McCartney, who had also lost his mother.

John's Aunt Mimi didn't approve of Lennon's love of music or his "little friend" Paul, who was a lower class. Paul's father also warned him of Lennon being nothing but a trouble-maker.

Paul McCartney (b. 1942) was born on June 18, 1942, also in Liverpool. He grew up in a modest home with his younger brother (Michael) and his mother Mary and father James, a trumpet player and former leader of the Jim Mac Jazz Band.

Paul was encouraged by his father to explore his love of music at a young age and take piano lessons, as there was one readily available in the front room of the home. Paul instead preferred to learn to play by ear.

When McCartney was 14 his mother suddenly passed away, which greatly affected the young and sensitive Paul. The following year he would become friends with John Lennon who had also lost his mother suddenly as a teen, a point of connection between the two.

Paul attended the Liverpool Institute and in 1954 while riding on the school bus he met George Harrison. The two quickly became friends as they realized they shared a similar love of rock and roll.

George Harrison (1943-2001) was born February 25, 1943 in Liverpool, the youngest of Harold and Louise Harrison's four children.

Even as a young child George was an enthusiastic fan of music, as was his mother. She introduced the youngster to the music of singer/actor/musician/ songwriter George Formby, gypsy swing jazz guitarist Django Reinhardt, and American composer and pianist

John Lennon

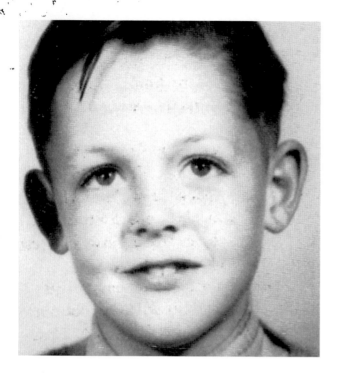

Paul McCartney

Hoagy Carmichael. George would later to grow to admire artists like Carl Perkins and Lonnie Donegan, loves that George would carry throughout his entire life.

While riding his bicycle in 1956 George heard Elvis Presley's "Heartbreak Hotel" and he became immediately smitten. He convinced his father to purchase him a guitar, which he would consistently practice with great encouragement of his mother.

As Paul McCartney was performing in the Quarrymen he suggested to John Lennon that he meet his friend George, who was becoming a very proficient player by 1958. Harrison first auditioned by playing Arthur "Guitar Boogie" Smith's "Guitar Boogie Shuffle," however Lennon thought George was just a kid and refused to let him join.

George later performed "Raunchy" for Lennon, who was duly impressed, but not enough to accept him as of yet. Eventually after socializing, rehearsing, and occasionally filling in with the group, George "became" an official band member even though it is possible he was never officially invited.

Ringo Starr (Richard Starkey b. 1940) was born in Liverpool on July 7, 1940 the only child of Elsie and Richard Starkey, Sr.

Both parents were fans of live music and dancing, until the birth of their son when Ringo's mother chose to stay home and raise her child. Meanwhile Ringo's father continued to "frolic around town" sometimes for days at a time.

The couple split when "Ritchie" was four years old. "Big Ritchie" failed to make an effort to bond with his young son, quickly losing touch.

Ringo was a sickly kid with several extended hospital stays which affected his scholastic progression and left him feeling very alienated from his peers. He frequently was truant and spent his free time alone.

At age 13, while being treated for tuberculosis, a nurse encouraged the young patient to remain active, join the hospital band, and "play music." Using a homemade mallet, Ringo would bang on tables and cabinets, and this exposure to music piqued his interest.

Also when Ringo was 13 his mother was remarried to a Londoner named Harry Graves. Ringo's stepfather was a fan of big band music and their vocalists, exposing a young Starkey to the sounds of American singer Sarah Vaughan. Ringo did not return to school, instead choosing to stay home and listen to big band music all day. Eventually he joined a machinist apprentice program, although he would not complete the full 5 years.

Unmotivated and unskilled, Ringo never kept a job for too long. However he was fascinated by melodies of all types, including skiffle which was a new and exciting style of music.

Ringo formed the Eddie Miles Band, later to be named Eddie Clayton and the Clayton Squares. With the band Ringo would play a washboard by running a metal thimble up and down the front of it, creating an unusually loud sound.

In 1957 Harry Graves (who Ringo says taught him gentleness) purchased a crude hand-me-down drum kit for Ringo as a Christmas gift. This facilitated Ringo's ability to proficiently perform with the Eddie Clayton band near the end of the skiffle craze in England, at a time when American rock and roll became the current trend in the U.K.

Al Caldwell's Texans were looking for a drummer with a full kit so they could make the transition from skiffle to standard rock and roll. To this end, they hired Starr in late 1959. The Raging Texans then became Jet Storm and the Raging Texans, finally becoming Rory Storm and the Hurricanes, who had become one of Liverpool's biggest acts by 1960.

Early 1960 is the best guess for when Ritchie Starkey became Ringo Starr, named after his stylish collection of rings. The nickname "Ringo" had a country and western sound, as in cowboy outlaw Johnny Ringo, who had been depicted in television, film, and comic books.

The Hurricanes would work an annual three-month residency at a Butlins holiday camp in Wales, followed by a run at Bruno Koschmider's Kaiserkeller where on October 1, 1960 Starr first met the Beatles. Later in the month Starr played a session with John Lennon, Paul McCartney, and George Harrison as they backed Hurricane member Lu Walters on "Summertime."

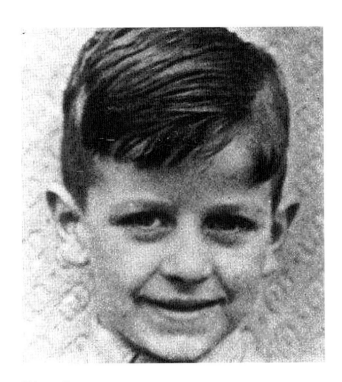

Ringo Starr

While the two bands would simultaneously perform in Germany, Ringo would occasionally "sit in" with the band and all four musicians immediately noticed the chemistry among them.

Also during this first Hamburg visit Ringo met Tony Sheridan, who valued Starr's drumming ability so much he convinced him to leave the Hurricanes to join his band in Hamburg. Starr left the Hurricanes for a brief time before returning to the band for a third season at Butlins camp, where Ringo's drum solos were referred to as "Starr time!"

On August 14, 1962 John Lennon asked Starr to join his band and Ringo anxiously accepted (always wanting to play with the best). He quickly made arrangements to permanently join his new band, and his first official show as a Beatle was August 18 at a horticultural society dance at Port Sunlight. The four quickly solidified their constantly consistent sound, which would of course be a combination that would affect music, fashion, culture, and the concept of popularity for decades, as well as the foreseeable future. ∎

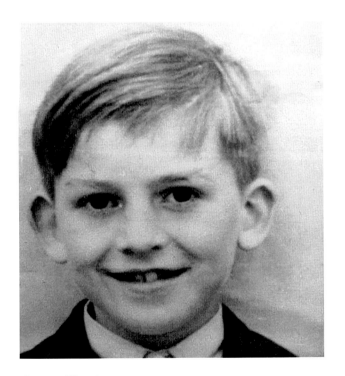

George Harrison

ACKNOWLEDGMENTS

ACKNOWLEDGMENTS

To begin, an extreme thank you to all of the people not singled out. The ones that have said good job or gave the thumbs up, the ones I have ever met without meeting and everyone else on the earth that made this possible.* With that being said, here is an extensive yet incomplete list of people I wish to thank in the long process of idea to holdable, readable book.

Big thanks to Dave Alderson for pointing out that I had run out of excuses, to Phil Angotti, Julie Rozewski, Chip Buerger, Tim Stovall, John San Juan, Dylan Woelfle (young Dylan) and Eric Keeley for their consistent encouragement, and for being top-notch A plus "students."

Thanks to Rich Krocker for listening to me talk Beatles more than anyone ever, Brother Michael Boyle for teaching me without dumbing it down, Toni Scavo for always being on my side, and for being MY Toni, Kit O' Toole for offering me advice on how to make this a real life book, as opposed to just an idea, Patrick Knasiak for being my late night go to guy when I needed brain tickling, Suzie Whitaker for always understanding how that brain works, Terri Hemmert for being my biggest fan, as well as the first, Kathy Posner for ALWAYS thinking that I'm great, Dan and Angie McKenzie for being a record-breaking great couple, Theodore Gray for all of your encouragement, thank you Aaron Grossi (my brutha) and sister Amy for getting it like few if any do.

Thank you Peter Denk and Chester Cross and Al Jones and Monique Fourie (my idol) and Tim Smith and Karen Cole and Kevin Budinger and Josh Link and Chris Tornow and Carla Donahue and Luke Sherridan and Kris Jackson and Mark Baker and Steve McMillan and Nick Hill and Scott and Kathy Jackson and Shawn Tassone and Shawn Carroll and Eric Hayes (cirE seyaH) and the dozens of other friends I have collected over the years, I hold a place in my heart for each of you.

Special thanks to my parents, Mike and Elaine Alexander, for always being fans of their greatest son, to Honey Pie, and to Kevin Walitalo Cunningham, MLNB.

Sincere and eternal gratitude to Joe McCardle, RAE Erving, MISTER Jimmy Fraser, Ron Ross, Marshall Stern, Gavin Carroll, Ken Sumka, Chris Cwiak, Marc Alghini, Bill Cochran, and Hal Sparks for their collective wisdom over the years.

Thanks to Marc Golde, Mike "Geppy" Gephart, Michael Boyle and drummer Dean Tassone for Father Mac, and all that we achieved.

Raise a glass to Otis and his assorted Alligators (as close to too much fun as possible), the Weavils, the Party of Clowns, Mark Olson, Bobby Evans and his Alimony Blues Band, and Andy and his Automatics for letting me inside the in crowd.

Mucho appreciation is headed the way of the entire Tributosaurus family for the rare and unique thrill of being able to "jam" with the band.

Double thanks to Norm Winer, Lin Brehmer, Frank E. Lee, Tom Marker, and my many friends at WXRT for being the only station where Professor Moptop could have ever been created.

Thank you to Donald Luksetich for encouraging my creativity, and to Puff for never leaving.

BIG thanks to Laura Veras Marran for turning a pile of words into a cohesive set of chapters, which makes up a real book, and thanks for the positivity too!

At a point when things seemed bleak Sara Greene joined forces with me and helped create in reality the book that I saw in my mind, all with very abstract descriptions and rather non-technical terminology.

I am eternally appreciative to Steve Gibson who designed all of the artwork for Beatle University, and is extremely effective with taking vague suggestions, and turning them into something remarkable, and a super nice dude!

Thank you to Kalyan Pathak for his infectious bright attitude and his kindness, to Markus Saulys for his vivid smile and warm thoughts, and to Dave Marran for always helping me dig for more knowledge.

Thanks to Stella Baiocchi and James Nolder for joining my ever expanding world, and thanks to Nanker Pheldge, you know who you are.

And finally without Mr. Dan Byrne, there may never have been the seed of ever putting my knowledge on paper. Thank you a billion times over for being a rare adult to treat a kid like an equal and for suggesting how about "howabouta Beatle book?" many years ago, this book is for you, Dan.

This book is dedicated to the memories of Todd Borsch, Jake Hartford, Bob Thomas, Ryan Van Ham, and "Happy" Jack Utley. As long as I think of your presence, you shall never truly be gone.

Please take note that Troy Miller is not part of the thank you list, as he has been a consistently huge disappointment over the last several decades.

KICKSTARTER

When it came time to make the book a reality, I utilized crowd sourcing, which gave me the boost of confidence I needed to move forward, and via Kickstarter I raised enough dough to really make this a serious project, instead of just a thing.

I wish to personally thank all who donated to the fund, and look forward to hearing reactions of friends who have been patient and understanding throughout this process. <u>**Sincere gratitude goes out to**</u>:

Rudy Rodriguez Jr. *(Official backer No. 1)*
Irma Rodela
Michael Rengel
Rob & Donna Lisec
Ken Fuehrmeyer
Frank Jackowiak *(Unofficial backer No. 1)*
Rod Homor
Pat Frederickson
Joe Cote
Billy Shears
Christopher Davis
Sean Stangland
Bill Bergman

Kenny Stevenson
Fabien Van Der Stappen
Dawn Tagtmeier
Debbie Bowsher
Chris Christenson
Kristina Coley *(say no more)*
Justin Kaminski
David Hayes
Amy Lyons
John Castellano
JC Heerdt and family
Gwen Strutzenberg
Ruth Kula

Robert E Olmsted

Chris Layton

Katherine Kirby

Jonathan Schwartz

Andrius Kudirka

Janet Boomer Kastruba

The Edwards Family *(Marsha, Jameson and Graham)*

Michael Luellen

The Leddy Family *(Tom, Amy and Sara)*

Emme Gil

Brian Bartleson

Sunny Riley *(who always observes kindness)*

Jackie Boyer

Sandra Ann Perez

Patrick Rose

John Hatmaker

Carly

Joanna Farris

Brian Allan

Duane Tomiak

Ed Manning

Evan Williams

Susan Allen

Erick Staresina

Tim Machnik

Richard Burgwinkel

Bryan Sannito and family

Lanea Stagg

Jon Fuchs

Ken Orth

Ann Lessick

Milan Spasovski

Mickey Milner

Judy Anderson

Dale Agogo

Michael Patrick Russell

Claudia Cuellar

Kevin Van Pelt

Dave DeMik

Steven Lux

Jenny Keeley

Karen Fouts

Monica Rodela

Jill J. Gardner

Kyle Kruszewski

Julie Brauneis

Tom Parkin

Gerard Anaszewicz

Lawrence Gualano

Kim Opalacz

Jack Taylor

Kent Desiderio

Gene DeMuro

Aaron Krerowicz

Julie

Sharon Scotellaro

Linda Bosy

Anita Byrne

Kathleen Danahy-Clesen

Bob Braschel

Terrence Flamm

Kurt Duerksen

Dennis Leise

Richard Milne

Edward Babush

Judy Parker

John Bezzini

Luke Havumaki

David Ingram

Neal Robinson

Paul Friend

John Schultz

Bob Esmail

Harvey Greenberg

Joe Whittaker

Debbie Blackwell

David Waun

Keith Moritz

Hope Kellman

Andy Sikorski

Jeri Petz

Danny Fahlgren

Clyde Rundle

Bruce Dornfeld

Dan Cihon

Roseanne Norten Webb

ABOUT THE AUTHOR

For almost his entire life Gregory Alexander has been obsessed with music, and at some point in his teens became fascinated by a band he always enjoyed, but never took the time to investigate.

After several years of intense studying he began his guise as Professor Moptop, who has taught Chicago listeners of WXRT college-level Beatle knowledge since 1999. With many scripts compiled and billions of thoughts, the Professor was finally convinced to put his "work" onto paper. Finally in 2016, with his cat Mary, the writing process began. Alexander has spent a great amount of time compiling as many details as possible into a cohesive and holdable book, which is presented to you now in 2018, we hope you enjoy.

I certainly hope everybody learns something, from the freshest Beatle fan in the world, to the most knowledgeable.

GREGORY ALEXANDER / PROFESSOR MOPTOP

SELECTED BIBLIOGRAPHY

BOOKS

Badman, Keith (2008). *The Beatles Off the Record*. London: Omnibus Press.

Bramwell, Tony (2005). *Magical Mystery Tours: My Life with the Beatles*. New York, NY: St. Martin's Griffin.

Bronson, Harold (2017). *My British Invasion*. Los Angeles: Rare Bird Books.

Brown, Peter and Steven Gaines (1983). *The Love You Make - An Insiders Story of the Beatles*. London: Macmillan Publishers Ltd.

Burger, Jeff (2017). *Lennon on Lennon: Conversations with John Lennon*. London: Omnibus Press.

Campbell, Colin and Allan Murphy (1980). *Things We Said Today: The Complete Lyrics and Concordance to the Beatles' Songs* 1962-1970. Ann Arbor, MI: Pierian Press.

Cooper, B. Lee and Frank W. Hoffmann (2015). *Novelty Records: A Topical Discography, 1900-2015*. CreateSpace Publishing.

Davies, Hunter (1968). *The Beatles: The Authorized Biography*. Portsmouth, NH: Heinemann Publishing.

Davies, Hunter (1985). *The Beatles Book*. London: Ebury Publishing.

Davies, Hunter (1975). *The Beatles Lyrics: The Stories Behind the Music*. New York, NY: Little, Brown and Company.

Dowlding, William J. (1989). *Beatlesongs*. New York, NY: Touchstone Publishing.

Emerick, Geoff (2005). *Here, There and Everywhere: My Life Recording the Music of the Beatles*. New York, NY: Gotham Books.

Epstein, Brian with Derek Taylor (1964). *A Cellarful of Noise*. Ann Arbor, MI: Pierian Press.

Hammack, Jerry (2017) *The Beatles Recording Reference Manual: Volume 1*. CreateSpace Publishing.

Harrison, George (1980). *I, Me, Mine*. Surrey, England: Genesis Publications.

Harry, Bill (2004). *The British Invasion: How the Beatles and Other UK Bands Conquered America*. New Malden, England: Chrome Dreams Publishing.

Hill, Tim (2007). *Beatles: Then There Was Music*. Cape Town, South Africa: New Holland Publishers.

Kane, Larry (2004). *A Ticket to Ride: Inside the Beatles' 1964 Tour That Changed the World*. London: Penguin Books.

Lewisohn, Mark (2013). *Tune In (The Beatles: All These Years, #1)*. New York, NY: Crown Publishing Group.

Lewisohn, Mark (2013). *The Complete Beatles Recording Sessions*. New York, NY: Harmony Books.

Macdonald, Ian (1994). *Revolution in the Head: The Beatles Records and the Sixties*. London: Fourth Estate Publishing.

Margotin, Philippe (2013). *All The Songs: The Story Behind Every Beatles Release*. New York, NY: Black Dog & Leventhal.

Martin, George with Jeremy Hornsby (1979). *All You Need Is Ears: The Inside Personal Story of the Genius Who Created the Beatle*s. London: Macmillan Publishers.

Miles, Barry (2007). B*eatles: A Diary: An Intimate Day by Day History*. Emmaus, PA: JG Press.

Norman, Philip (2016). *Paul McCartney: The Life*. London: Orion Publishing Group, Ltd.

Norman, Philip (1981). *Shout! The Beatles in Their Generation*. London: Elm Tree Books.

Otfinoski, Steven (2000). *The Golden Age of Novelty Songs*. New York, NY: Billboard Books.

Riley, Tim (1988). *Tell Me Why: The Beatles: Album by Album, Song by Song, The Sixties and After*. Boston: Da Capo Press.

Robertson, John (2004). *Complete Guide to the Music of the Beatles*. London: Omnibus Press.

Spitz, Bob (2005). *The Beatles: The Biography*. New York, NY¬: Little, Brown and Company.

Stark, Steven D. (2005). *Meet the Beatles: A Cultural History of the Band That Shook Youth, Gender, and the World*. New York, NY: HarperCollins.

Taylor, Derek (1973). *As Time Goes By: Living in the Sixties*. San Francisco: Straight Arrow Books.

The Beatles (2000). *Anthology*. San Francisco: Chronicle Books.

Turner, Steve (1994). *A Hard Day's Write*. New York, NY: HarperCollins.

Turner, Steve (2006). *The Gospel According to the Beatles*. Louisville, KY: Westminster John Knox Press,.

Whitburn, Joel (1972). *Top Pop Singles, 1940-1955*. Milwaukee, WI: Hal Leonard Performing Arts Publishing.

Whitburn, Joel (1988). *Joel Whitburn's Top R & B Singles 1942-1988*. Menomonee Falls, WI: Record Research Inc.

Whitburn, Joel (1989). *Joel Whitburn's Top Country Singles, 1944-1988*. Milwaukee, WI: Hal Leonard Performing Arts Publishing.

Whitburn, Joel (1995). *Joel Whitburn Presents Billboard Pop Charts: 1955-1959*. Milwaukee, WI: Hal Leonard Performing Arts Publishing.

Whitburn, Joel (1995). *Joel Whitburn presents the Billboard Hot 100 Charts: The Sixties.* Milwaukee, WI: Hal Leonard Performing Arts Publishing.

Whitburn, Joel (1999). *Joel Whitburn Presents a Century of Pop Music 1940-1999.* Menomonee Falls, WI: Record Research Inc.

Whiticker, Alan J. (2014). B*ritish Pop Invasion: How British Music Conquered the Sixties.* London: New Holland Publishers.

Womack, Kenneth (2017). *Maximum Volume : The Life of Beatles Producer George Martin, The Early Years, 1926–1966.* Chicago, IL: Chicago Review Press.

WEBSITES

45Cat.com

45Worlds.com

Discogs.com

Google.com

Wikipedia.com

Made in the USA
Monee, IL
18 September 2019